IMAGES
of America

DELAWARE COUNTY

On the Cover: Shortly after the Ford Model T became available, industrious farmers came up with ways to convert the automobile into an early version of a farm tractor. This photograph is from a glass negative by Otto Sellers. A second Sellers glass negative features what appears to be the same unidentified driver and kit-assembled automobile. A Sellers logbook has an entry with the subject "building tractor co" for Feeny Manufacturing Company in March 1918. Another entry under Farmer Tractor Co. also appears to refer to Delaware County photographs. (Courtesy of the Delaware County Historical Society.)

IMAGES
of America

DELAWARE COUNTY

Norma Lasley and the
Delaware County Historical Society

ARCADIA
PUBLISHING

ISBN 978-0-7385-9430-9

Published by Arcadia Publishing
Charleston, South Carolina

Printed in the United States of America

Library of Congress Control Number: 2012942212

For all general information, please contact Arcadia Publishing:
Telephone 843-853-2070
Fax 843-853-0044
E-mail sales@arcadiapublishing.com
For customer service and orders:
Toll-Free 1-888-313-2665

Visit us on the Internet at www.arcadiapublishing.com

To all those who work to preserve local history

Contents

ACKNOWLEDGMENTS

Appreciation for the assistance of all those who helped in collecting the photographs and information for this book is extended to the following: Thomas R. Tomlinson, scanning and photography expert, for all his work and patience; Michael Mavis for his knowledge of Albany and Muncie locations and history, plus his expertise in reading the intricate details of fire maps; Jeffrey Koenker for his collection of photographic postcards of Delaware County scenes; Larry Campbell for his collection of photographs and knowledge of Delaware County railroads; Rev. Gary McManus for his photographs and activities in the preservation of Daleville history; the Eaton Public Library for sharing their photographs of local history; Muncie Public Library and Beth Kroehler for their photographs, collections, and research materials; Minnetrista Heritage Collection and Susan Smith for their assistance and sharing photographs in their collections; Kathy Lee for her proofreading assistance; the Liberty Township Historical Society members for their interest and helpfulness; those individuals who shared their family photographs for the book; and all others who provided support.

An abbreviation for the Delaware County Historical Society (DCHS) has been used in the captions and courtesy lines.

INTRODUCTION

Delaware County was organized in 1827, and Muncie was chosen to be the county seat. As the railroad came east from Indianapolis in the 1850s, local citizens regarded it with interest and enthusiasm, recognizing this great advance in making the area accessible to the rest of the state and country. The area was heavily wooded, and poles were one of the first products sent out, with grain and other crops following as agriculture developed and became important in the economy.

Many Delaware County men served in the Civil War, some of them in the famous Iron Brigade, the 19th Indiana Regiment. The railroad development after the Civil War connected the villages with the outside world and, along with the gas boom in the 1890s, lead to a period of high growth across the county.

The gas boom era began in 1886 when the Eaton commercial gas well was successfully drilled. The Trenton gas field was the largest known gas field in the world at that time. Huge flares burned day and night, attracting spectators from miles around to view them. By February 1896, there were 127 oil leases on record at the courthouse for territory in Delaware, Niles, Union, and Hamilton Townships, the northeastern part of the county. There was much wasting of the gas, though, and the wells began to fail about 1900. Some places were able to sustain the surge of industrial growth and its contraction better than others.

The automobile era saw a surge in creativity and invention in the county with the building of cars and experimentation with systems and parts a "garage industry" before there were garages. Home workshops developed into the later garages for automobile repair. Automotive industries became the primary employment in the county with Chevrolet Muncie, Delco Battery, and Warner Gear located in Muncie.

The lawlessness of the 1920s brought speakeasies and liquor running to the county. During the Depression, some without jobs turned to small local burglaries and thefts. Others were more ruthless and used nitroglycerin to rob small town banks such as those in Eaton, sometimes terrorizing the citizens. As local budgets allowed, new police cars, updated weapons, and eventually radios helped law enforcement gain control.

From the first events leading to World War II, the county participated in the war effort. The home front was well organized to support the defense of the nation, with manufacturing to the fore. Workers in munitions plants and other war-related industries kept the military supplies flowing while dealing with rationing and shortages.

The importance of education was seen first in the classes held in settlers' homes in the 1830s. A normal school for teachers was established in the county in 1875. The 20th century saw the development of what became Ball State Teachers College, now Ball State University. Becoming one of the largest employers in the county, the university has provided cultural opportunities that add greatly to the community's attractions.

Agriculture has continued to thrive in the county through the years and remains an important part of the economy. Mechanization from threshing machines, hay bailers, and tractors to dairy operations rolled across the county in successive waves.

The postwar years of the 1950s and 1960s were generally prosperous. More recently, small machine shops and small businesses helped to alleviate the shifting economy as it became more service oriented. The decline of employment in the automobile-related industries made an enormous difference to the county at the turn of the 21st century. Manufacturing still exists but uses a much smaller labor force. Ball State University and IU Health Ball Memorial Hospital became the largest employers in the county.

Muncie, having acquired suburbs and appendages, is larger than the other towns and is now a city. However, it still has problems in common with the rest of the county, with each area responding in its own way to events and changes.

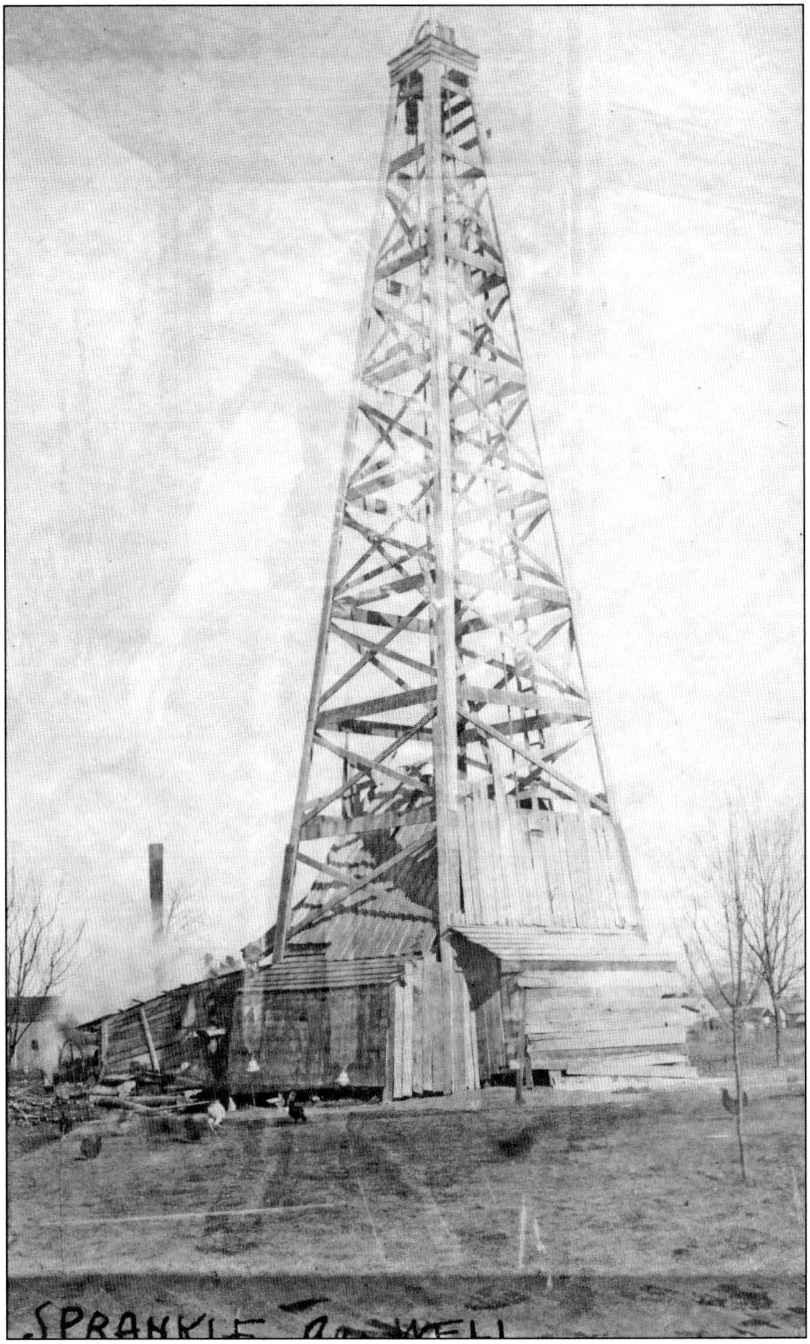

James R. Sprankle and his father, Rudolph Sprankle, were from Cleveland, Ohio, where they had become known as shippers of grain and other commodities to the ports of the United States. After they had disposed of their business interests in Cleveland and James Sprankle came to Muncie, he built steam flouring mills on High Street in 1887. The Sprankles organized the Delaware County Bank as a state bank in Muncie about 1887, and they reorganized it as a national bank with capital stock of $100,000 in 1892. The gas well in this photograph was one of the Sprankle investments in Delaware County. (Michael Mavis.)

One

Albany

The land on which Albany is situated was purchased from the land office in 1832 by Andrew Kennedy, who sold the land to William Venard. Albany had its beginning in 1833 when Venard divided part of his purchase into town lots. Located near the then navigable Mississinewa River, Albany became a trading and shipping center for that part of Delaware County. Albany was also on the trail from Union City to Marion that partly followed the Mississinewa River. The pioneers who traveled this trail considered Half Way Creek to be about halfway on their route northward. Memories of these people linger near Albany in Strong Cemetery, where travelers and their children were buried when they became ill and died along the way.

The advent of the railroad provided expedited shipping of wares to and from the area. After the Civil War, local businesses expanded to include liveries, groceries, clothing shops, and others serving those in and around town.

After gas was found in the area in the late 1880s, free gas was offered to encourage industries to come to Albany. The town expanded rapidly with the development of an industrial area east of town. But the gas began to run out in the early 1900s, and some of those companies fell by the wayside.

In the 1890s, a fire destroyed the Speiker Block and threatened other downtown buildings. The town then organized a firefighting operation, and businesses rebuilt.

As the state road system developed, Albany found itself near the intersection of State Road 67 and State Road 28. Local businesses benefited from the passage of State Road 28 through the downtown. As business patterns changed, so did Albany and other Delaware County towns. Both Delaware Township to the south and Niles Township to the north are good agricultural lands, and Albany has continued to be a trading center for the northeast corner of Delaware County.

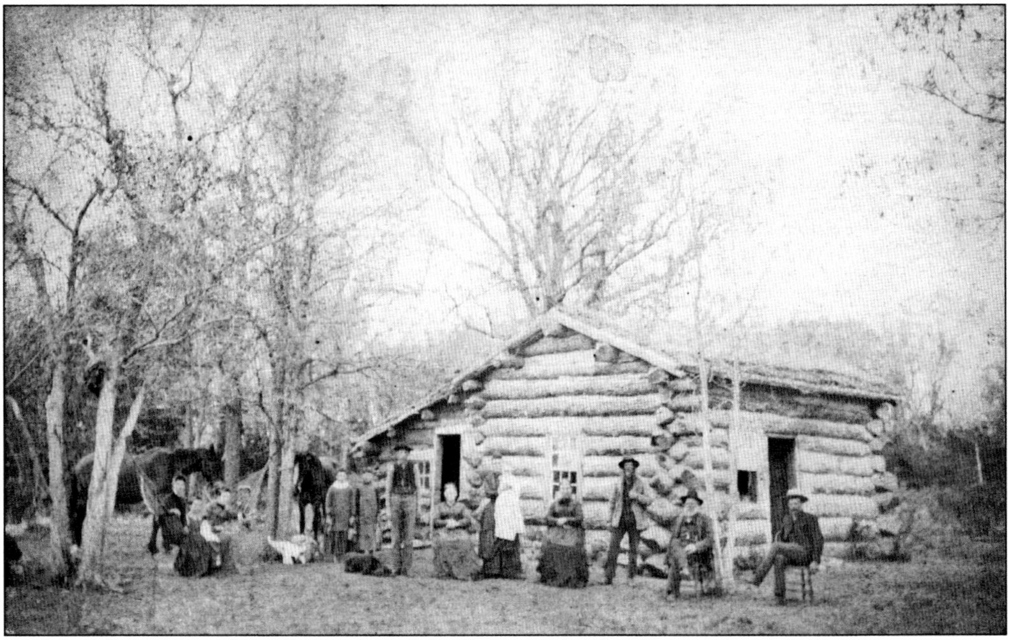

In 1834, Reuben Strong settled his family near Albany on land entered in his name. Strong died about 18 months later, and the homestead was occupied by his son Alfred B. Strong. John W. Strong, another son, settled on land south of the homestead. This early photograph of a family at a log cabin was found in the Strong family's memorabilia. (Michael Mavis.)

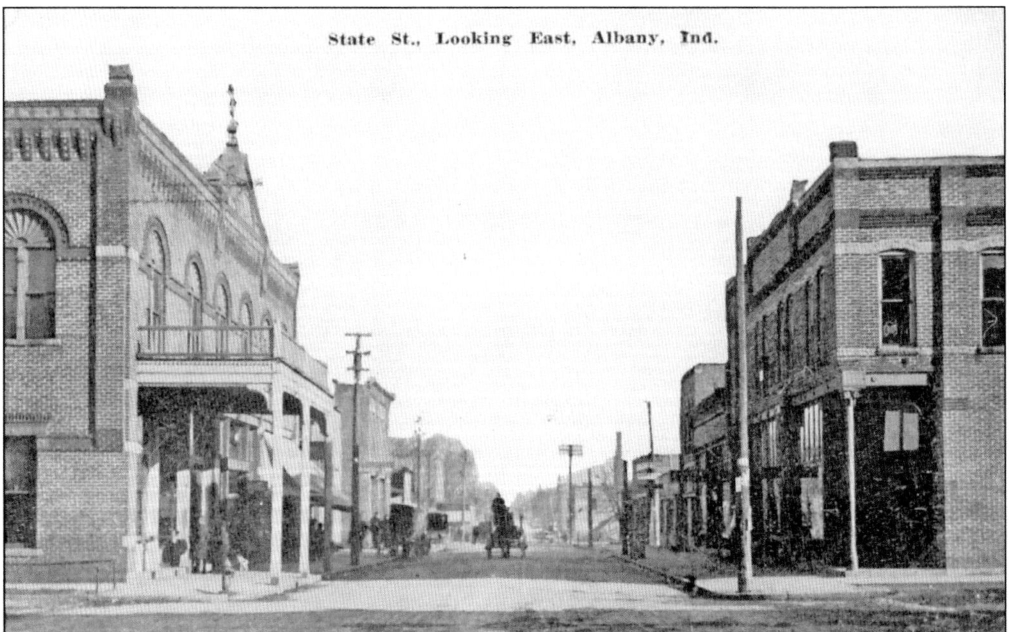

The electrical and telephone poles and wires in this east-facing view of Albany's main thoroughfare, State Street, indicate that the photograph was probably taken around 1900. The Bartlett Hotel is on the left corner, and the Albany State Bank is on the right corner. (Jeffrey Koenker.)

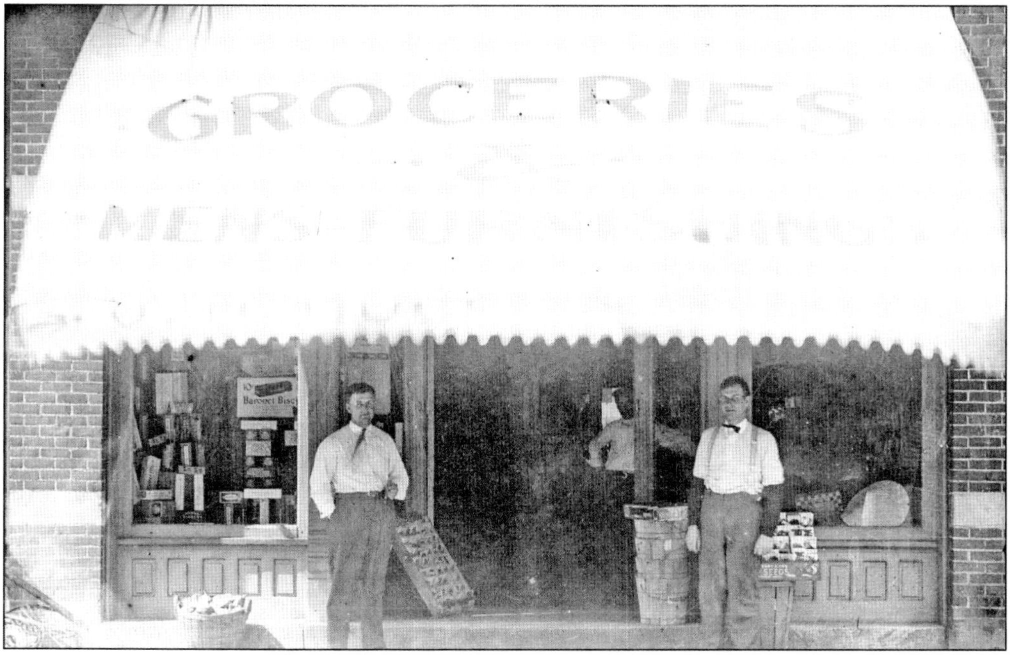

"Groceries & Men's Furnishings" is a combination that may seem a bit unusual from a modern perspective. The business model was successful, though. Groceries were on the right side, and clothing was displayed on the left side of the shop's central door. This 1890s photograph appears to have been taken in the spring, as there are seed packets for sale. (Jeffrey Koenker.)

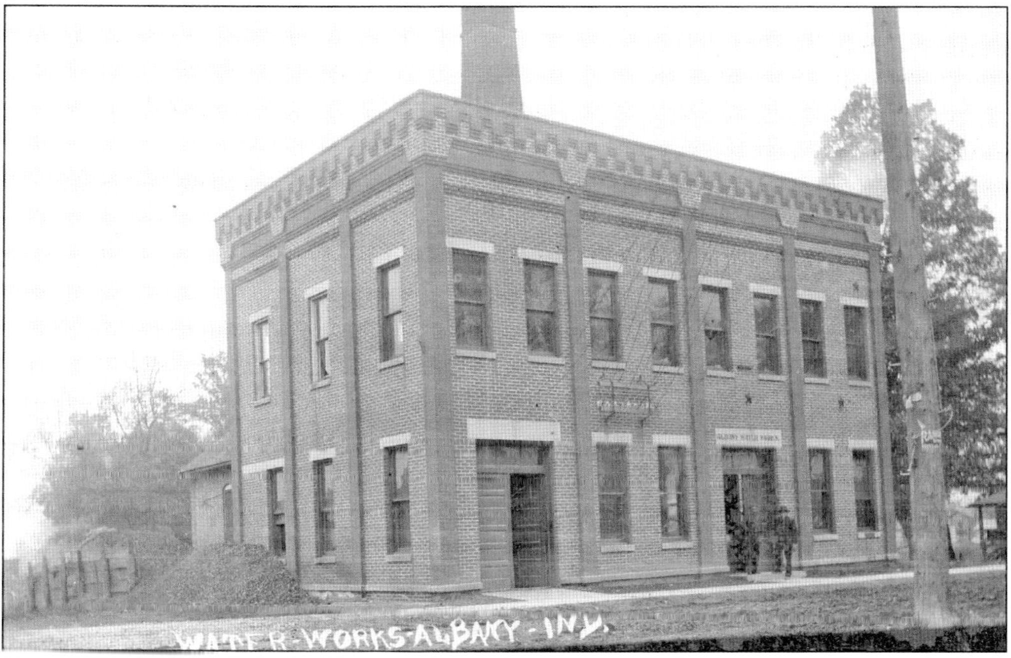

The Albany Water Works Building was located next to the park where the wells were located, and it has continued in use at this location. Water service was first offered in 1899, the same year electrical service was also first offered. The park occupies an area to the south behind the building and is heavily used for various activities. (Michael Mavis.)

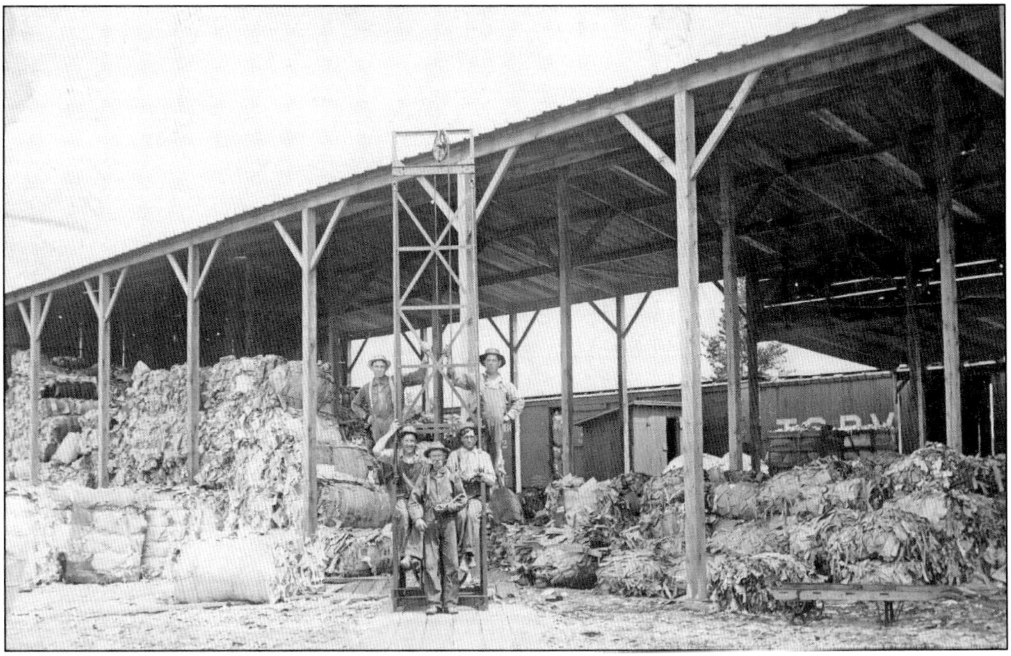

The Albany Paper Company was a strawboard factory that produced paper from straw purchased from local farmers. *Yesteryear Albany* reports, "In 1898, 65 tons of paper a week was being produced for the paper carton industry." These workers appear to be straw packers. (Michael Mavis.)

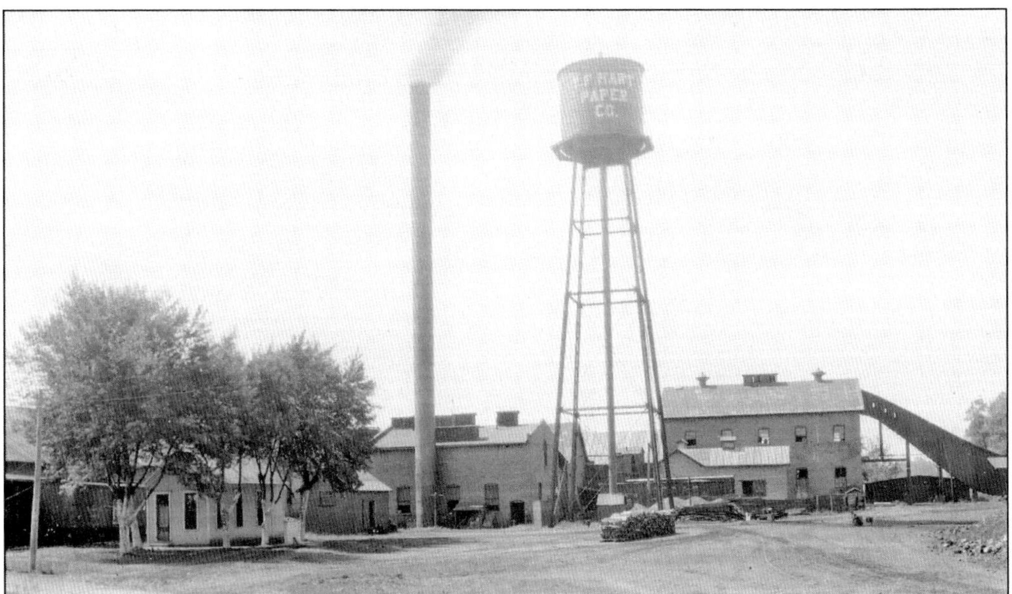

The Albany Paper Mill was taken over by the T.F. Hart Paper Company in 1916. Charles M. Smith was superintendent of the plant for many years. This c. 1920 view of the factory shows their water tower and an expanded set of buildings, as the plant prospered during this era. (Jeffrey Koenker.)

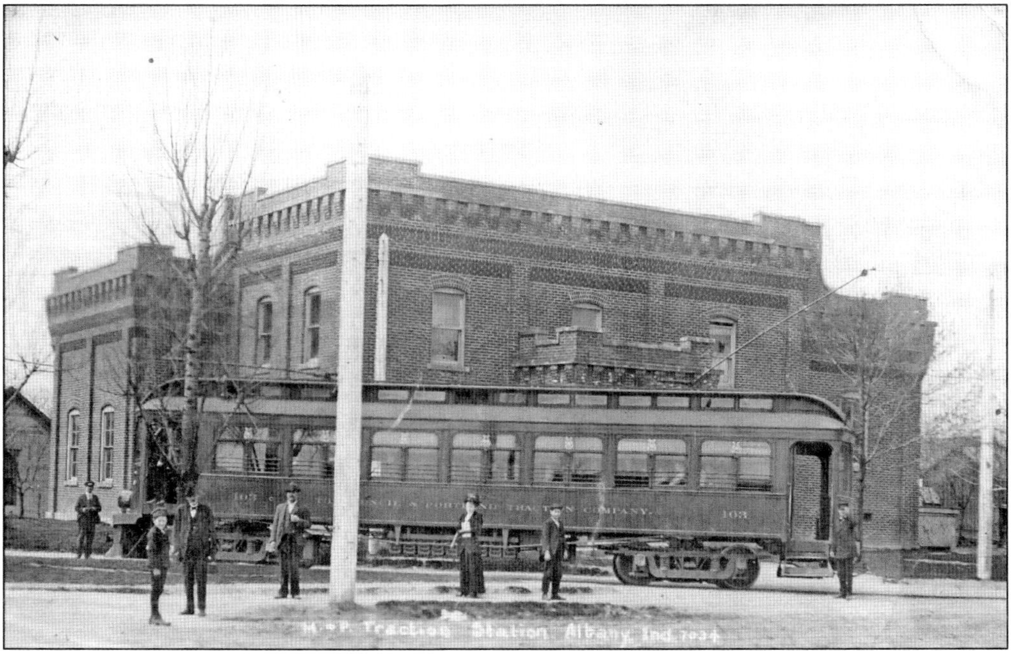

The side of the car reads "Muncie & Portland Traction Company" as it sits in front of the company traction terminal built in 1906. That company was purchased by the Union Traction Company and then sold to the Indiana Railway in early 1930. Unfortunately it then went out of service in September 1930. (Jeffrey Koenker.)

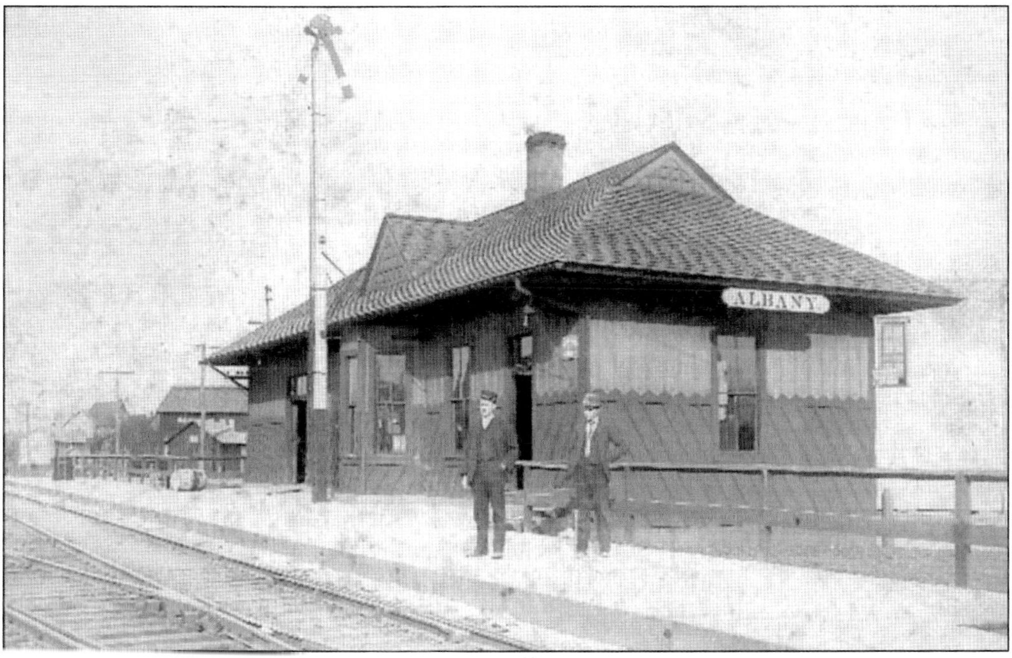

The gas boom in the 1890s and the subsequent offering of free gas brought a new industrial area to the east side of town. In 1894, the railroad moved its station to the industrial east side. There were many retail and customer protests in the downtown area, resulting in this Lake Erie & Western Railroad depot on the west side of town in 1903. (Jeffrey Koenker.)

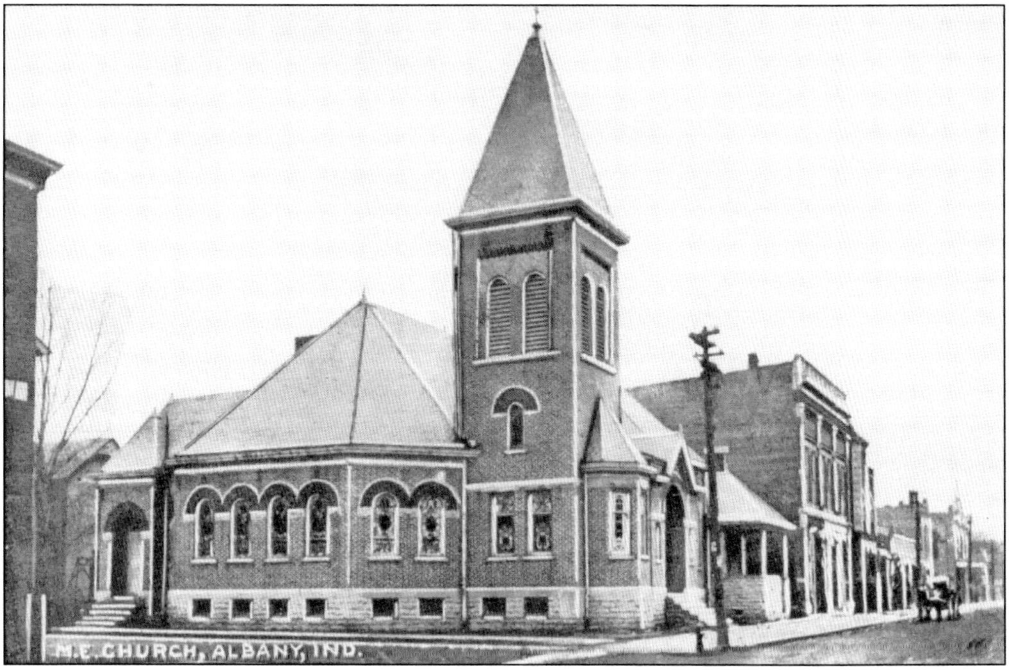

Albany Methodist Episcopal Church was first organized in 1835 at the house of Jacob Pendroy. It was moved to a log house built by John W. Strong, then later relocated to a frame structure in town. A brick church was constructed at the present site in 1876. That building was replaced in 1898 by the present church. (Jeffrey Koenker.)

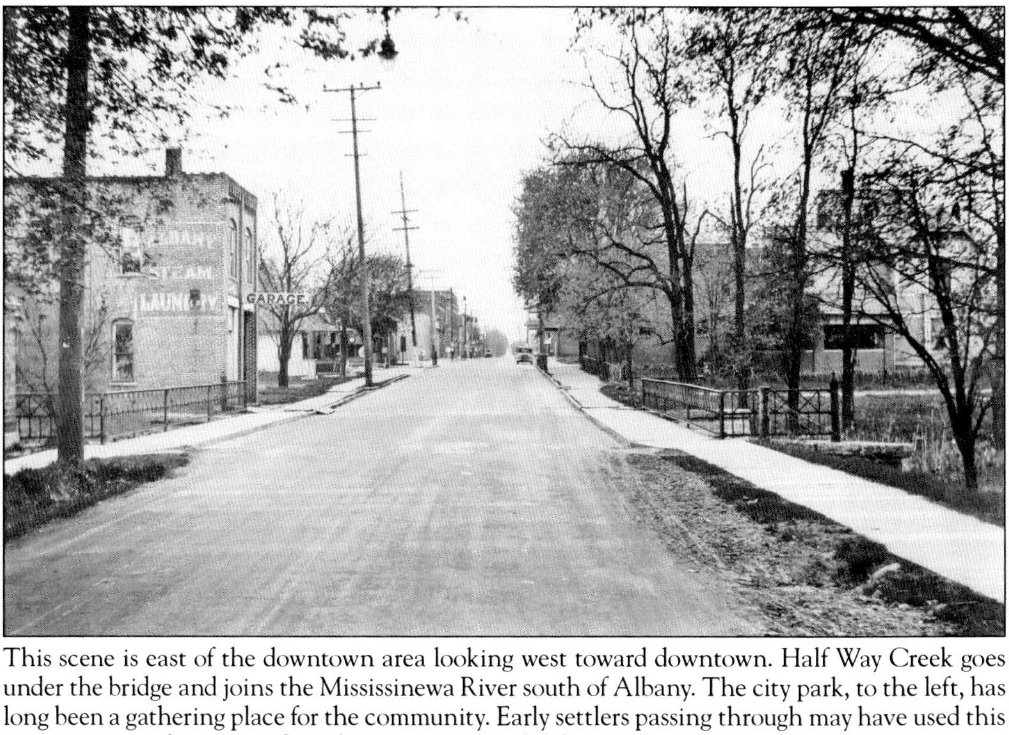

This scene is east of the downtown area looking west toward downtown. Half Way Creek goes under the bridge and joins the Mississinewa River south of Albany. The city park, to the left, has long been a gathering place for the community. Early settlers passing through may have used this area to rest on the way to their destinations. (Michael Mavis.)

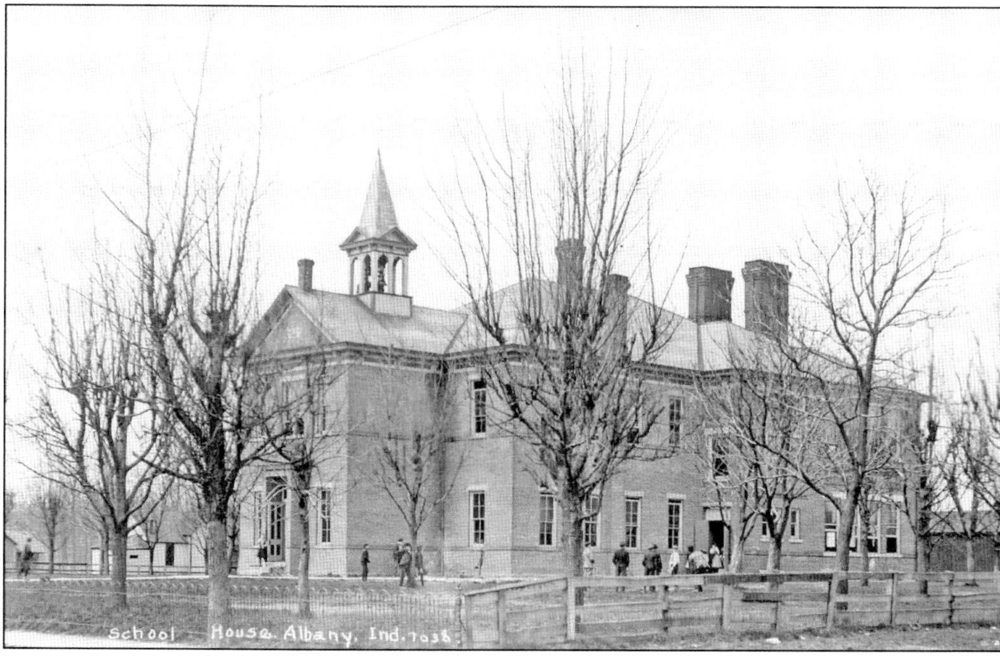

Part of this school building was constructed in 1889. An addition was built after the gas boom brought more families to Albany. The school was demolished and replaced in 1914–1915. During construction of the new school, classes were relocated to various buildings around town, including a garage. (Jeffrey Koenker.)

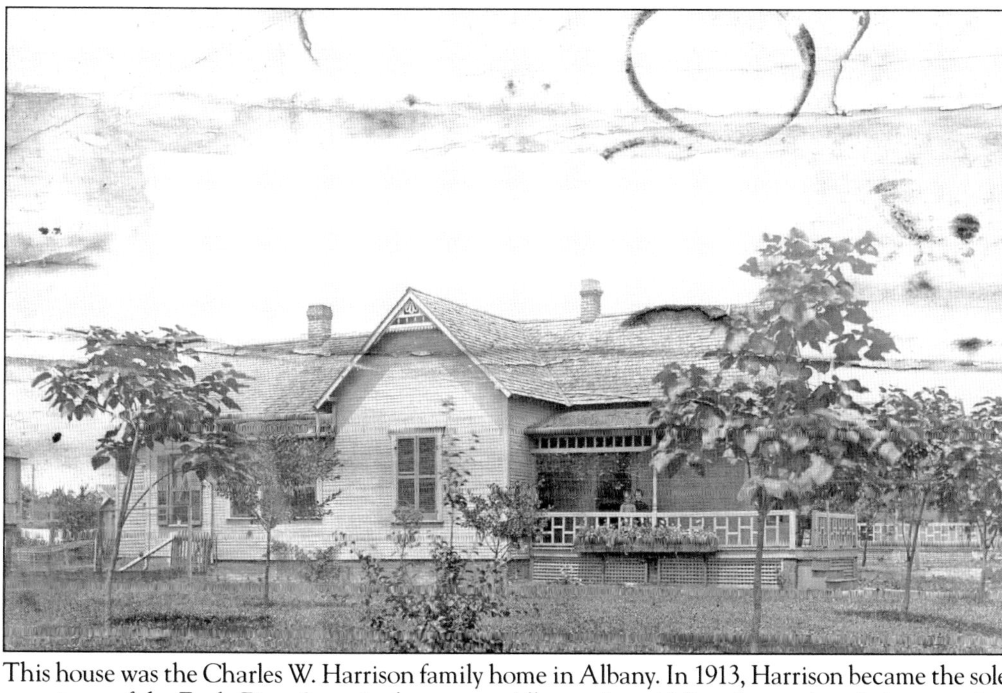

This house was the Charles W. Harrison family home in Albany. In 1913, Harrison became the sole proprietor of the Eagle Drug Store in downtown Albany. As a sideline, he produced photographic postcards of many local sites and had them for sale in his drugstore. (Michael Mavis.)

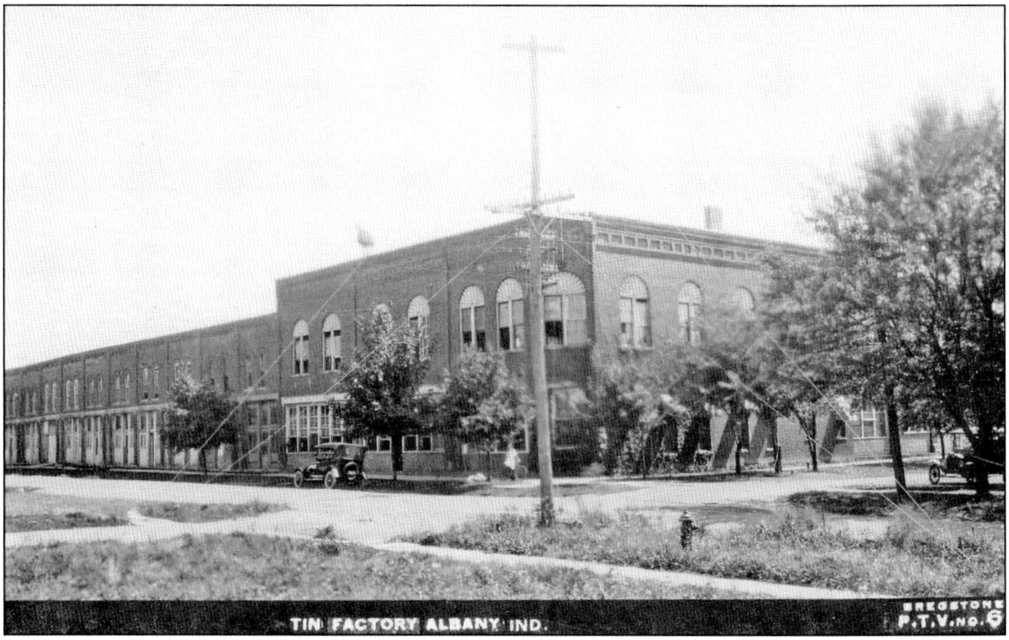

The former bank building on the corner was purchased by McCormick Brothers in 1910. The rest of the building was purchased later, and tin accessories for kitchen cabinets were manufactured here. McCormick Brothers first came to Albany in 1907 and opened a hardware store in a downtown building, which they sold in 1912. (Jeffrey Koenker.)

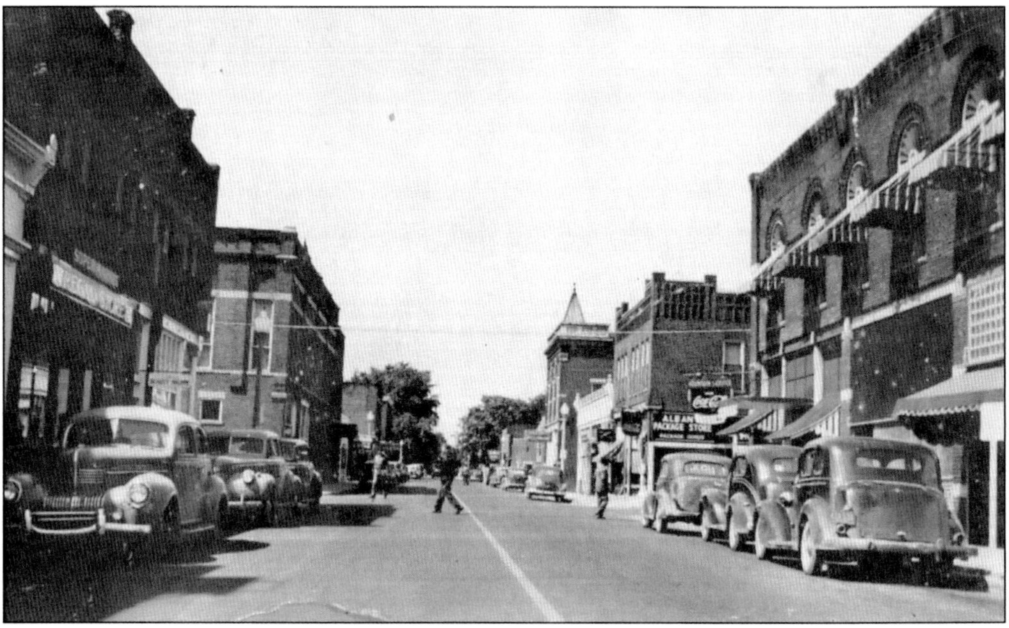

State Road 28 has been routed through downtown Albany from its establishment to the present day. The spire of the Albany Methodist Episcopal Church is visible at center right. The former Bartlett Hotel is on the right, and on the left are the Regal Store and the Beauty Shoppe. (Michael Mavis.)

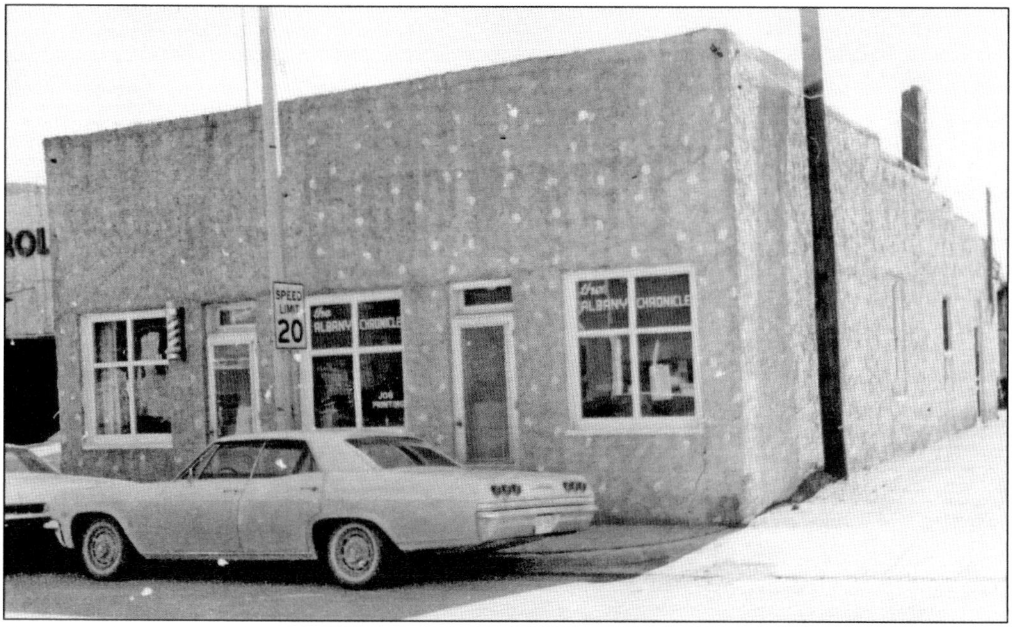

This nondescript building was for many years the home of the *Albany Chronicle*, later known simply as the *Chronicle*. Although not the first newspaper published in Albany, it ran the longest, from about 1902 to 1972. It then merged with the *Journal* of Yorktown under the name *Delaware County Suburban*, which ceased publication in 1974. (Jeffrey Koenker.)

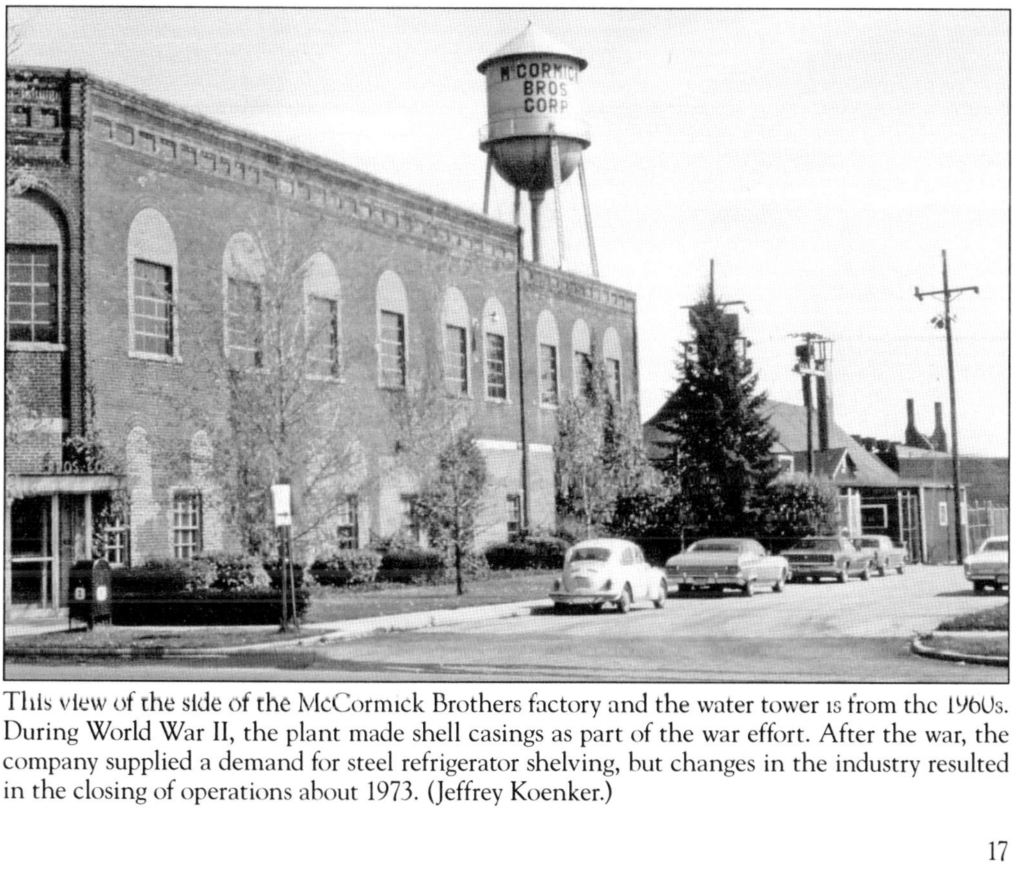

This view of the side of the McCormick Brothers factory and the water tower is from the 1960s. During World War II, the plant made shell casings as part of the war effort. After the war, the company supplied a demand for steel refrigerator shelving, but changes in the industry resulted in the closing of operations about 1973. (Jeffrey Koenker.)

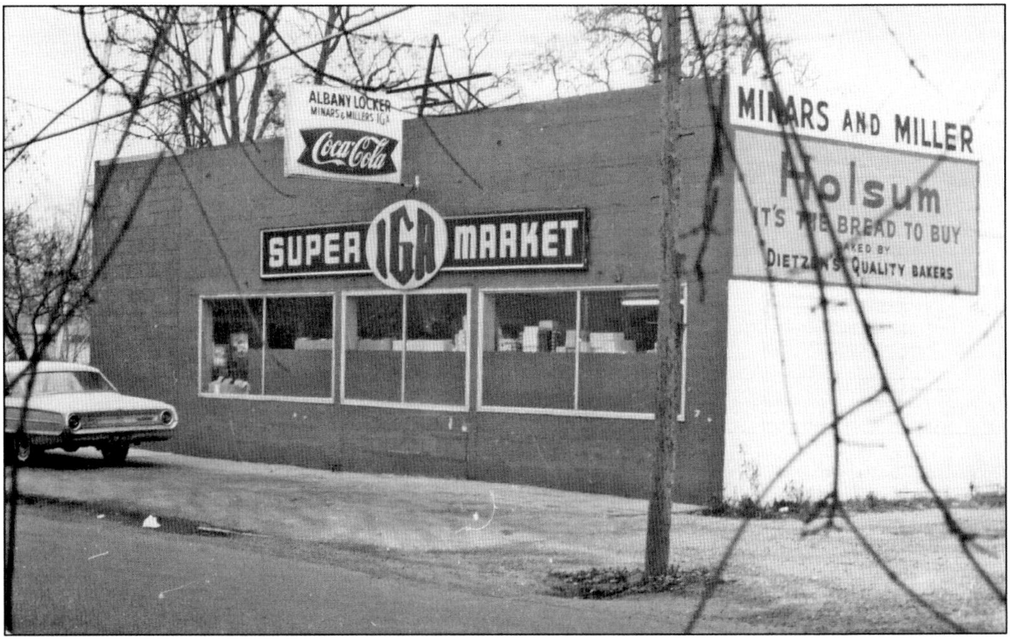

The Albany Locker store offered a popular service in the 1950s. Before home freezers, locker stores provided a way to freeze and store vegetables, fruits, and especially meats in an affordable and convenient way. An animal could be butchered, cut, and packaged in appropriate sizes and stored in a locker to provide a family with meat over several months. Minar's Grocery continues service to customers in 2012. (Jeffrey Koenker.)

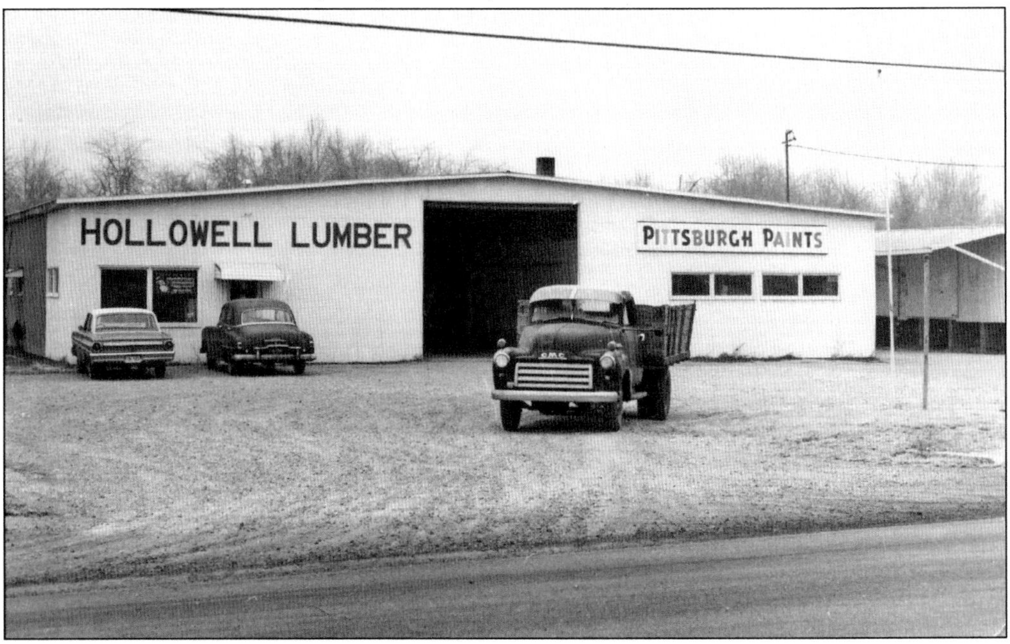

This building on the highway at the west edge of Albany was constructed after a structure on another site was destroyed by fire in 1959. Rev. Otto Hollowell and his sons began the operation in 1936 on North Broadway. Business patterns changed in the 1970s and 1980s, and this lumberyard was closed in 1985. (Jeffrey Koenker.)

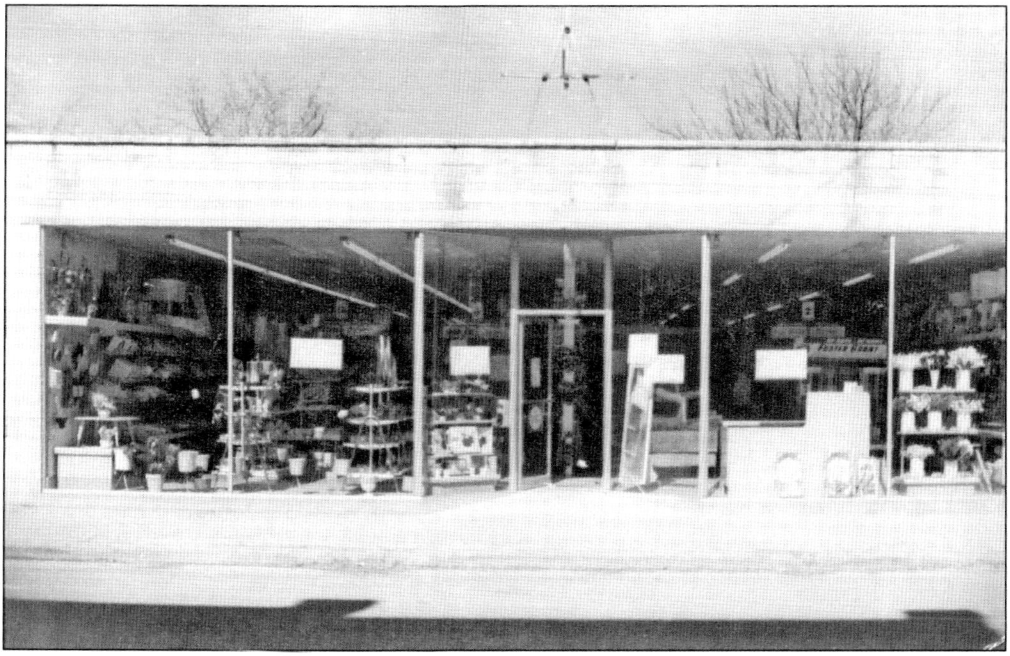

Although it was renamed the Albany Dime Store, this store was known as McCord's 5 & 10 for many years. Through passing generations, it has remained a reminder of the old-fashioned dime store, with its wooden floors, bulk candy, craft and sewing supplies, hardware, and miscellaneous collection of items to meet household needs. (Michael Mavis.)

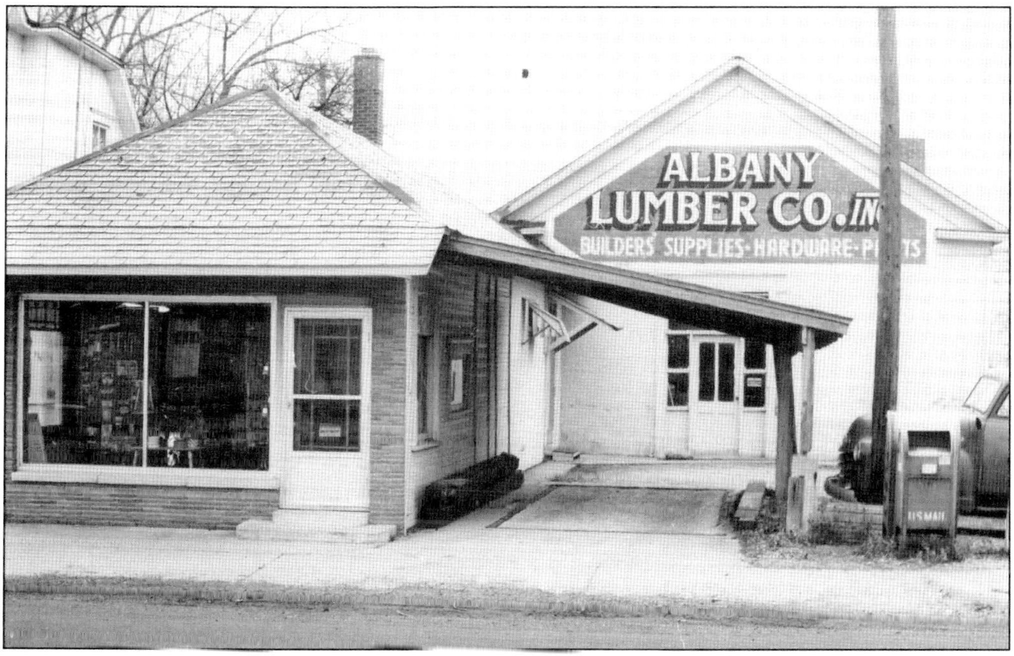

Part of this building started as a German Reform church. The lumber company was operated by L.N. Way for about 35 years before he retired in 1945. It was operated by William Barley for several years, then by Ralph Craw. The office area later was turned into the Flower Box Shop, operated by Donna Mavis. The building has been demolished. (Michael Mavis.)

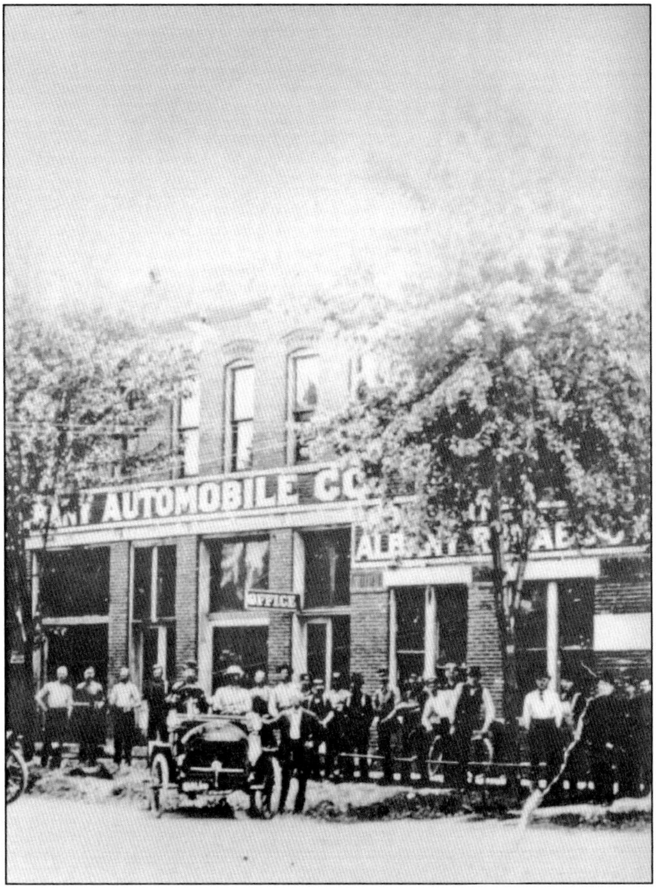

The Albany Automobile Company was established by John L. Tulley in the early 1900s after various experiments with automobile components. The factory's 44 employees built some 1,400 cars priced between $600 and $750. Tulley also served as engineer for water and light plants in Indiana and Illinois. (Minnetrista Heritage Collection, Muncie, Indiana.)

This steel bridge crossed over the Mississinewa as part of the Albany-Desoto Pike. The interurban bridge is in the background. The area to the southwest of Albany, where the Mississinewa River winds through wooded areas, is particularly scenic in the fall. (Michael Mavis.)

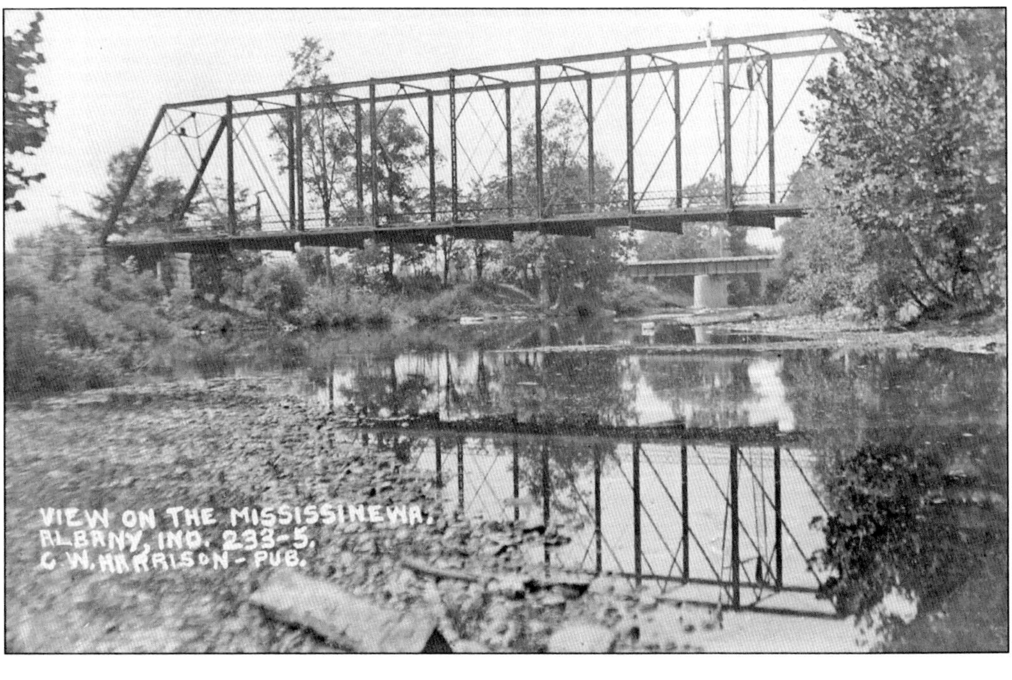

Two

Daleville

Daleville was platted in 1838 by Revolutionary War veteran Campbell Dale. Its position on the roads from Muncie to Indianapolis was an advantage, as was its location on the railroad that was built from Indianapolis to Bellefontaine, Ohio, in the early 1850s. A canal was planned and some construction took place before these plans failed, along with other canal plans in the state, as the developing railroads became the leading mode of transportation.

Gas was discovered here in 1888, and a glass factory soon appeared along with other industries. Some survived after the gas supply failed, and some did not. A stove foundry, a lumberyard, a tile factory, a brick factory, and a canning factory were among the Daleville industries. The cannery continued longer than most and burned in 1977.

Historic buildings are scattered across the town. The Daleville Christian Church, a brick structure built about 1900, continues to serve the community. The original downtown area still has buildings from 100 years ago, although it is no longer a shopping area. The town's old dirt streets eventually were paved over. The traction line was as important to Daleville as to the other communities around. It allowed people to visit relatives, shop, or find entertainment in other towns in east central Indiana or in Indianapolis.

Many people in the county remember the Top Hat Restaurant on State Road 32, a favorite place to eat; it burned down in 1974. State Road 32 is the major street in the old downtown. State Road 67 on the south edge of town is also a well-traveled highway.

Interstate 69 was built at the west edge of Daleville in the 1960s, and the area has seen many changes. A trucking company established near the highway was very successful. Although a nearby retail mall failed, it was successfully converted to the Heartland Business Center. These companies and businesses, along with various amenities for travelers, have made this a thriving growth area.

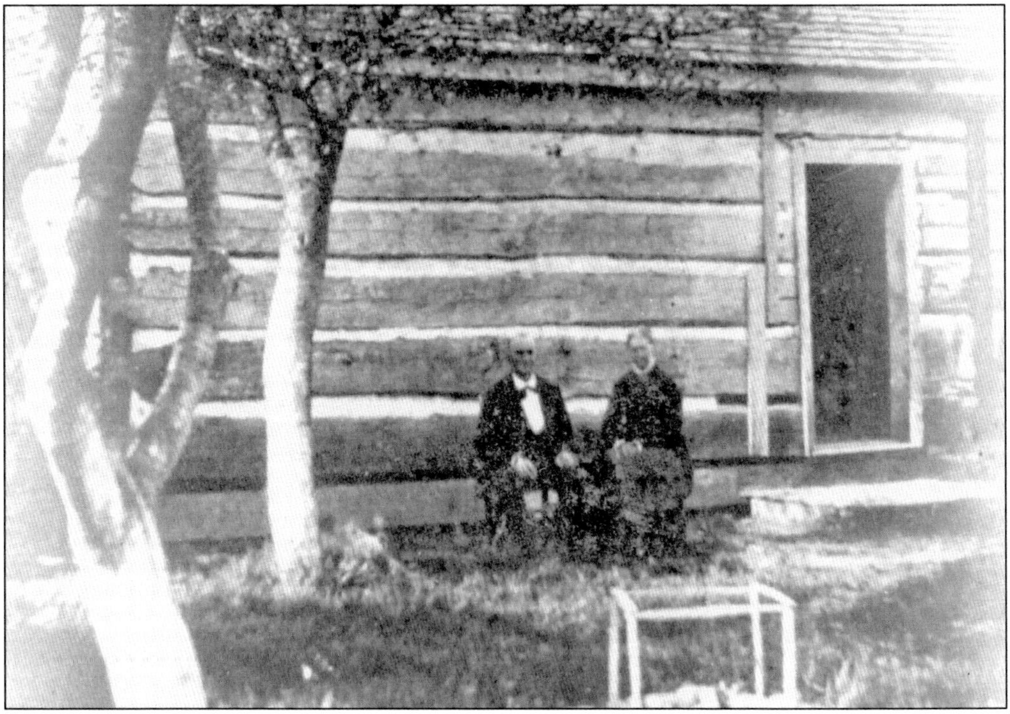

This unidentified couple settled near Daleville in their log cabin, possibly as early as the 1830s. The cabin appears to be quite sturdy, with its squared-off logs. The old pioneers frequently revisited their former cabin homes after they had moved into a better constructed frame house. Such old memories revisited served to remind them of the comforts of a settled community. (Rev. Gary McManus.)

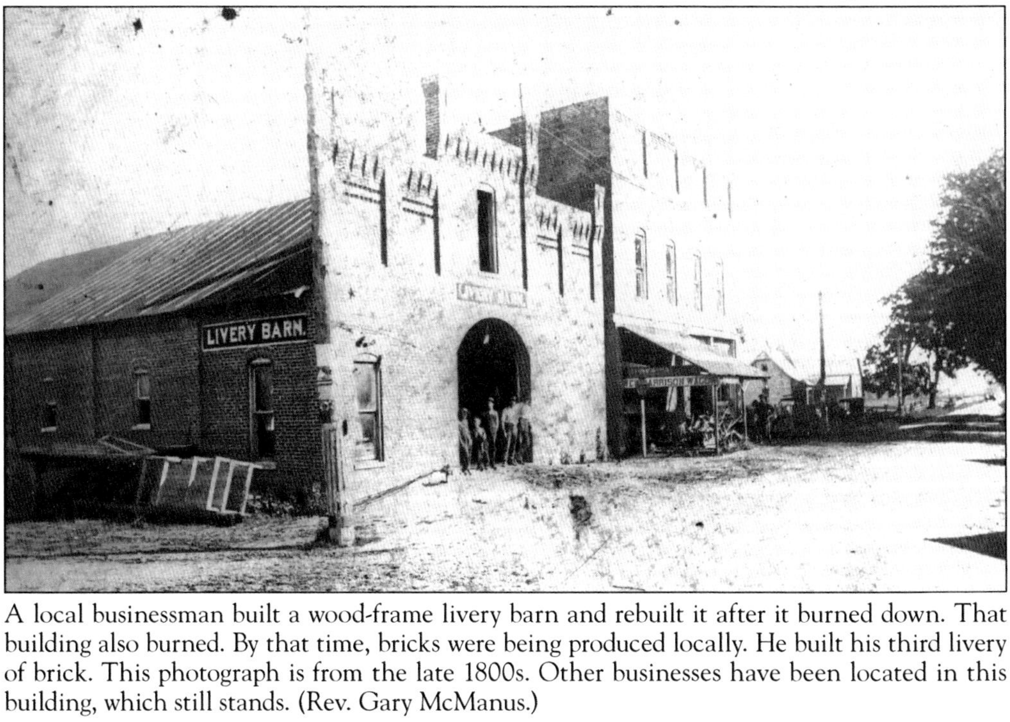

A local businessman built a wood-frame livery barn and rebuilt it after it burned down. That building also burned. By that time, bricks were being produced locally. He built his third livery of brick. This photograph is from the late 1800s. Other businesses have been located in this building, which still stands. (Rev. Gary McManus.)

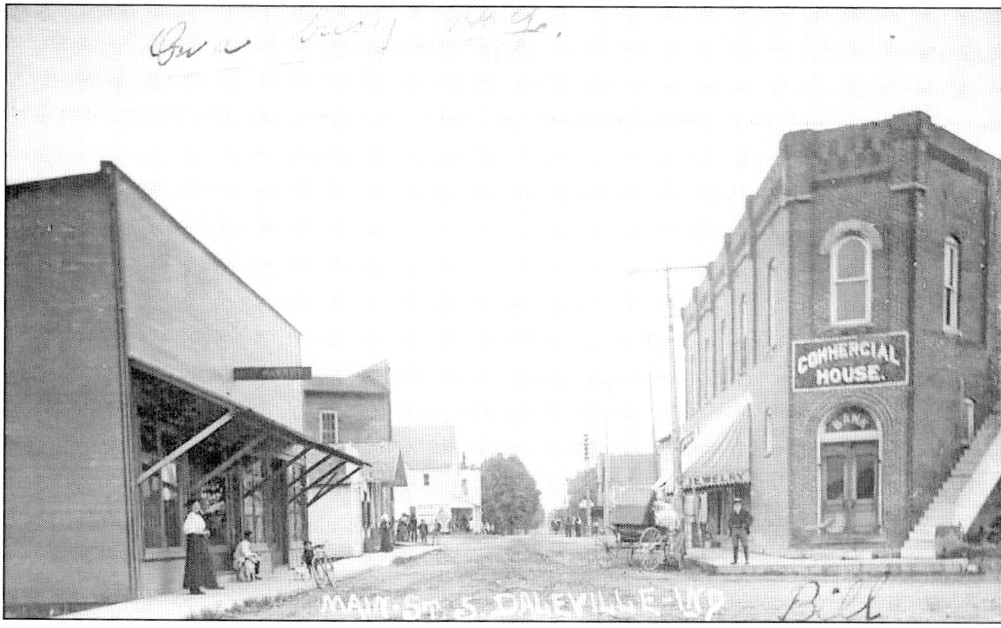

This view of Main Street looking south shows the distinctive corner building on the right that still stands today. At the time of this photograph, it was a hotel called the Commercial House. At left center is the old Opera House on the far side of the railroad tracks. The postcard sender, "Bill," also wrote the note: "On a busy day." (Jeffrey Koenker.)

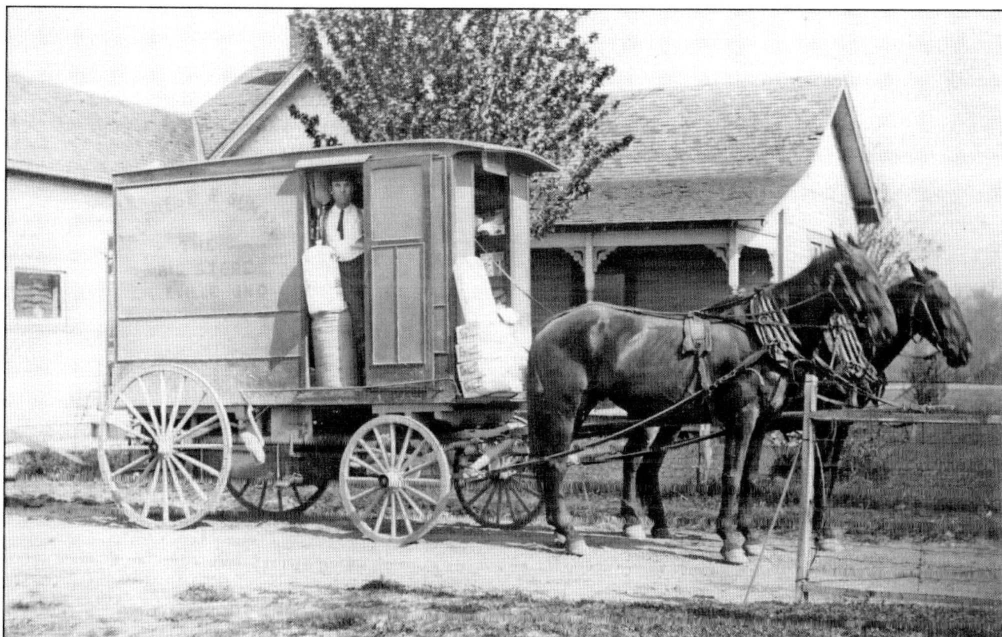

This Forrest & Suman delivery wagon would have represented a great convenience to the rural customers at whose doors the wagon stopped. In a time when travel was difficult, housewives greatly appreciated the chance to greet the wagon driver and examine his goods. (Minnetrista Heritage Collection, Muncie, Indiana.)

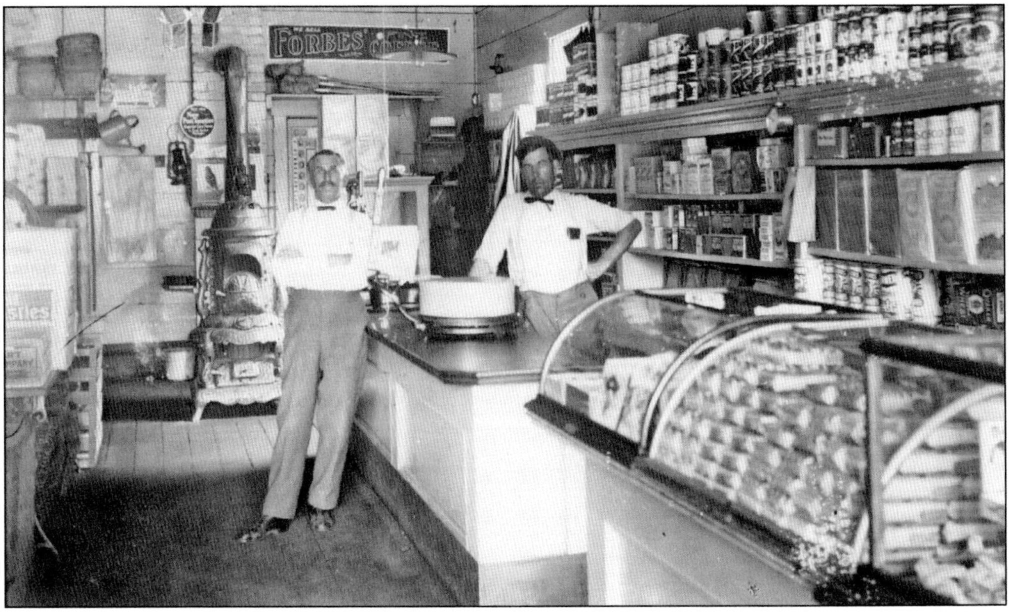

This photograph of the Daleville grocery, owned by Frank Daniels, shows the owner, at left, in front of the stove. Behind the counter is the clerk, Will Chandler. On the far left is a carton of Post Toasties. The round sign to the left of the stovepipe says, "Try the New Post Toasties." (Minnetrista Heritage Collection, Muncie, Indiana.)

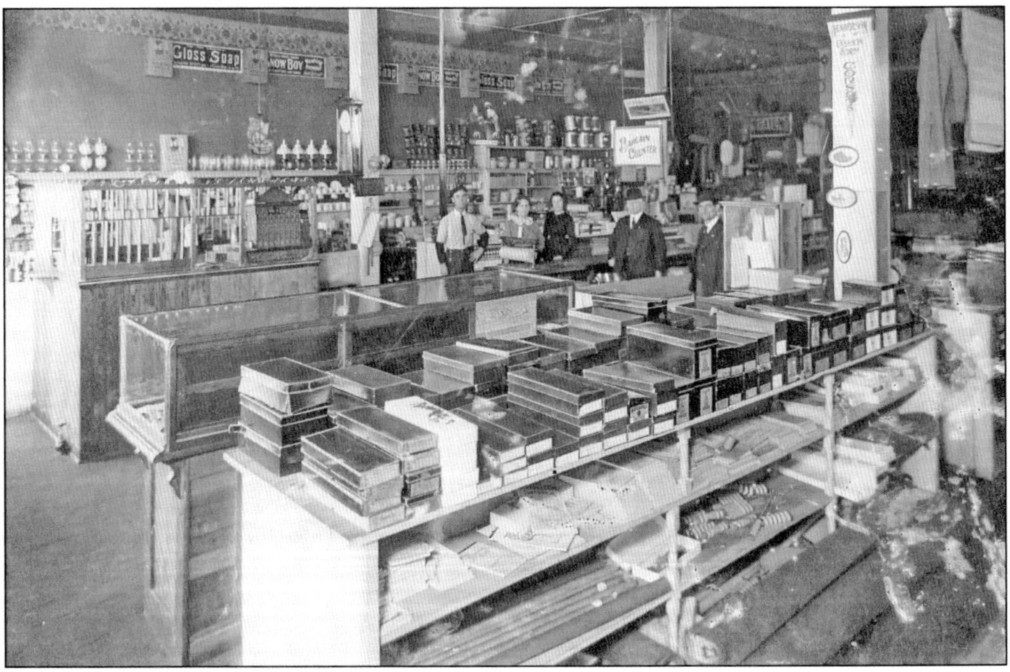

In the 1890s, George Suman had a large store with groceries, dry goods, and notions. This view of the store shows some of the merchandise, from lamps on the left back wall to the "Bargain Counter" at the right rear. Gloss soap and Snow Boy Washing Powder are advertised, along with Henderson Fashion Form Corsets. A hotel was located on the second floor of this building. (Larry Campbell.)

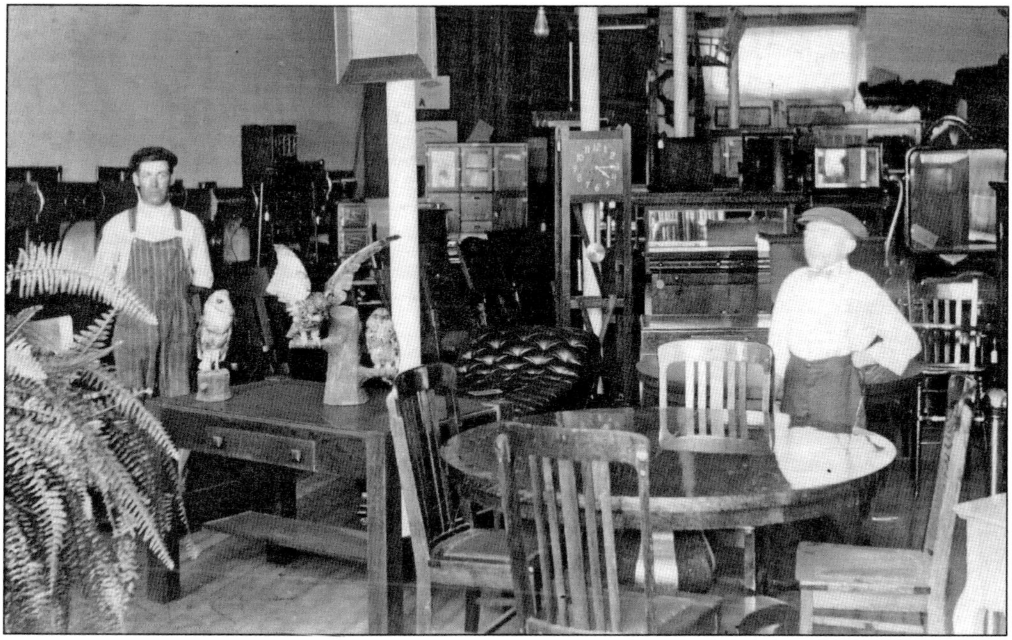

The combination of undertaker and furniture store was quite common in the 1880s through the first decade or so of the 1900s. Initially, wooden caskets and clothing for burials were supplied, with making furniture and/or selling furniture being the primary business. (Jeffrey Koenker.)

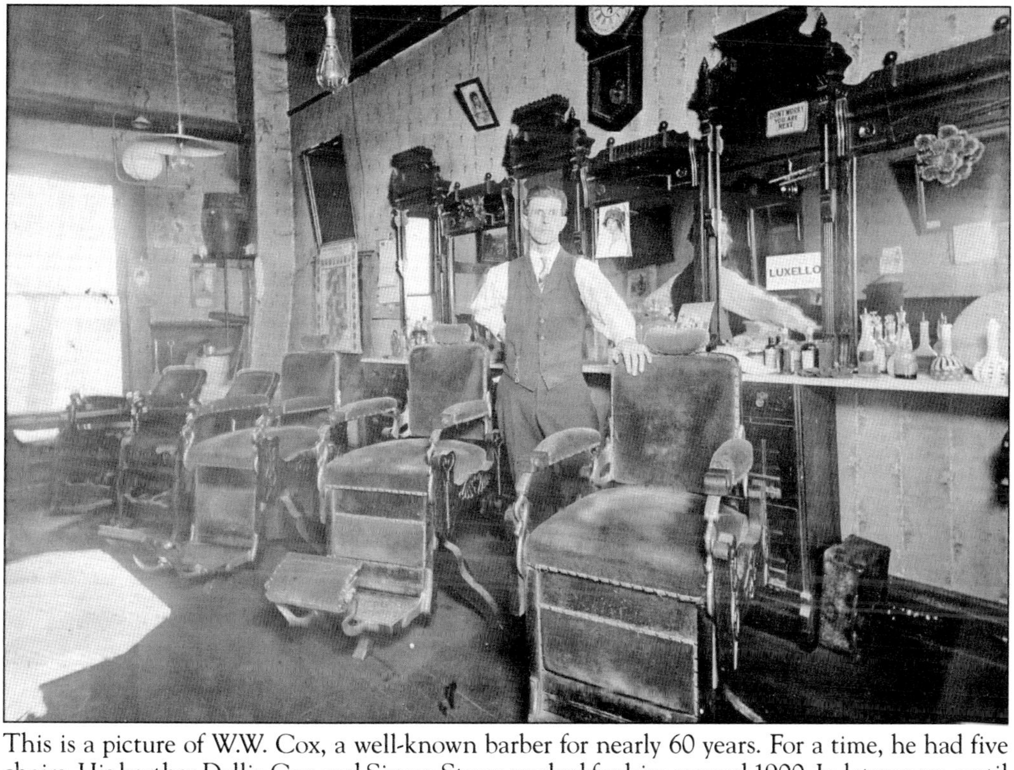

This is a picture of W.W. Cox, a well-known barber for nearly 60 years. For a time, he had five chairs. His brother Dellie Cox and Simon Steers worked for him around 1900. In later years, until his death at the age of 86, he worked alone. (Larry Campbell.)

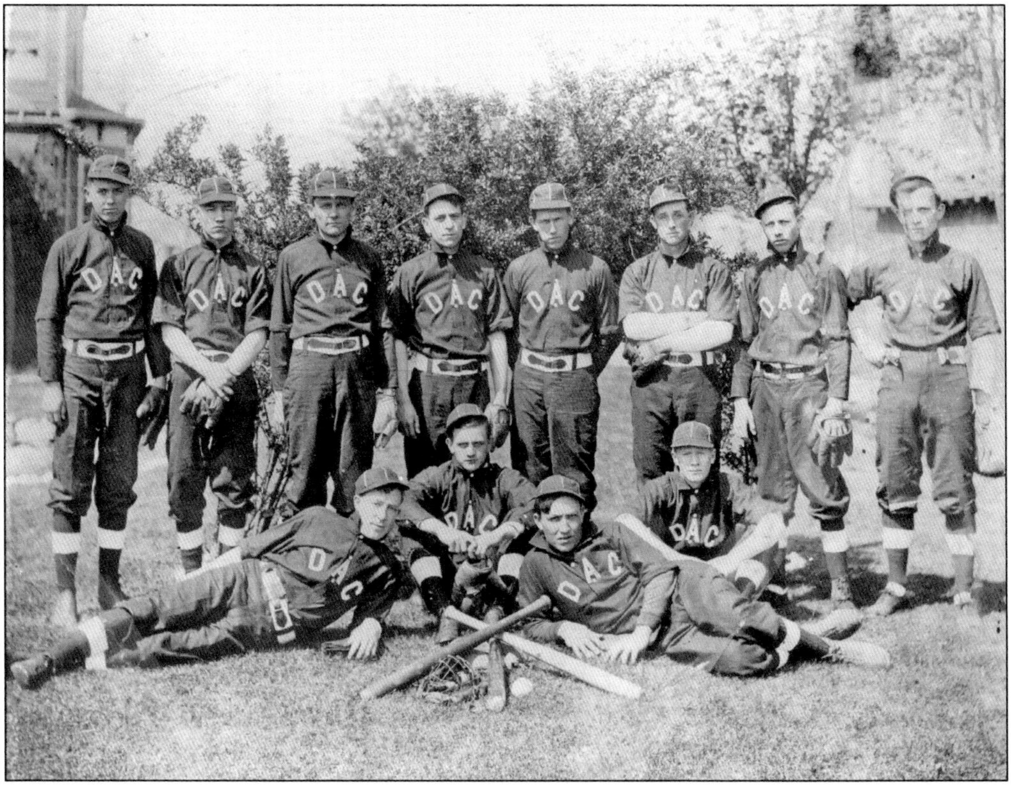

The Daleville Athletic Club baseball team is pictured around 1910. Although individual members are not identified, Berryman Hurley commented, "Our baseball team was hard to beat. In the line-up was a fine pitcher, Perry "Pee Wee" Stewart, [and] Sim Steers [was] the catcher." (Rev. Gary McManus.)

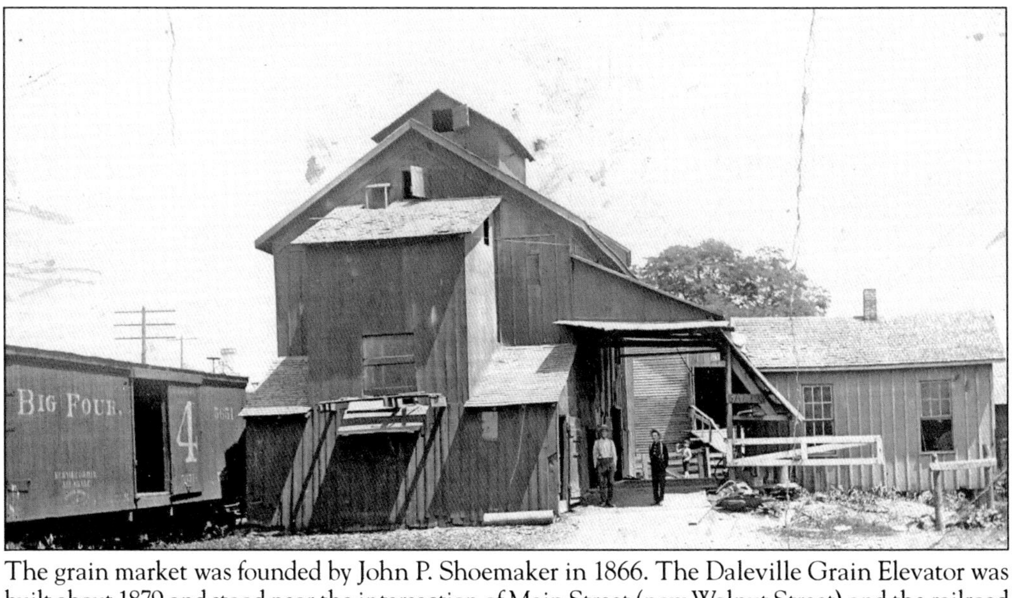

The grain market was founded by John P. Shoemaker in 1866. The Daleville Grain Elevator was built about 1879 and stood near the intersection of Main Street (now Walnut Street) and the railroad line. It is no longer there today but was in place as recently as 1996. (Rev. Gary McManus.)

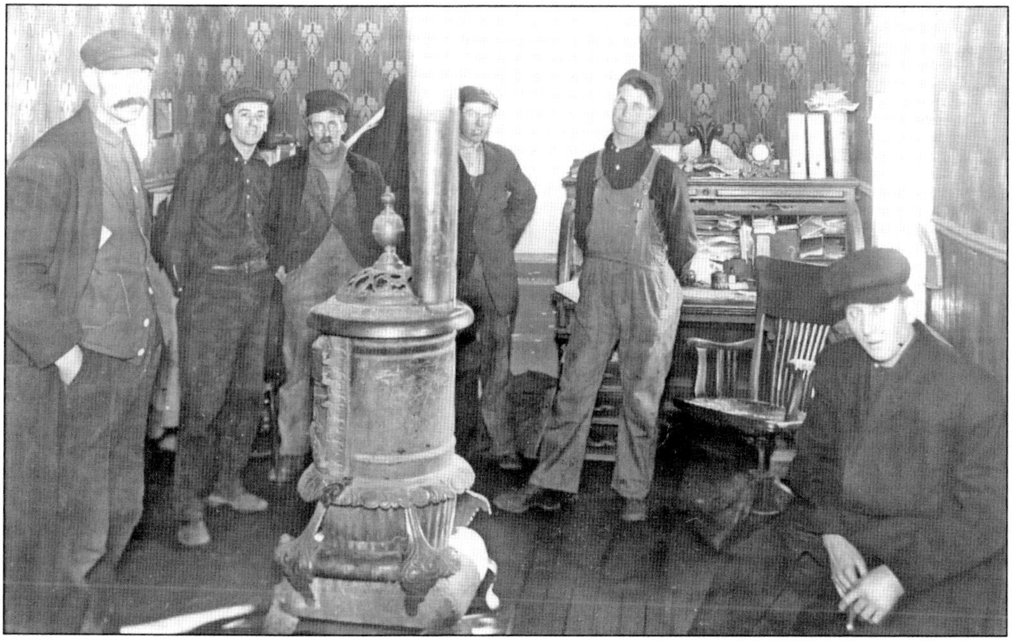

The Daleville Feed Mill interior is shown here about 1915 with, from left to right, Albert McCordle, Todd Feely, ? Hahn, unidentified, Alva Betterton, and unidentified. John Shoemaker was the owner of the elevator in 1914, and Alva Betterton was an employee. (Rev. Gary McManus.)

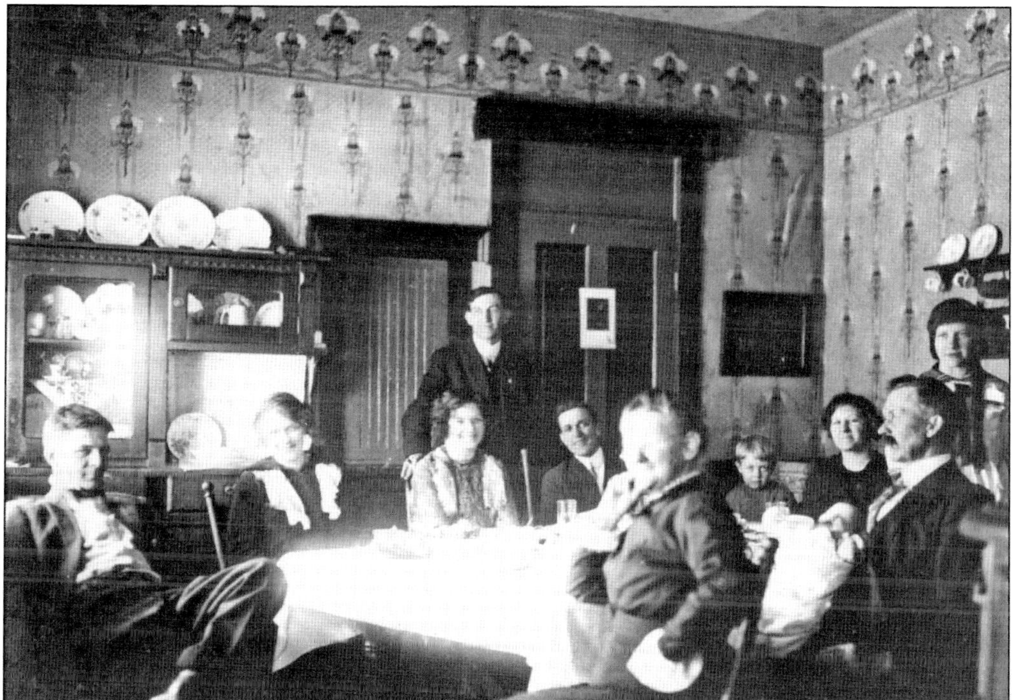

The Fenwick family celebrated Christmas of 1913 with this family gathering. James Fenwick came to Delaware County in 1832 and settled east of Daleville. Members of the family were carpenters and bricklayers and built various houses and barns in the community. (Rev. Gary McManus.)

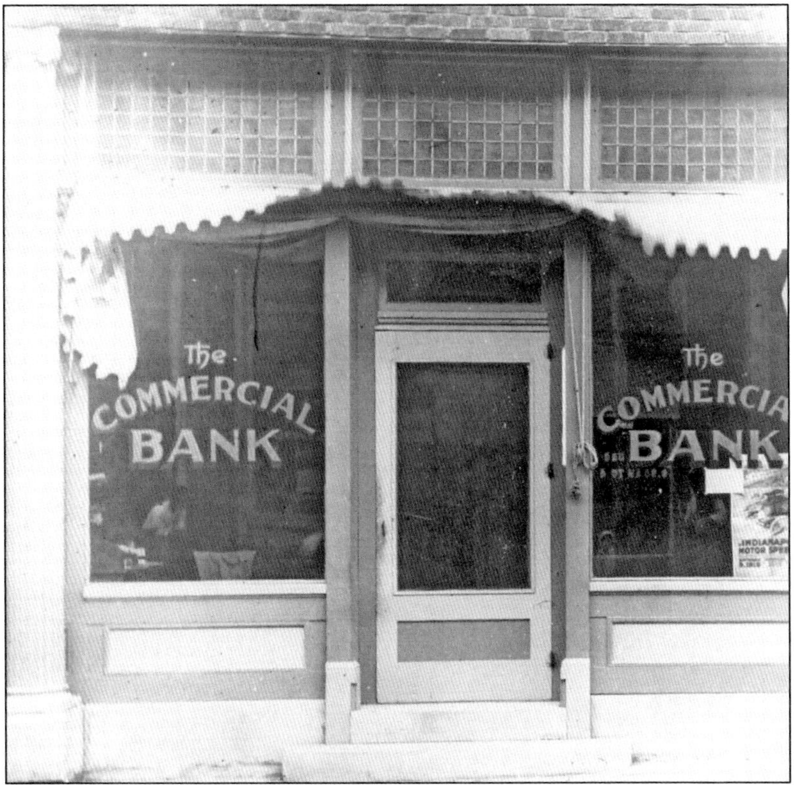

This is the bank that John Dillinger held up on Monday, July 17, 1933. The bank had already been held up once before in 1930. Over the years, the bank was held up four times. It was originally formed by J.N. Barnard in the early 1900s and was probably the first bank in Daleville. The building has been demolished. (Rev. Gary McManus.)

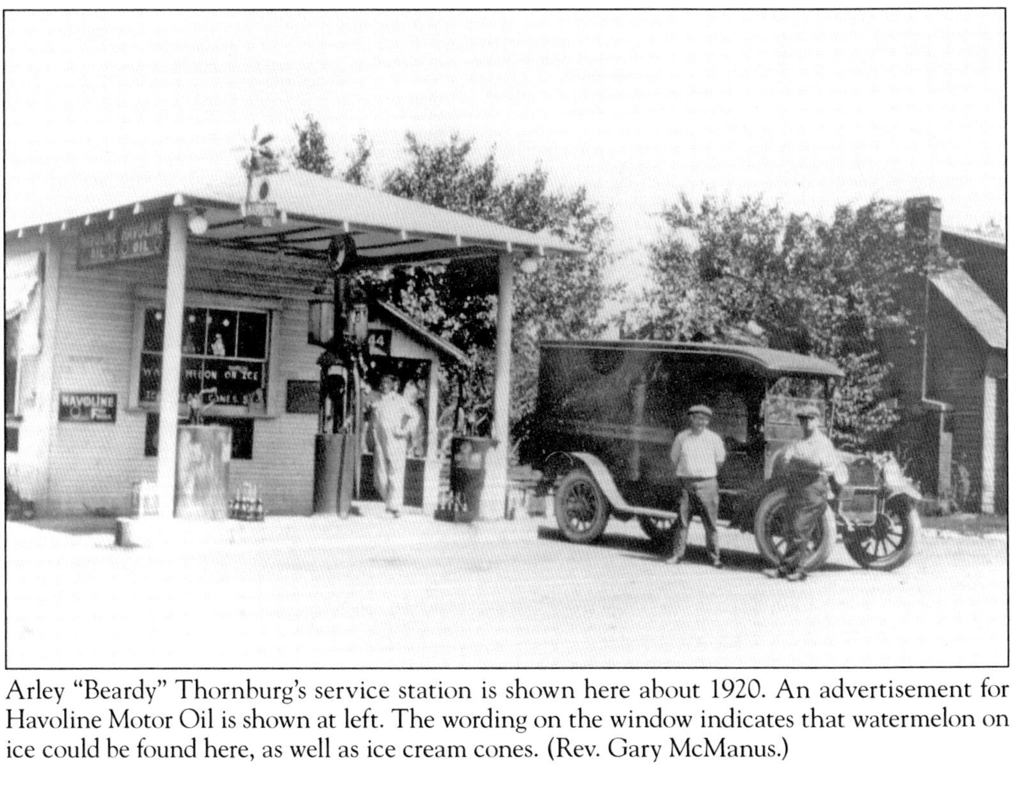

Arley "Beardy" Thornburg's service station is shown here about 1920. An advertisement for Havoline Motor Oil is shown at left. The wording on the window indicates that watermelon on ice could be found here, as well as ice cream cones. (Rev. Gary McManus.)

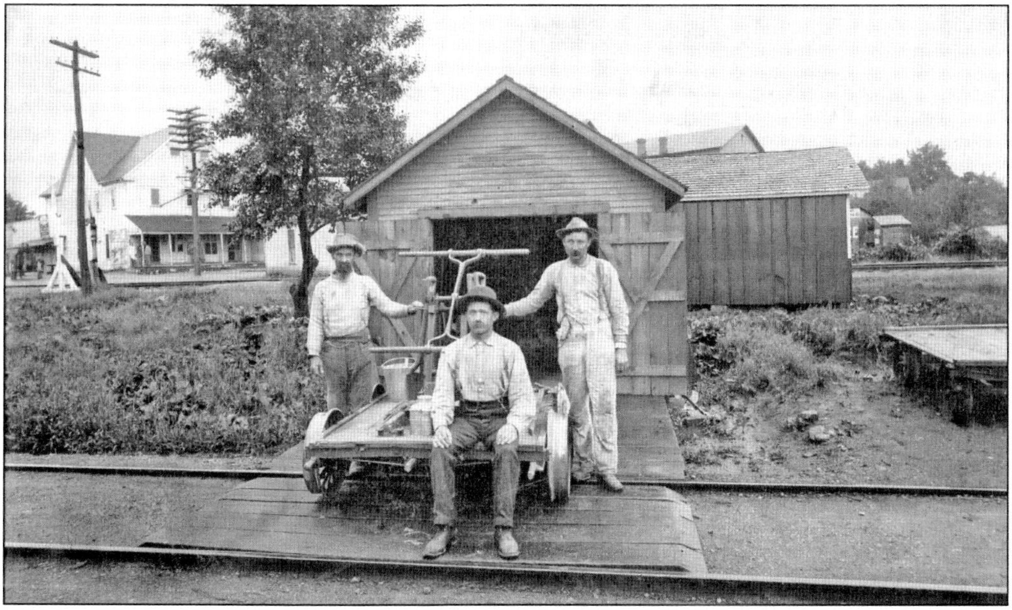

The traction station's handcar is show here with, from left to right, section boss Charles Dooley, ? Essex (sitting), and unidentified. In the background, at left across the railroad tracks, is the old two-story Opera House. Traveling shows gave performances on the second floor at one time. It was also used for dances and roller-skating. (Larry Campbell.)

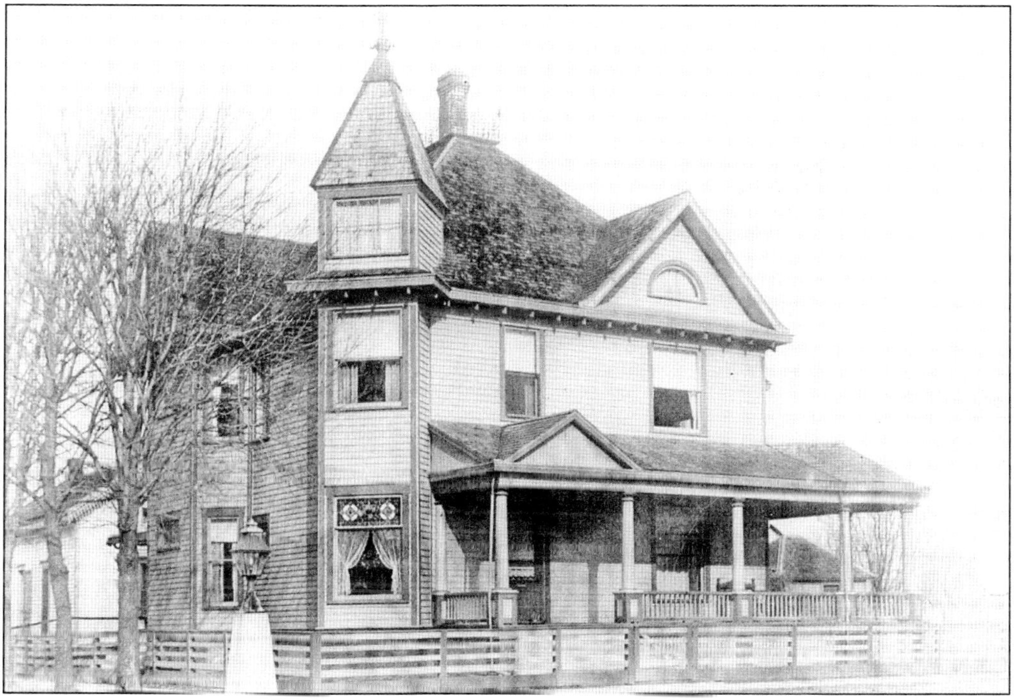

This beautiful Victorian house was once owned and occupied by Frank Daniels and his family. He not only owned a grocery, but had a flour mill at one time in partnership with Joe Overman. The house and its corner stained-glass window still stand in a residential area of Daleville. (Rev. Gary McManus.)

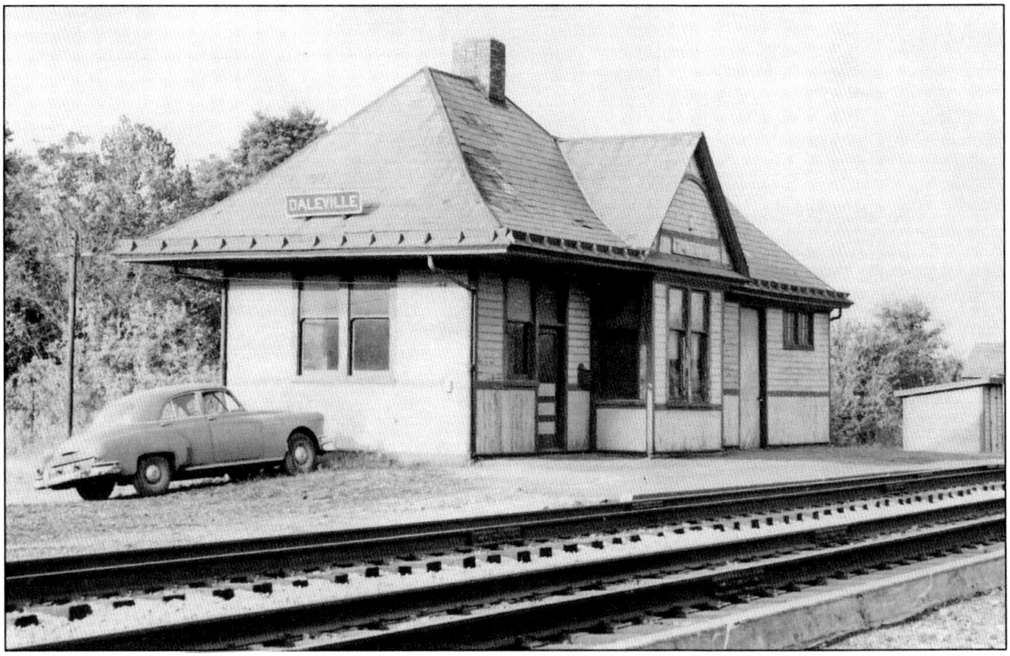

The railroad first came to Daleville in the early 1850s. The Cleveland, Columbus, Cincinnati & Indianapolis Railroad, so named in 1868, was better known as the "Bee Line." Berryman Hurley, in *Daleville Long Ago*, wrote that the old iron rails were replaced with steel rails in 1892, allowing speeds to increase from 20 to 50 miles per hour. (Jeffrey Koenker.)

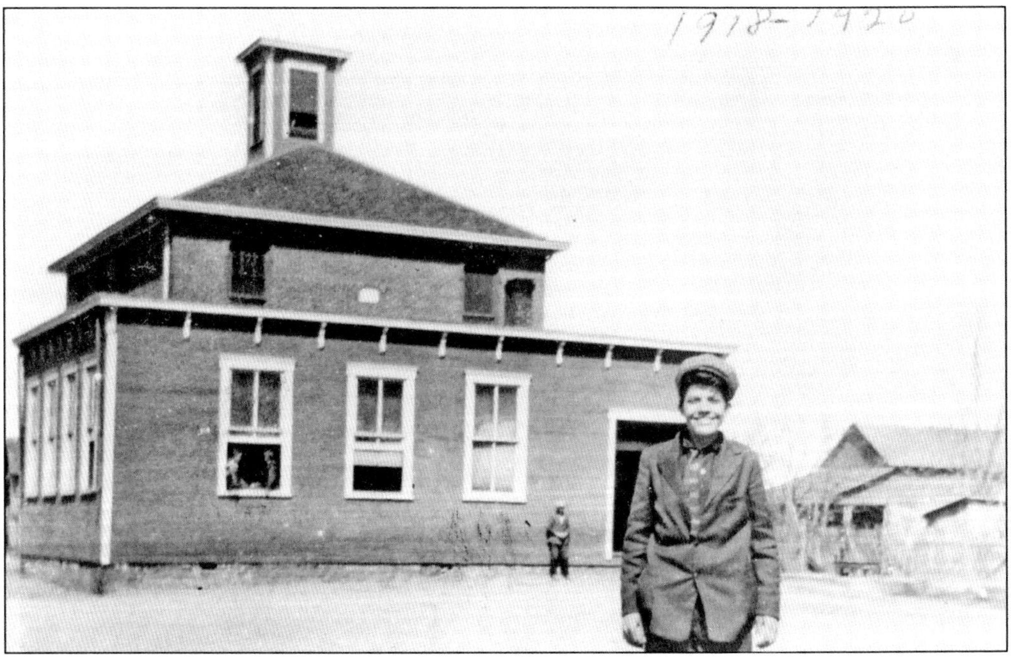

In this c. 1918 image, John Whetstone stands in the school yard at Cross Roads School. The brick building at the rear was probably constructed in the 1880s. Cross Roads had a store as early as 1838 when one was opened by William and Erasmus Moffitt, but after several years the stock was closed out. Cross Roads had a post office from 1879 to 1895. (Rev. Gary McManus.)

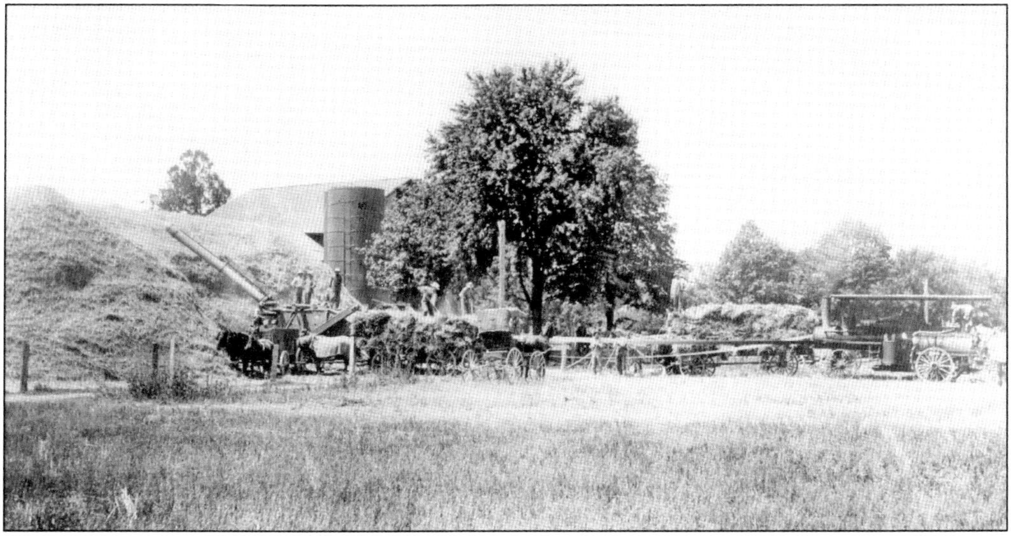

This threshing scene took place on the A.A. Van Matre Farm, about one mile west and three-quarters of a mile south of Cross Roads, near the Salem–Monroe township line. The entire threshing operation can be seen here from end to end. The equipment is conveniently near the silo and barn, which can be seen in the background at left. (Rev. Gary McManus.)

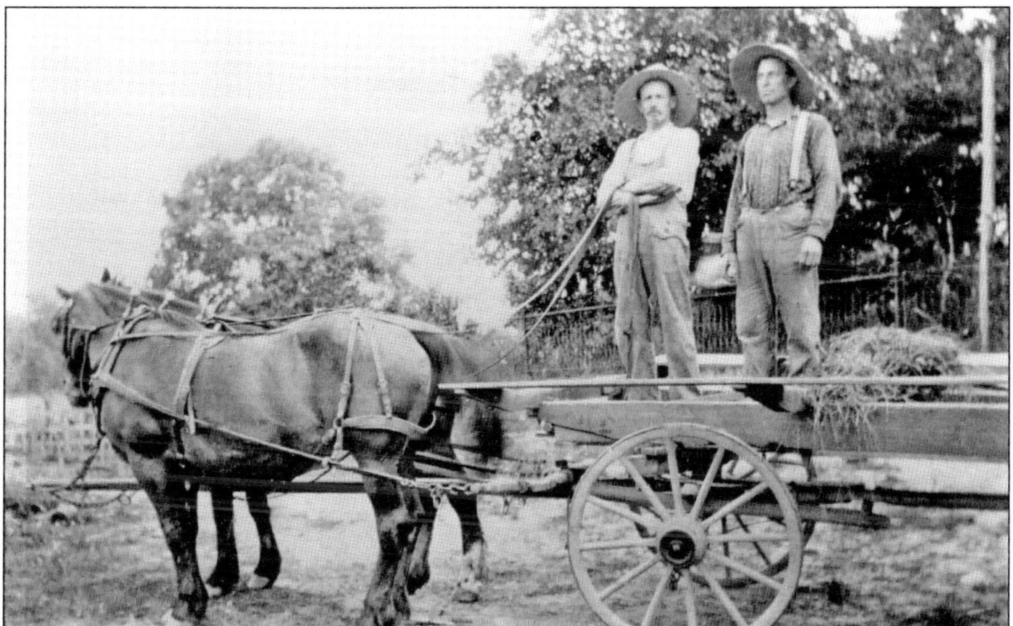

This hay wagon was on the Shirey farm near Cross Roads about 1918. Pictured on the wagon are Warren C. Shirey (left) and George Reedy. Hay was piled high on the wagon and taken to the barn. A double fork was plunged into the hay and the bundle hauled on a pulley through the hay mow door by horse or tractor. The advent of baling eliminated such labor. (Rev. Gary McManus.)

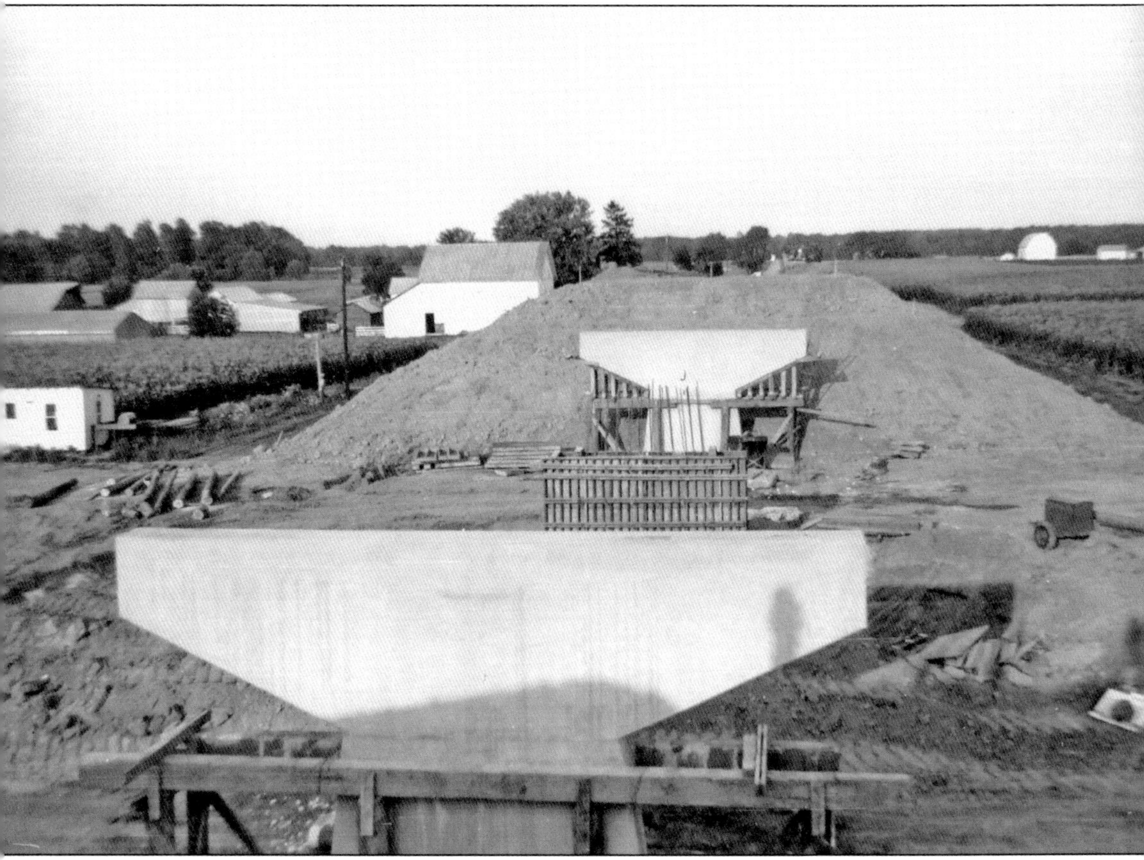

Construction of Interstate 69 near the west side of Daleville brought many changes to the area as businesses took advantage of the new highway. Travel to Indianapolis and Fort Wayne is greatly facilitated by the interstate. Amenities for travelers and a flea market continue to be attractions around the State Road 67 and State Road 32 interchange. The retail shopping mall initially set up at this interstate exit began to fail, but a conversion into business offices and services was successful. This area continues to thrive and grow in the new millennium. (Rev. Gary McManus.)

Three

Eaton

Although Eaton was platted in 1854, it grew very little in the early years. Eaton was located just west of Union Corners or Henpeck, as it was locally known, at the junction of the Fort Wayne state road and the Greenville and Marion state road. The ford over the Mississinewa River was near Henpeck, so the Eaton site was off this traveled route. The railroad was completed in 1869 when there were only four or five families living in Eaton. The town grew in the 1870s. Area businesses included stone quarries and mills for grains and flour as well as sawmills and other small factories.

The first commercial gas well was drilled at Eaton in 1886 and introduced a new prosperity to the town. As in other towns of the county, free gas was offered to industries. The town became an industrial center as companies took advantage of the ready fuel. As the population grew, schools needed to be enlarged and many organizations and businesses profited from the continuing influx of workers. One of the longer lasting businesses was the canning factory, which grew under different owners and was generally known as Butterfield's in the postwar era.

In the early 1900s, the interurban railroad grew and provided transportation to and from the area. The Eaton Riverside Park, an interurban park, drew visitors to the bustling town and its businesses. As the years passed, the interurban became less important as families prospered and had automobiles to take them on both pleasure and shopping expeditions.

Near the end of World War II, labor from prisoners of war was available to some industries. For a few months, the Eaton Canning Company had a prisoner-of-war camp near the factory. A small group of German prisoners worked for the cannery.

Eaton continued to have industries after the war, including a paper company and RockTenn, a producer of insulation.

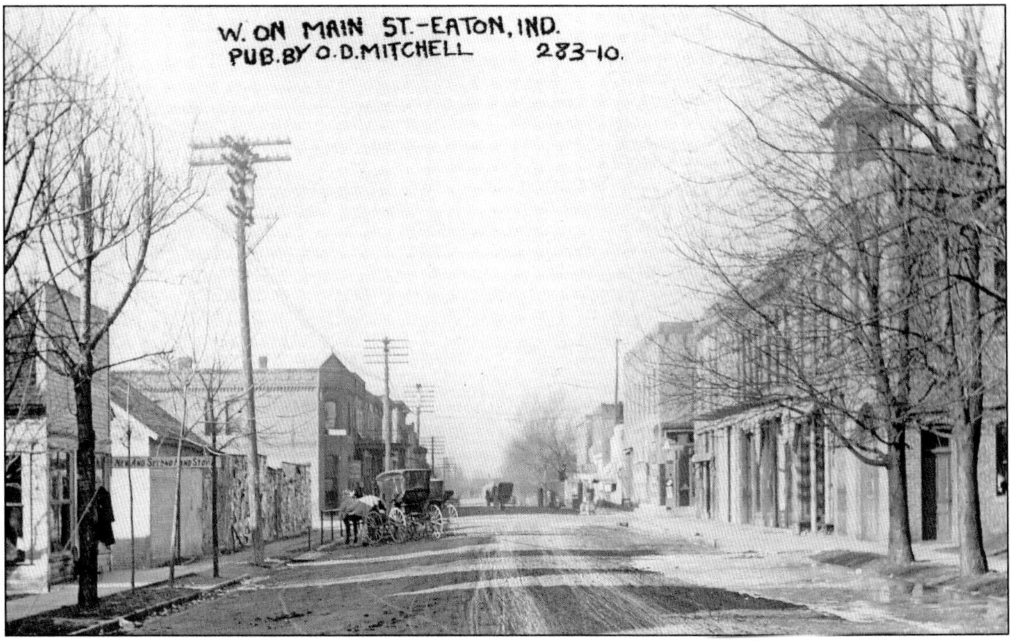

This view looking west on Eaton's main thoroughfare, Harris Street, is probably from the 1890s. On the left is a sign for a "New and Second Hand Store." Behind the horse and buggy is the Farmers State Bank. The windowed tower at right is on the town hall. (Jeffrey Koenker.)

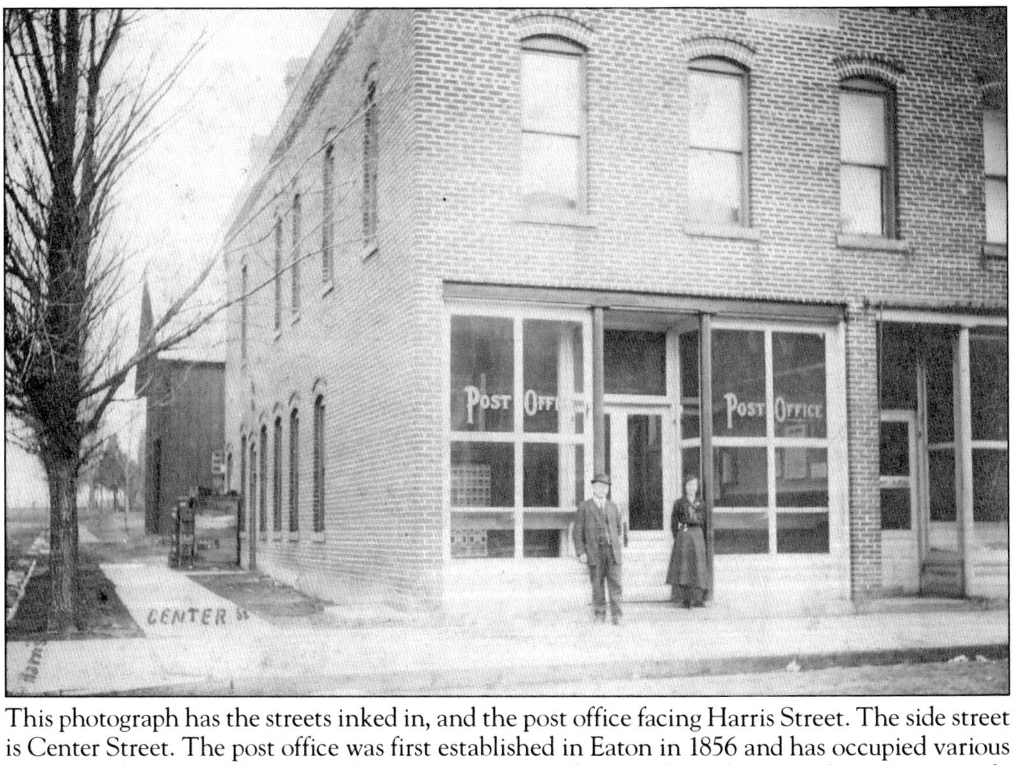

This photograph has the streets inked in, and the post office facing Harris Street. The side street is Center Street. The post office was first established in Eaton in 1856 and has occupied various sites over the years. The woman's costume suggests this may have been in the 1910s or early 1920s. (Eaton Public Library.)

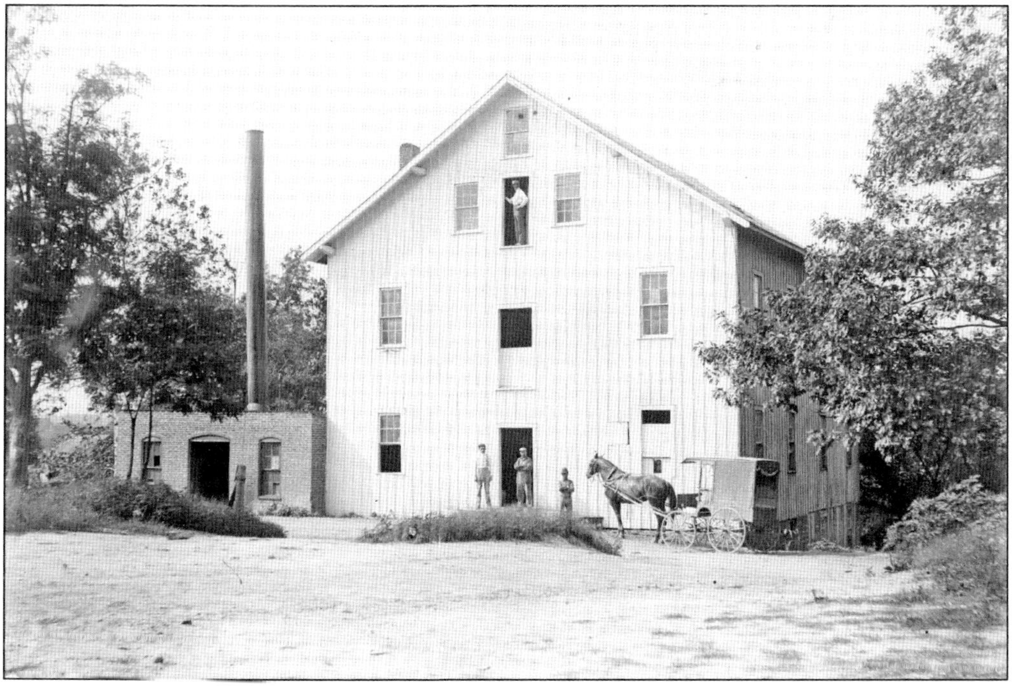

The first mill in the county was established at Eaton in 1831. It was known as Carter's Mill; the Carter brothers owned it for many years and rebuilt it after a fire. This appears to be the four-story flour mill, which was built a little farther west. The mill also did carding (of wool) and, eventually, general woolen manufacturing. (Eaton Public Library.)

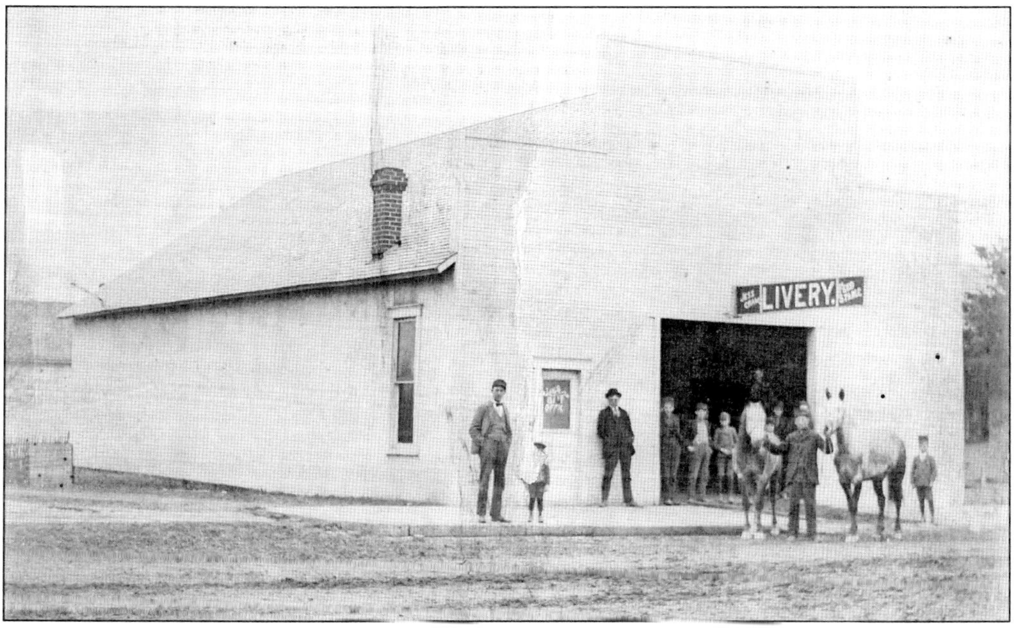

This is Jess Craw's livery, pictured sometime between 1890 and 1905. His office is through the door on the left front of the building. Craw was listed in the 1900 census with his wife, Anna, and four children, Myrtle, Edgar, Clara, and Eilene. The Craw family was among the early settlers in the area. (Eaton Public Library.)

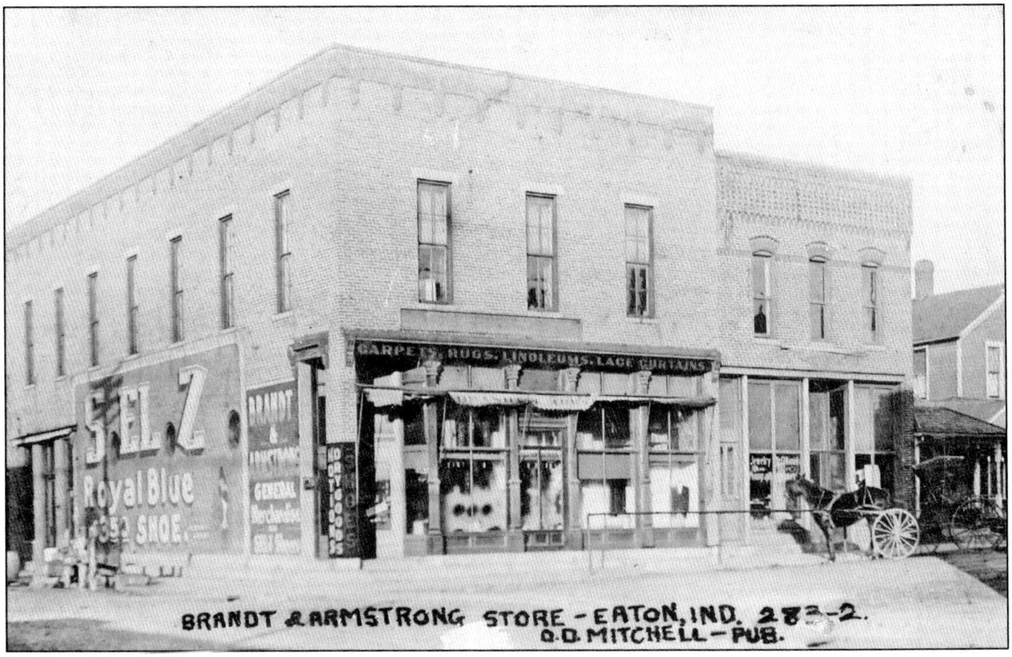

David Brandt was an early settler and merchant in Union Township. His son Robert continued business in Eaton. This view of the store appears to be from the 1890s or early 1900s, with carpets, rugs, linoleums, lace, and curtains specified in the sign over the store. (Jeffrey Koenker.)

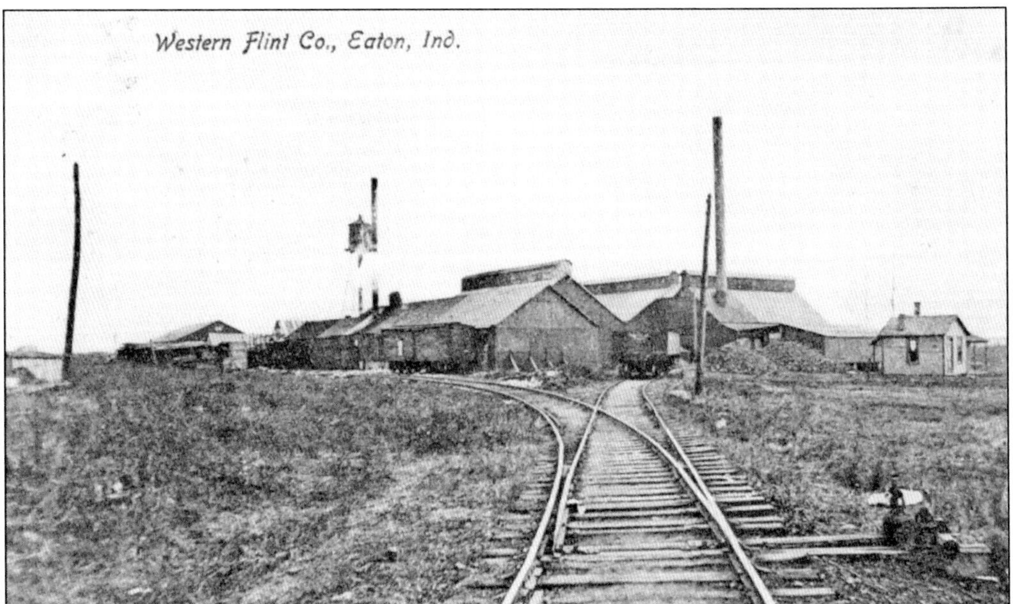

The Western Flint Company was one of the industries attracted to Eaton in the gas boom days. The company suffered severe fire damage in 1901; the engine room and box shops were destroyed. In 1904, three rooms of the glass house burned. (Jeffrey Koenker.)

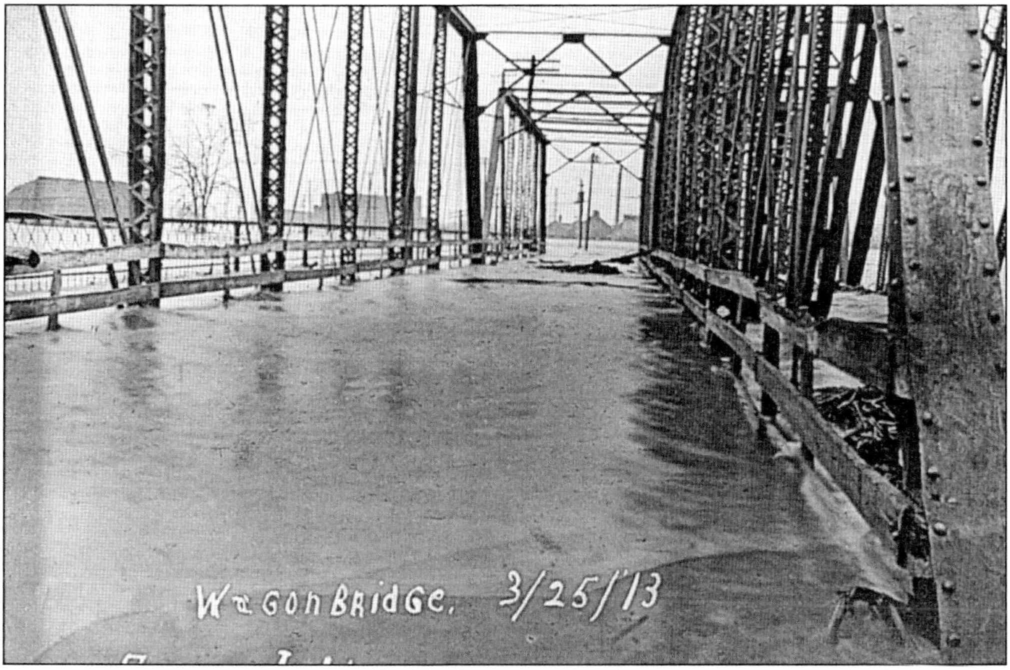

This bridge at the south edge of Eaton shows the height of the 1913 flood that badly damaged many areas of the county. This steel bridge was near the later location of the RockTenn plant. (Eaton Public Library.)

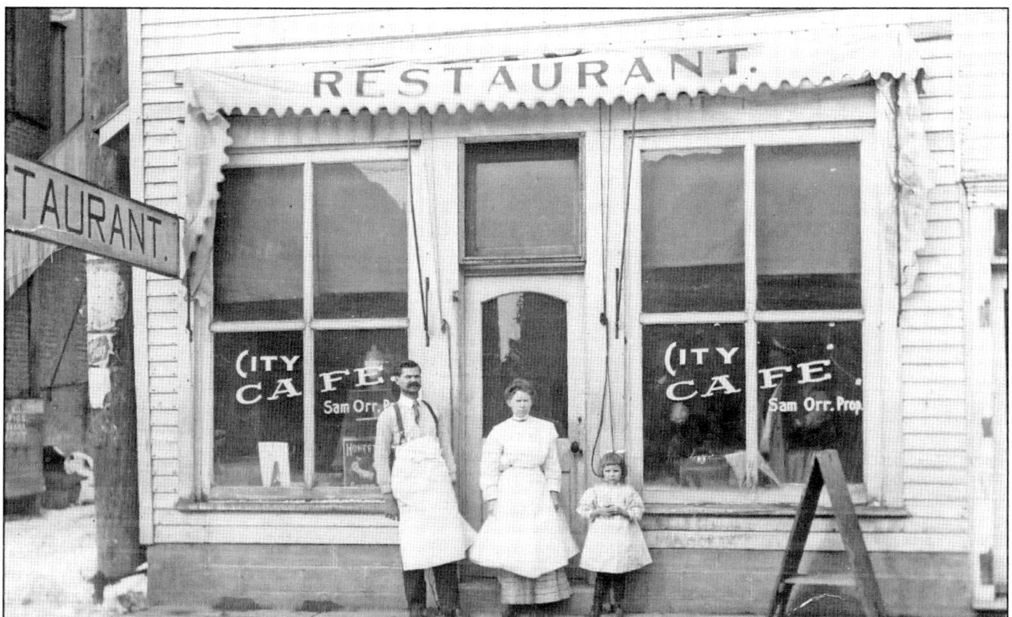

This c. 1909 view of the City Café shows proprietor Samuel Orr with his wife, Pearl, and their daughter Mildred. The restaurant was probably on Harris Street. In the 1910 census, Samuel Orr was listed in Eaton as a merchant with a restaurant. Listed also were his wife and a daughter, age five. Mildred later married Ralph Butterfield, a partner in the Butterfield Canning Company. (Jeffrey Koenker.)

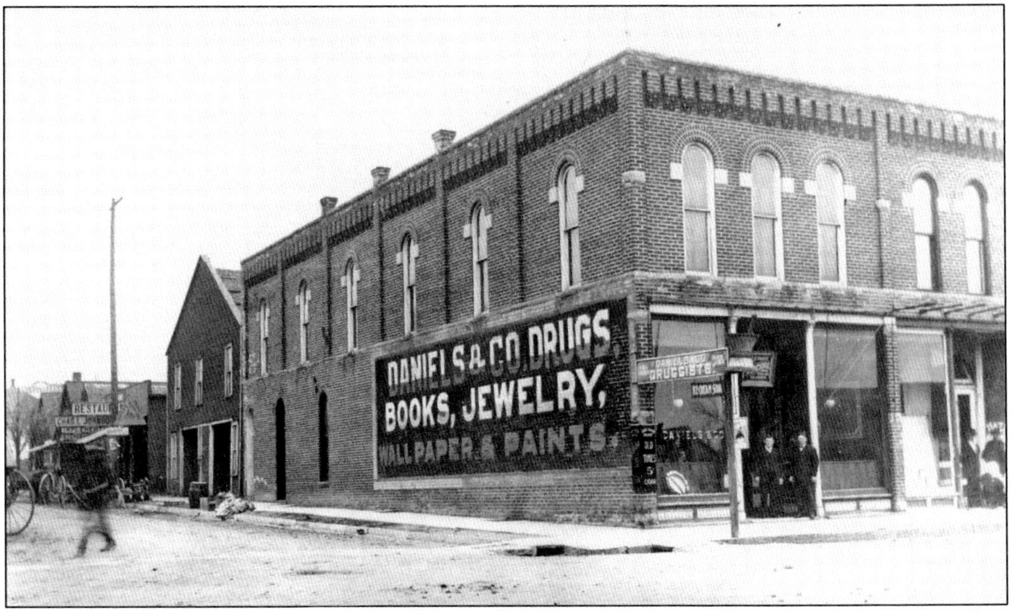

Daniels and Company had a wide range of products, including wallpaper and paints—a somewhat unusual combination for druggists, even for the early 1900s. There certainly would have been a demand for these products, especially in the high-growth times of the gas boom and industrialization. Also advertised were Old Times 5¢ cigars and ice cream sodas. (Michael Mavis.)

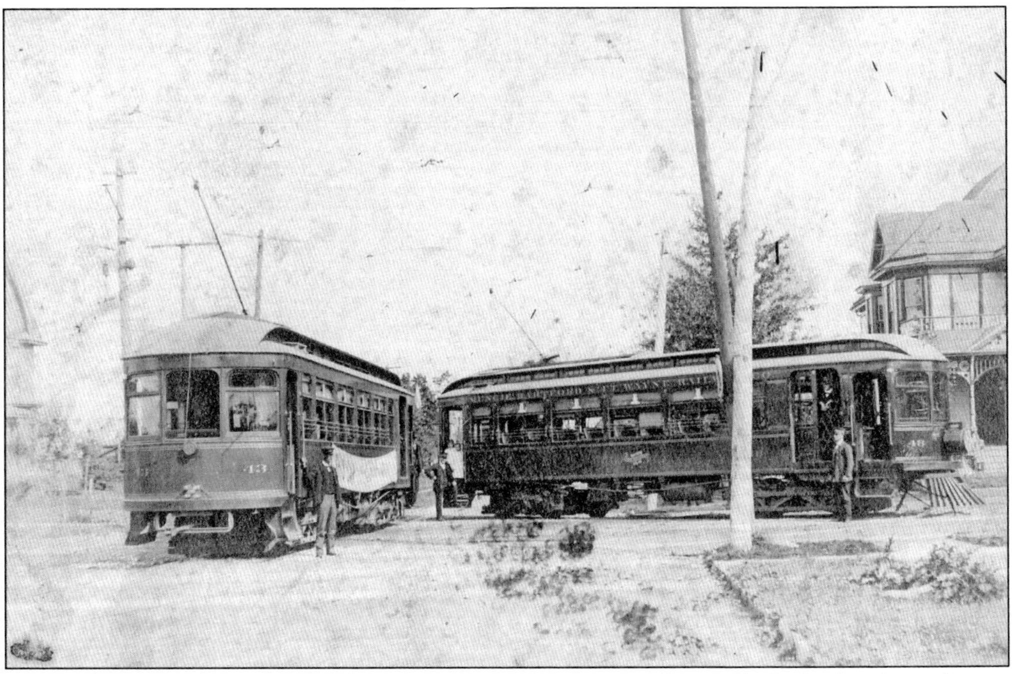

In this photograph, the car at left is on the spur that went to Riverside Park. On the right is a Muncie, Hartford & Fort Wayne Railway Company car. Hartford City was apparently truncated to "Hartford" for the railroad car sign. The Indiana Union Traction System map in the 1907–1908 *Emerson's Muncie Directory* shows Eaton on the major route from Muncie to Bluffton. (Eaton Public Library.)

Albert Palmer (left), a lawyer, poses with an unidentified client. Palmer was listed in the 1900 census as a farmer born in 1868 in Ohio. He was listed as a lawyer in the 1910 census. Also listed were his wife, Myrtle, and two daughters. (Eaton Public Library.)

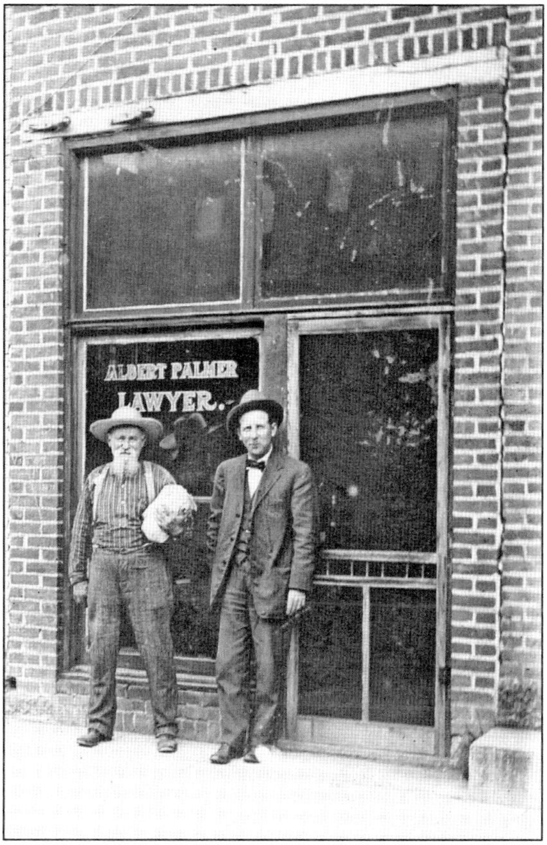

These unidentified men in a traction crew have either not started their day, or perhaps already finished their day, and are posing for the photographer. The presence of a small child with the work crew raises intriguing questions. Shovels appear to be the major work tool here. (Jane Swingley Racer.)

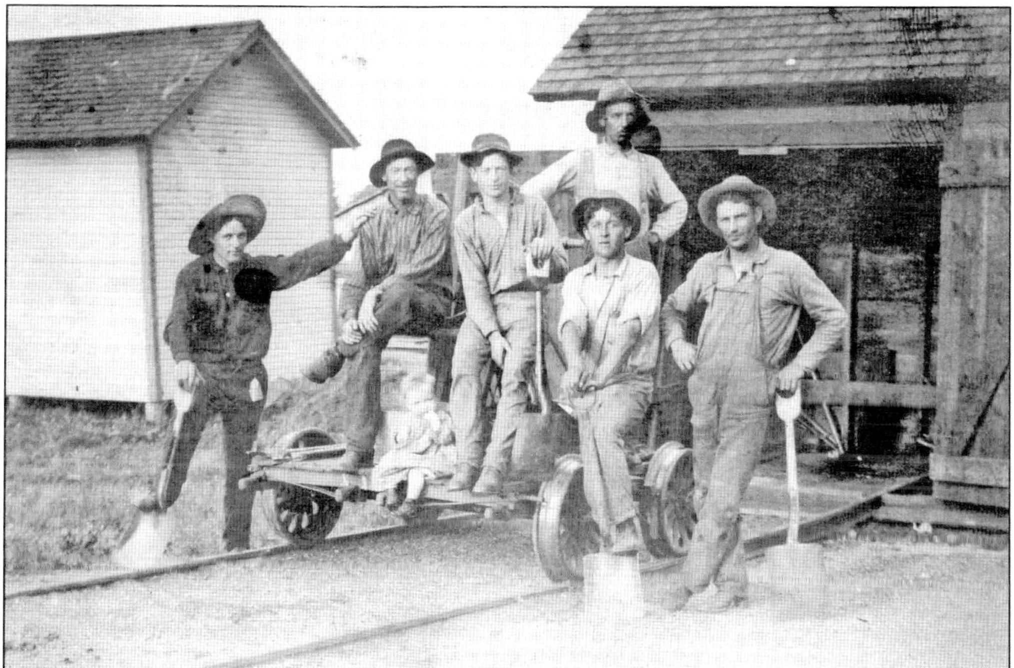

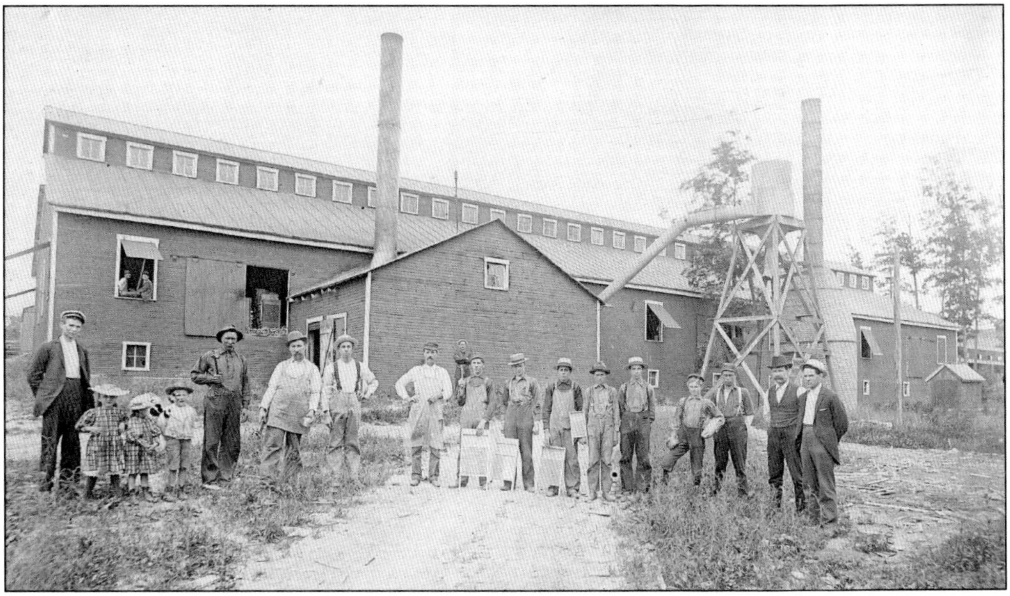

The Standard Manufacturing Company, later McCormick and Sons, was established in Eaton by Walter P. McCormick and his sons. Washboards were the product of the plant. These workers and others on the scene are standing next to the office with several washboards of various sizes. (Eaton Public Library.)

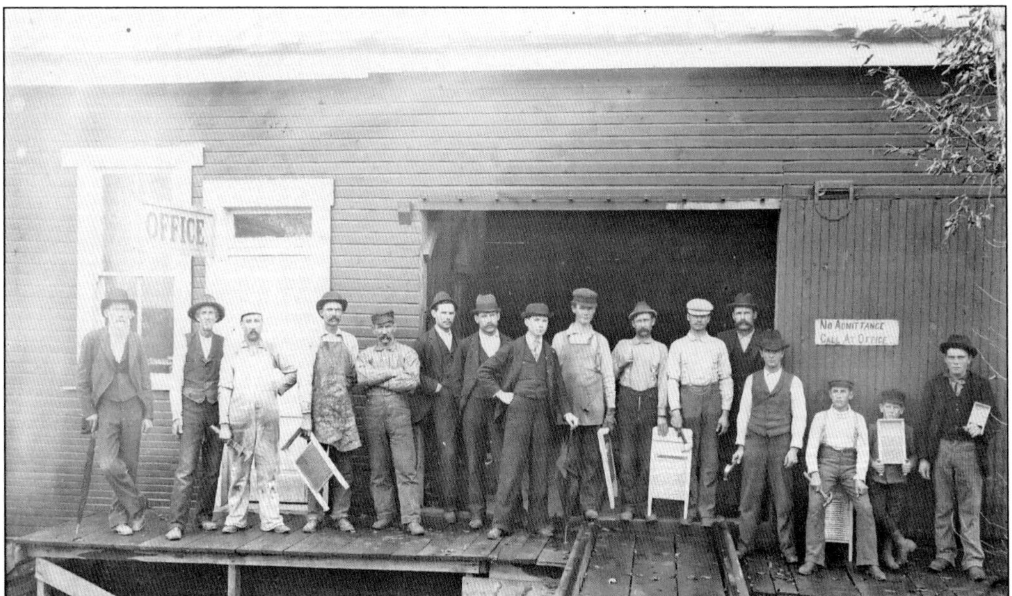

More of the washboard factory is pictured here, with a group of workers and bystanders alongside. The plant was sold to Emil Baur, a native of Switzerland, who reorganized the business as the Standard Wash Board Company. The McCormick family moved to Albany, where they began a hardware store and tin manufactory. (Eaton Public Library.)

This photograph of Bert Deeter and his daughter Margaret is labeled "His biggest crop was in 1914." His daughter was only a few months old, and the giant sized rutabagas were from their garden. The Deeters were living in Eaton at the time of this photograph, but they later moved to Selma. Margaret Deeter was Jane Swingley Racer's mother. (Jane Swingley Racer.)

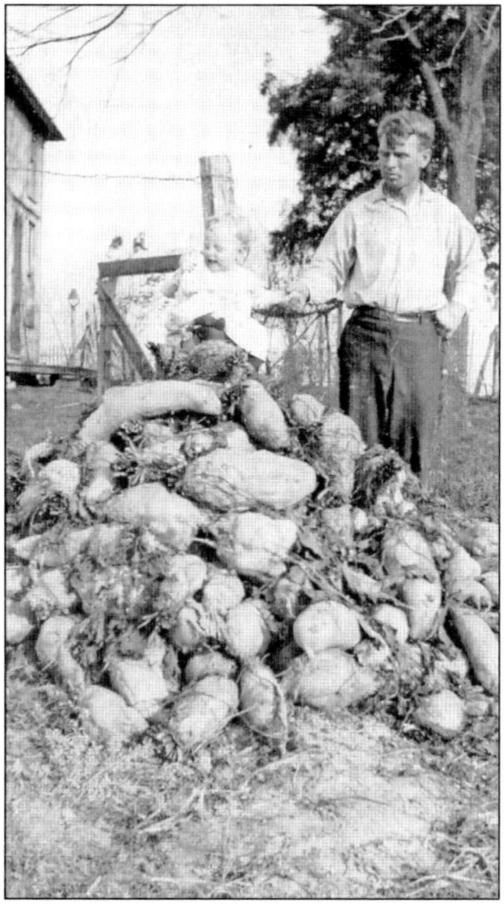

This Eaton High School building was constructed in 1908, during a high growth period in Eaton. In four years, the enrollment went from 68 to 169, necessitating the addition of more space. The building was demolished in 1976. (Jeffrey Koenker.)

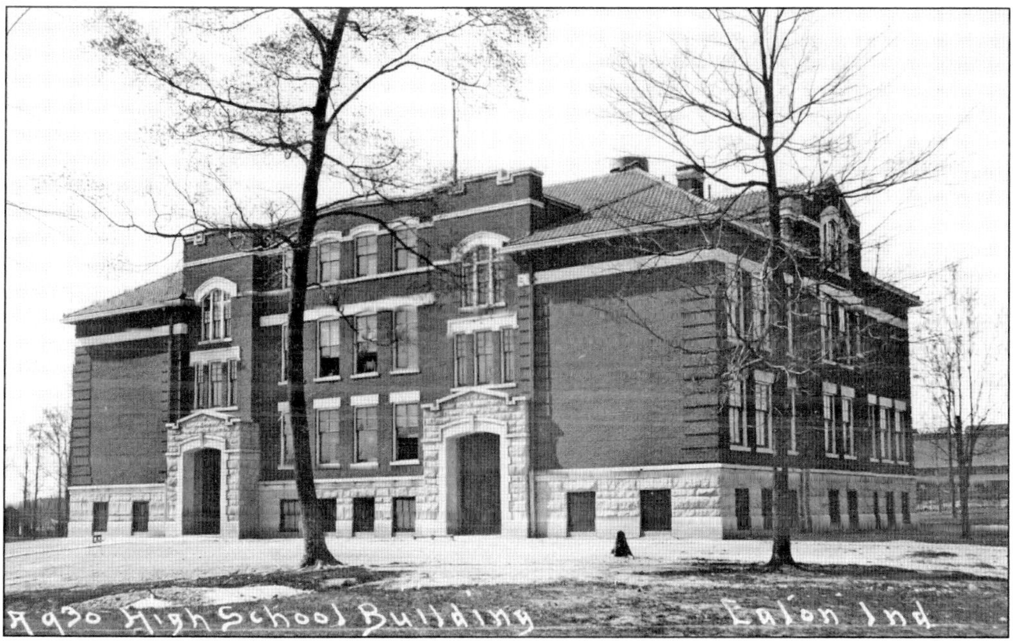

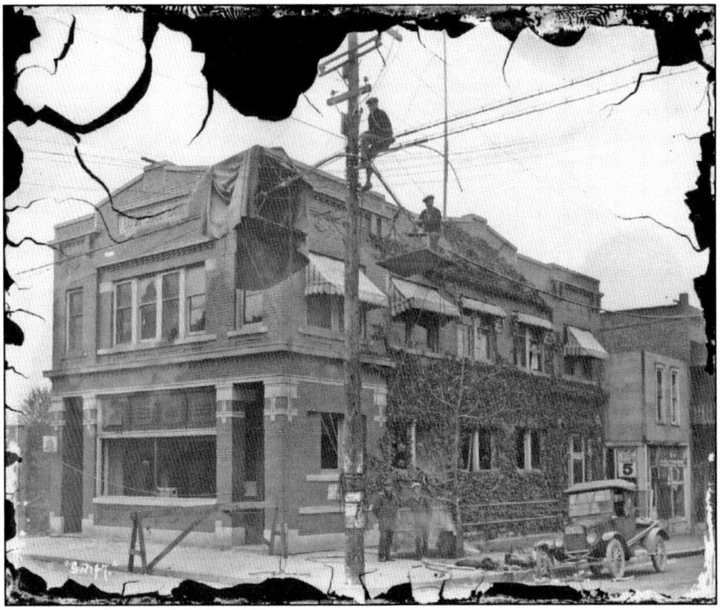

Eaton had two banks, both of which were robbed; Farmers' State Bank in 1924 and Eaton State Bank in 1925. This May 1925 view of the Eaton State Bank was photographed during the aftermath of the robbery. The repairmen were on site and beginning work on the damaged bank building. The bandits shot at some citizens, but there were no injuries. (Minnetrista Heritage Collection, Muncie, Indiana.)

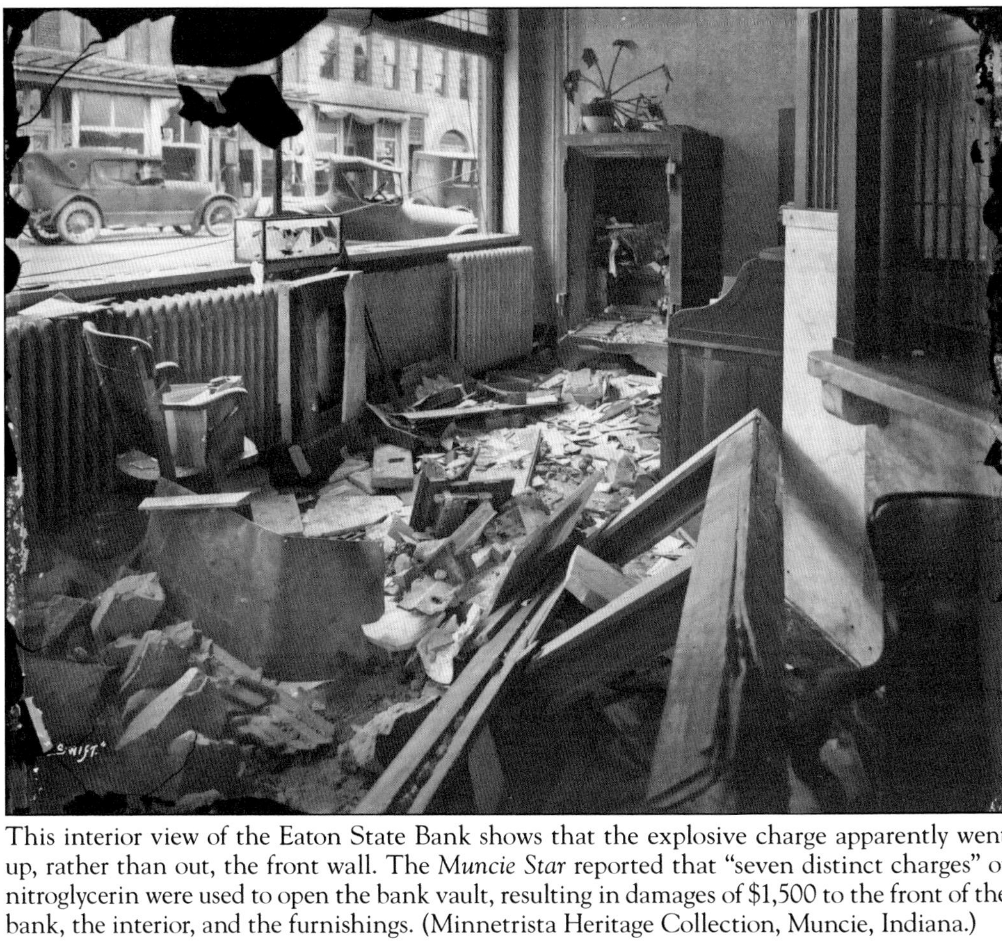

This interior view of the Eaton State Bank shows that the explosive charge apparently went up, rather than out, the front wall. The *Muncie Star* reported that "seven distinct charges" of nitroglycerin were used to open the bank vault, resulting in damages of $1,500 to the front of the bank, the interior, and the furnishings. (Minnetrista Heritage Collection, Muncie, Indiana.)

This photograph of the Eaton Canning Company appears to be from the 1930s. The Butterfield family began the cannery at Eaton in 1924, with tomatoes being a major product. At one time, they would can special orders for local producers of various vegetables. Tomato canneries of various companies were scattered around East Central Indiana. The Butterfield cannery was locally owned and operated. (Jeffrey Koenker.)

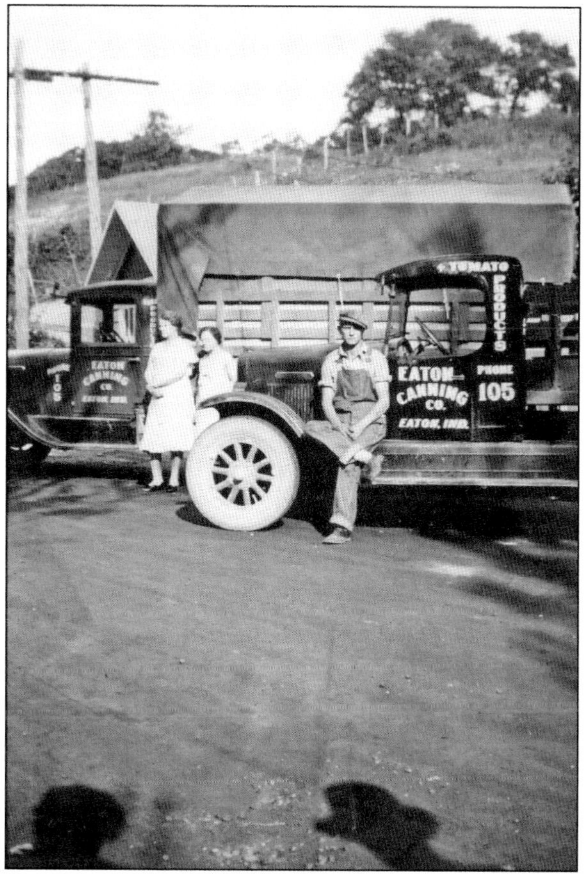

There was a German prisoner-of-war camp at Eaton near the end of World War II. During the summer of 1945, the camp at Windfall sent 10 prisoners to the Butterfield Canning Company. Butterfield's made arrangements to have a temporary camp in Eaton and donated a 17-acre field northeast of the factory. (Eaton Public Library.)

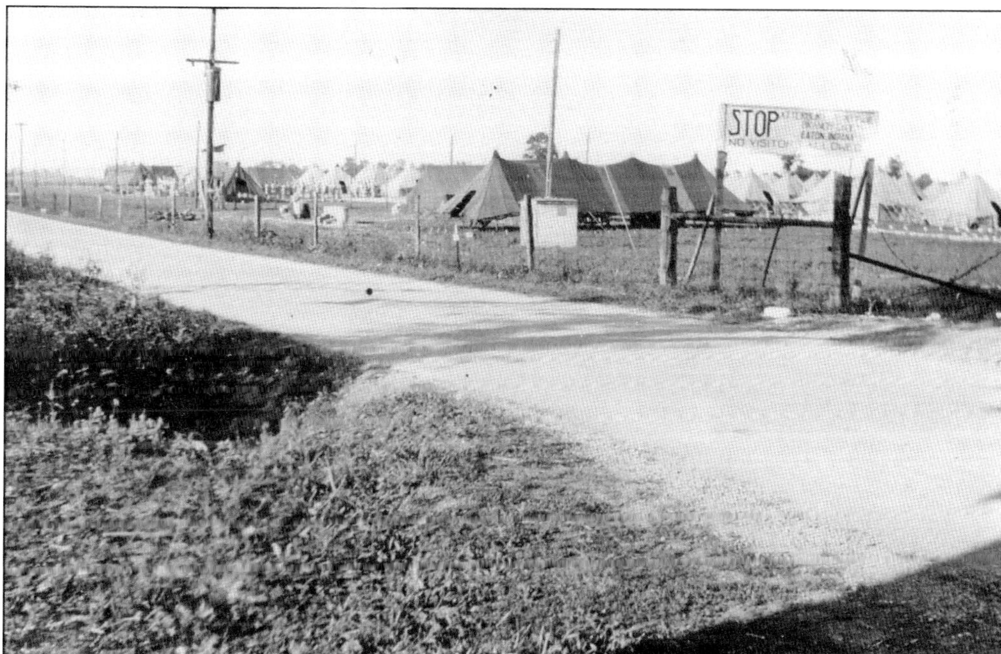

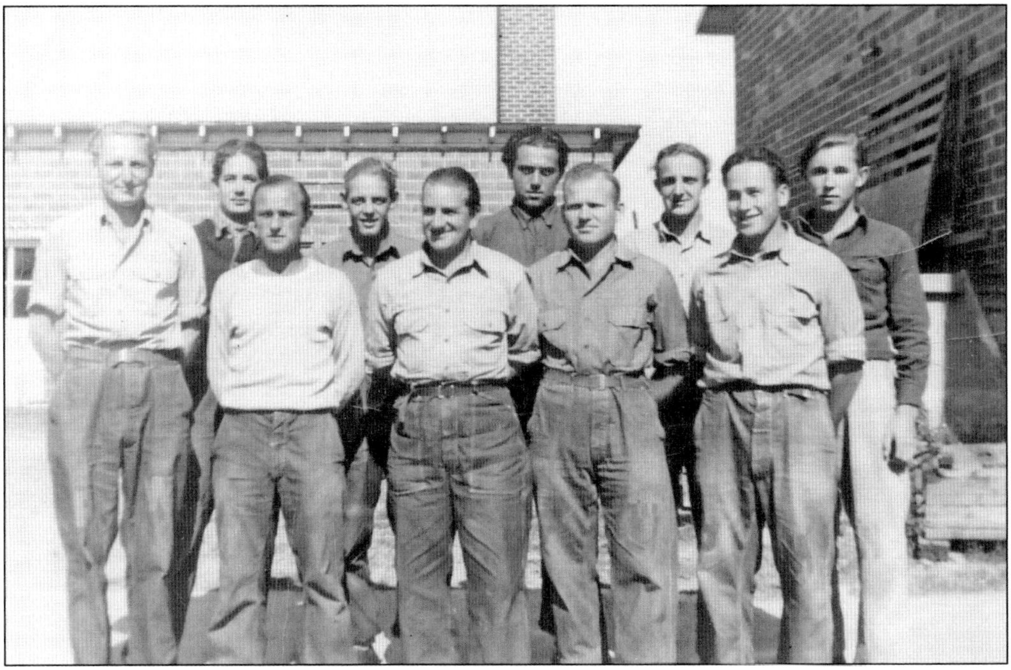

These German prisoners of war lived in Branch Camp 4 at Eaton and worked for the cannery. From left to right are (first row) Erhard Albrecht, Reinhold Kurka, Ernst Kurbjuhn, Hans Luebker, and Gebhard Biehl; (second row) Bruno Walter, Kurt Roehmuss, Ernst Huck, Siegfried Dzenisch, and Karl Wiedmer. At least one of them corresponded with the Butterfields after he returned to Germany. (DCHS, Butterfield Collection.)

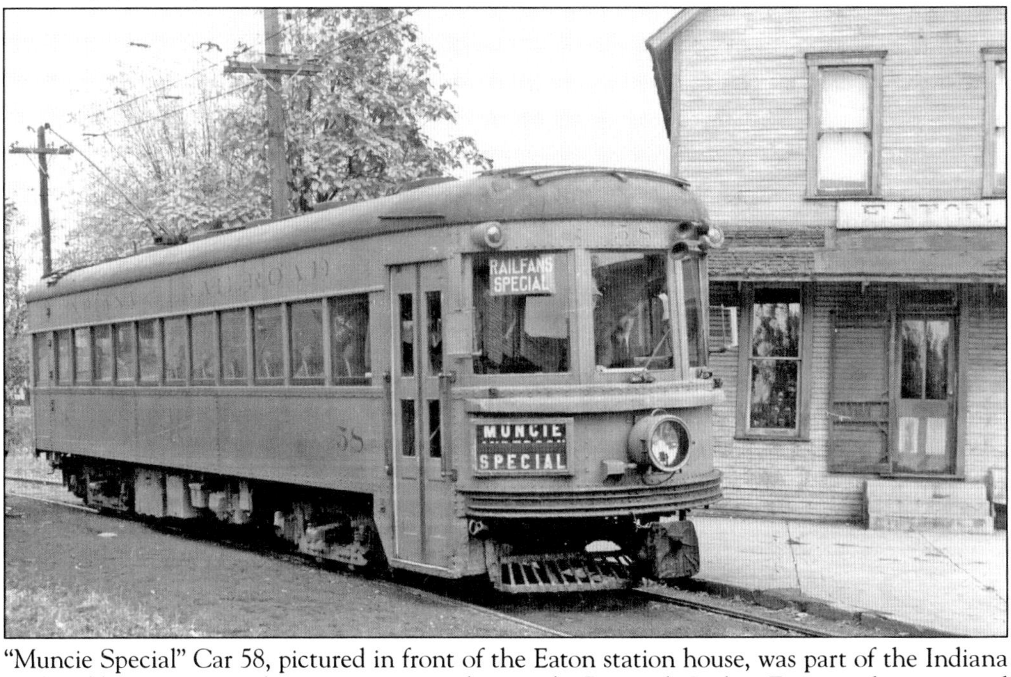

"Muncie Special" Car 58, pictured in front of the Eaton station house, was part of the Indiana Railroad line. It attracted entertainment seekers to the Riverside Park at Eaton and transported Eatonians to various destinations along the line. (Jeffrey Koenker.)

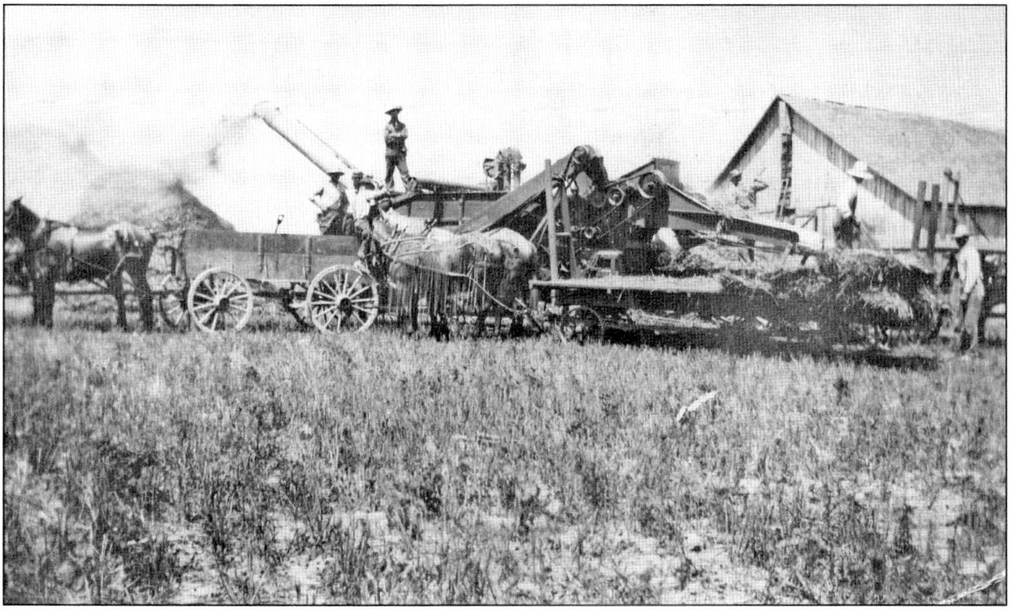

Edgar B. Craw did custom threshing for many farmers in the area. The investment in such equipment provided a way to make a living for the family. Farmers arranged for the thresher and crew to come to their fields for harvesting. (Eaton Public Library.)

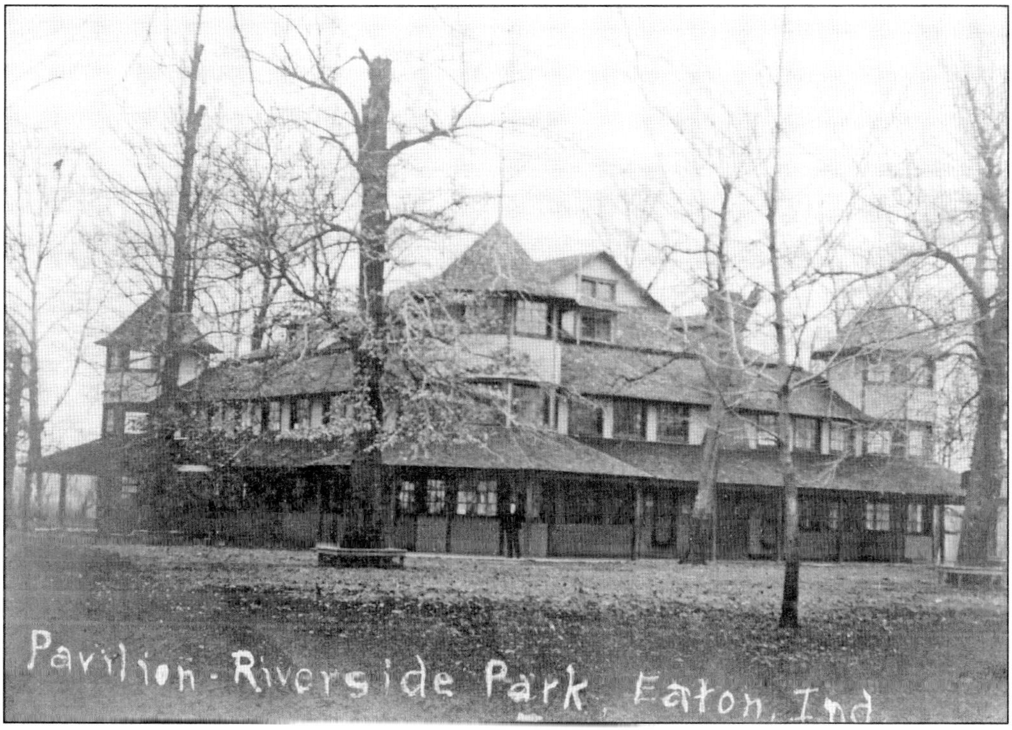

In the early 1900s, Riverside Park at Eaton was developed as a traction line destination, as was Westside Park in Muncie. Riverside Park was developed on land east of Eaton in the former Henpeck area along the Mississinewa River, which was navigable at that time. The pavilion provided space for family reunions, lodge events, and other gatherings. (Jeffrey Koenker.)

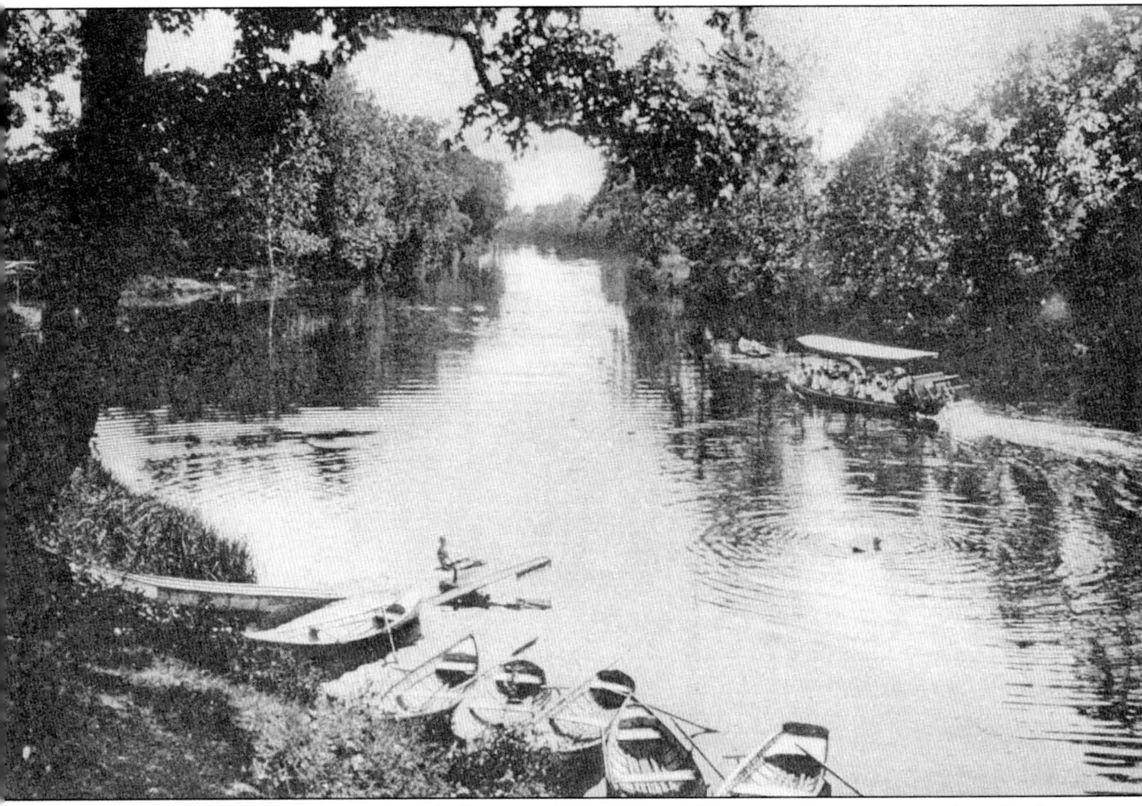

The first run on the Muncie, Bluffton, and Fort Wayne Traction Company track took place in 1901. The company soon established destination parks with all kinds of family entertainment to attract customers. At Eaton, there was a track spur that passengers transferred onto that took them to Riverside Park on the east side of Eaton. A steamboat called the *Mayflower* went on moonlight cruises, and rowboats provided entertainment for the more athletically inclined. The setting at the bend of the Mississinewa River had many beautiful oak and beech trees. There was a hotel for people who stayed for the weekend. The park was an attraction for many miles around. On Sundays, horse-drawn vehicles occupied the two-acre parking lot. (Jeffrey Koenker.)

Four

GASTON

The county histories say that Gaston was platted as New Corner by David L. Jones in 1855. An earlier settlement called Snagtown was apparently absorbed in the development of new houses at the corner. The deed records show Jones selling pieces of land as small as .59 of an acre in 1855 in sections 33 and 34, where New Corner (later Gaston) was located. He does not describe these as part of a plat for the developing town, as was commonly done in other settlements. Gas wells were drilled near the village in the 1890s, and people began thinking about a new name for the town. In 1904, there was a vote in favor of incorporating as Gaston.

The railroad arrived later in New Corner than in some of the other county communities, but it was greeted with a great celebration in the summer of 1901. A Cincinnati, Richmond & Muncie Railroad train arrived at the town station with an engine, two flats, and a boxcar. While horses and buggies occupied a field, those so conveyed to the occasion were served lemonade. The gas wells brought industry to Gaston, such as a tile factory and a canning company. A bank was established, and a hotel was in a specially built, two-story frame structure. Churches established included Methodist Episcopal, United Brethren, Methodist Protestant, Christian, Nazarene, and Wesleyan Methodist.

A physical feature of Washington Township is the Old Prairie Swamp, a large peat upland depression, or wetland prairie. Drainage of the area has made good farming land in this part of the county. Gaston's location near the southern line of Washington Township has made it a retail center for both Washington and Harrison Townships. Some of the smaller villages around the area have been Stockport, Grey Eagle, Elizabethtown, Gilman, and Bethel. Elizabethtown had hopes of becoming a county seat but was bypassed in the organization of the counties. Harrison was platted by Job Garner in Harrison Township, but the planned town never grew.

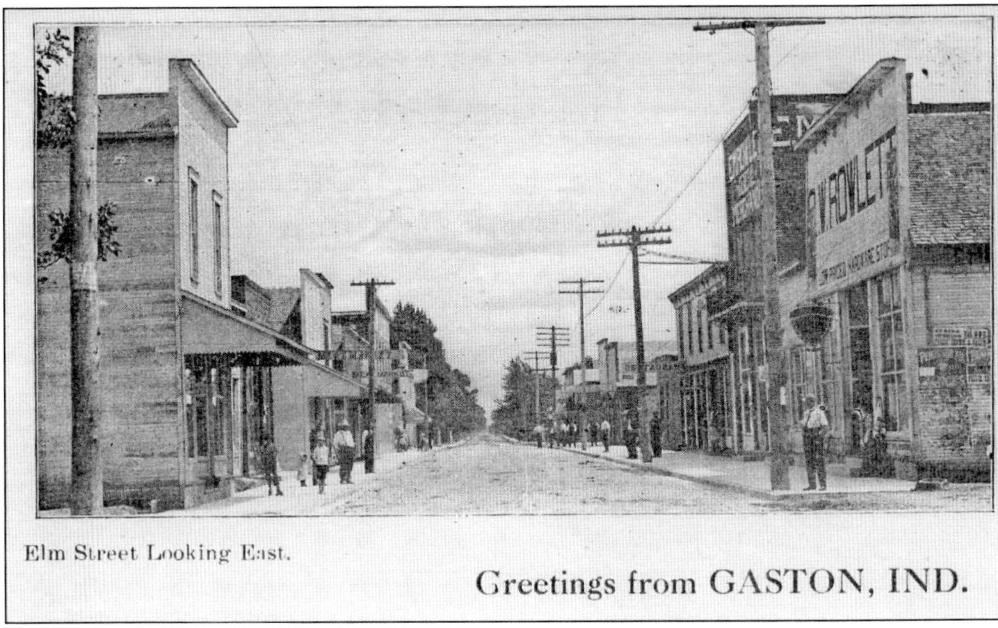

In this view of Elm Street looking east, the citizens have come out on the sidewalks for the photographer. At left are a meat market and another market, and at right center is a restaurant. Rowlett Low Priced Hardware Store is on the far right. (Jeffrey Koenker.)

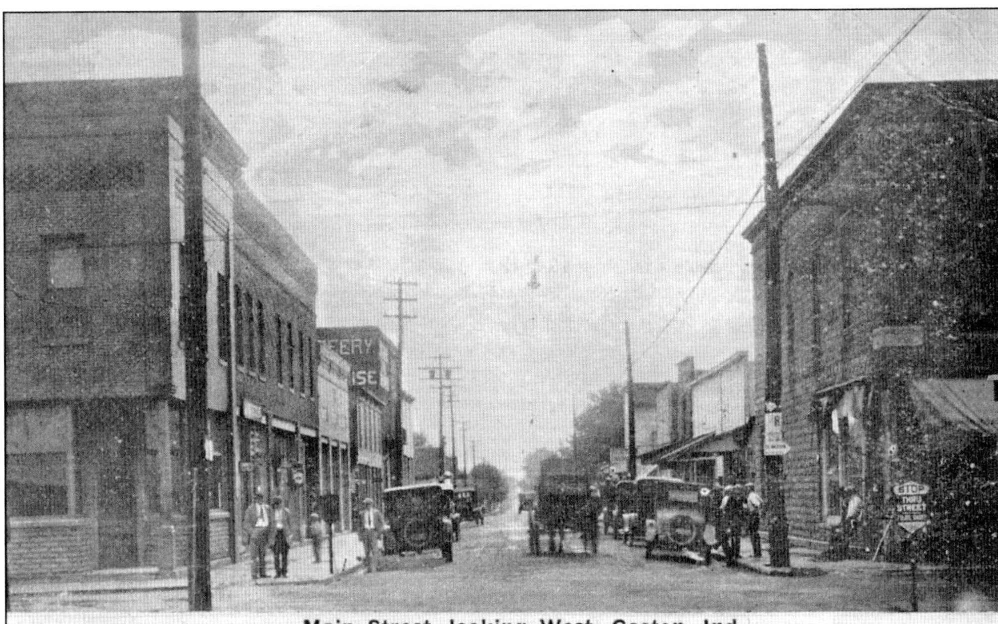

Both motor vehicles and a horse-drawn wagon can be seen in this view of Gaston's main street, Elm Street. The downtown area appears to be having a busy day. (Minnetrista Heritage Collection, Muncie, Indiana.)

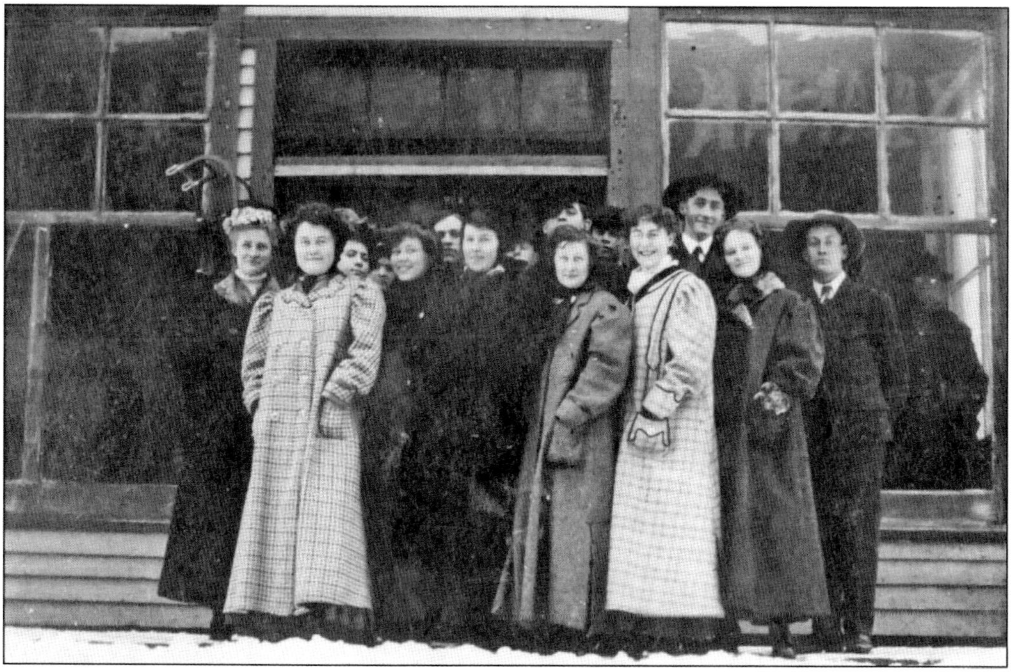

This unidentified group is pictured in front of the Markle drugstore on December 21, 1906. Samuel E. Markle came to Gaston about 1898. He purchased the drugstore business about 1901 after the death of Jesse S. Munsey, for whom he had worked. (Minnetrista Heritage Collection, Muncie, Indiana.)

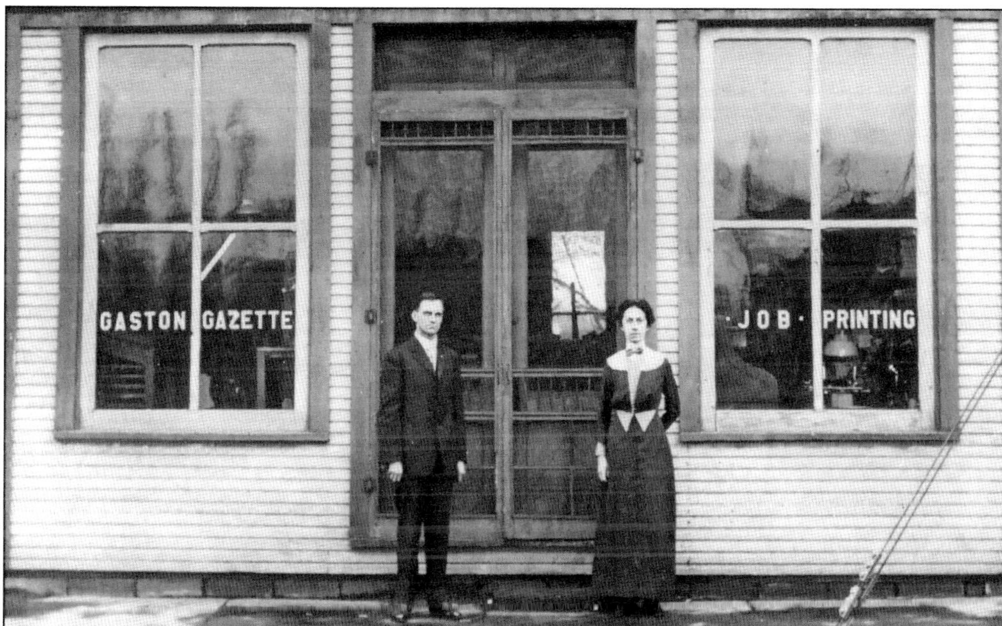

A newspaper was first published in Gaston by C.W. McIntosh & Son beginning in 1897. The 1900 census shows Charles W., wife Alice, and son Frederic as printers. The 1920 census shows Charles McIntosh at the post office and Fred McIntosh as a publisher. The newspaper had probably ceased publication by that time. (Jeffrey Koenker.)

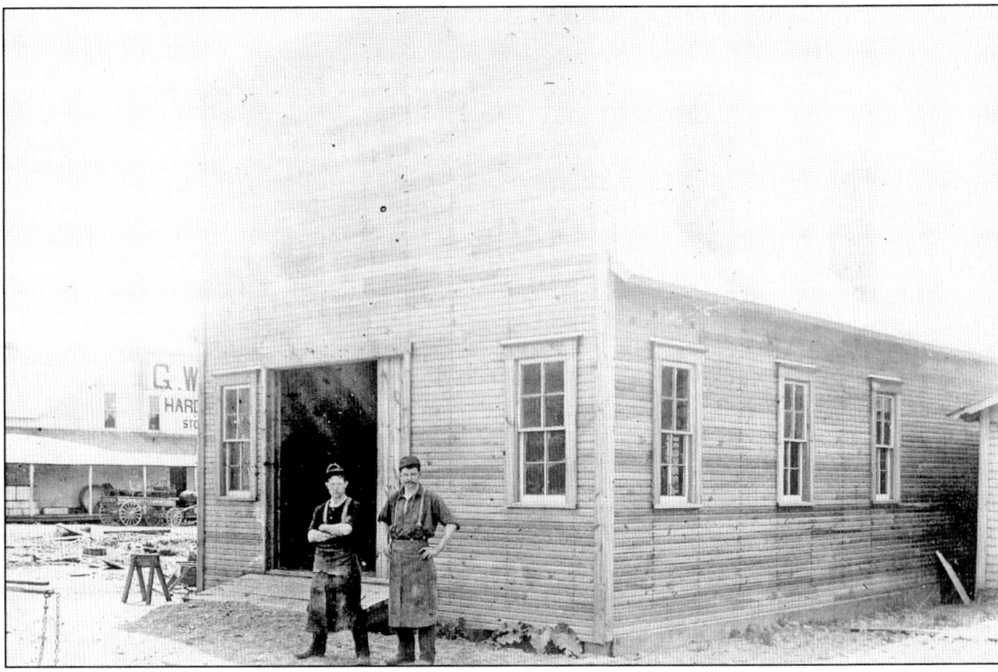

In this photograph of the blacksmith shop in Gaston are George Holiday (left) and Charles Ullum. Ullum was an uncle to Lawrence Nicklin, who was orphaned when he was about nine years old. Lawrence was sent from his family in Martinsburg, West Virginia, to live with Charles Ullum. (DCHS, donated by Mrs. Lawrence Nicklin.)

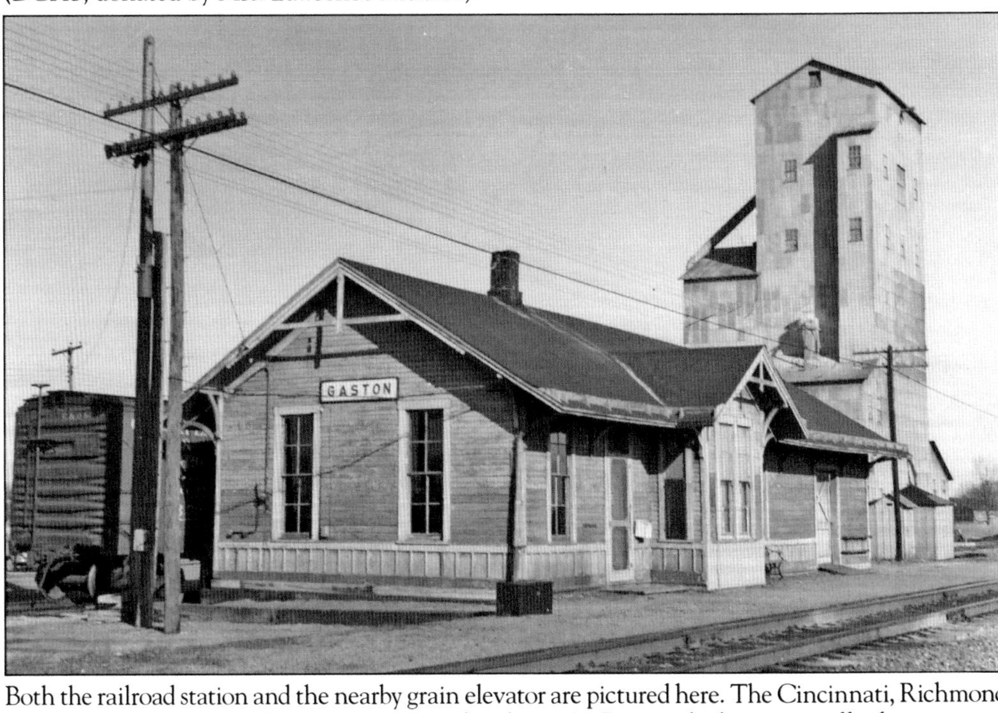

Both the railroad station and the nearby grain elevator are pictured here. The Cincinnati, Richmond & Muncie Railroad, later the C&O, was completed in 1901. During the heaviest traffic days, as many as 200 people were on the afternoon trains from Gaston to Muncie. (Jeffrey Koenker.)

In the early settlement times, the entire area was covered with trees. As the trees were cut down and the land cleared, there were fewer and fewer trees to be hauled to the sawmill and made into lumber. The local sawmills began to disappear and were replaced by lumberyards. (Jeffrey Koenker.)

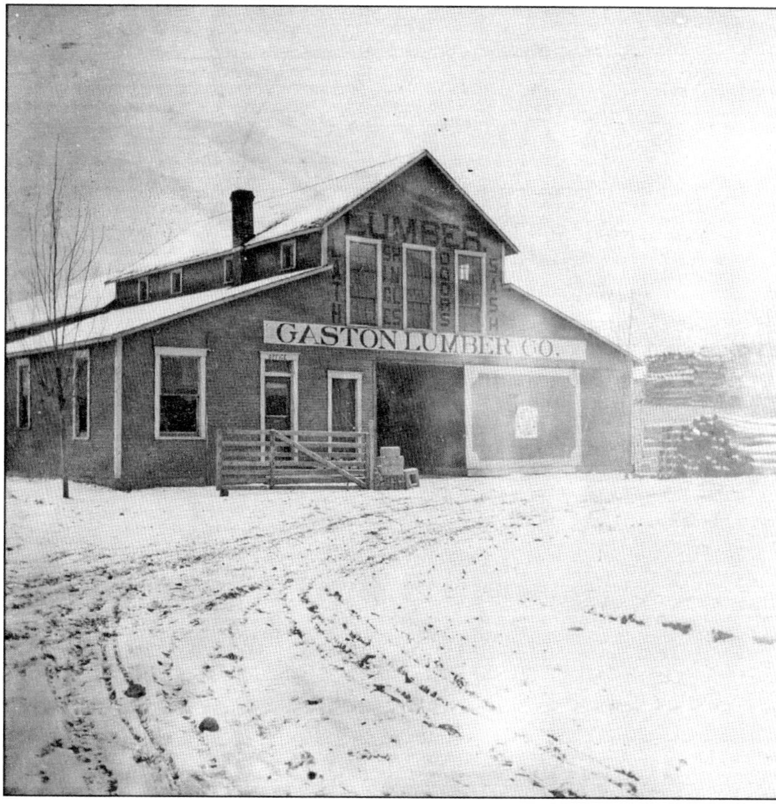

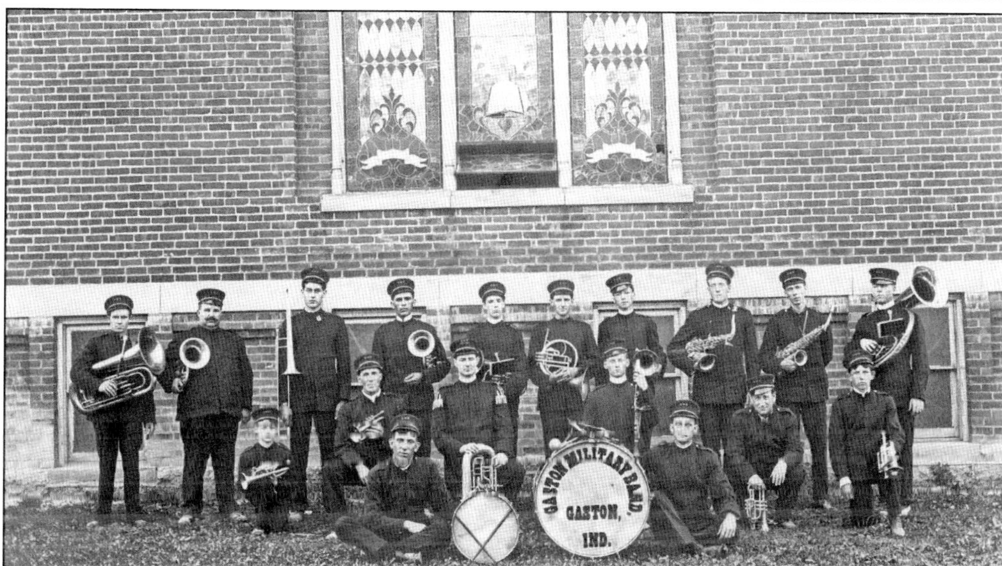

Small bands were very much a part of town and village life as a way to create entertainment for both the bands and their audiences. This Gaston Military Band photograph was taken with the Gaston Methodist Episcopal Church, later the Gaston United Methodist Church, as the background. The church was built in 1903 at a cost of $10,000 and dedicated in February 1904. (Jeffrey Koenker.)

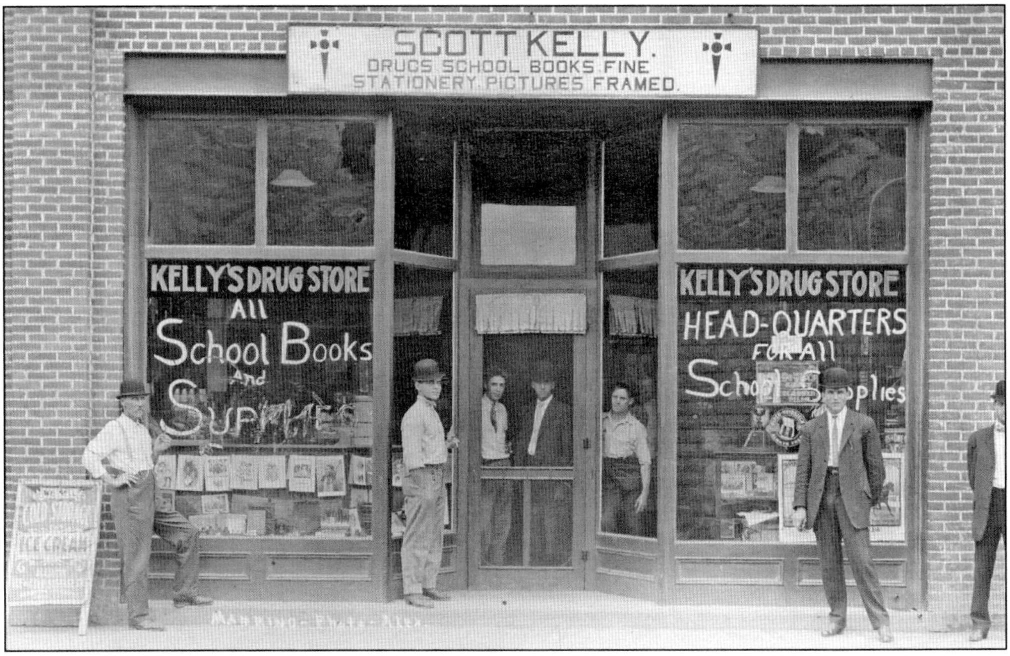

This photograph was probably taken about the time the new school year began. School supplies made a good sideline for a druggist. The 1920 census lists Scott Kelly as a druggist owning his store. He is listed with his wife, Iva, and a nine-year-old son. (Jeffrey Koenker.)

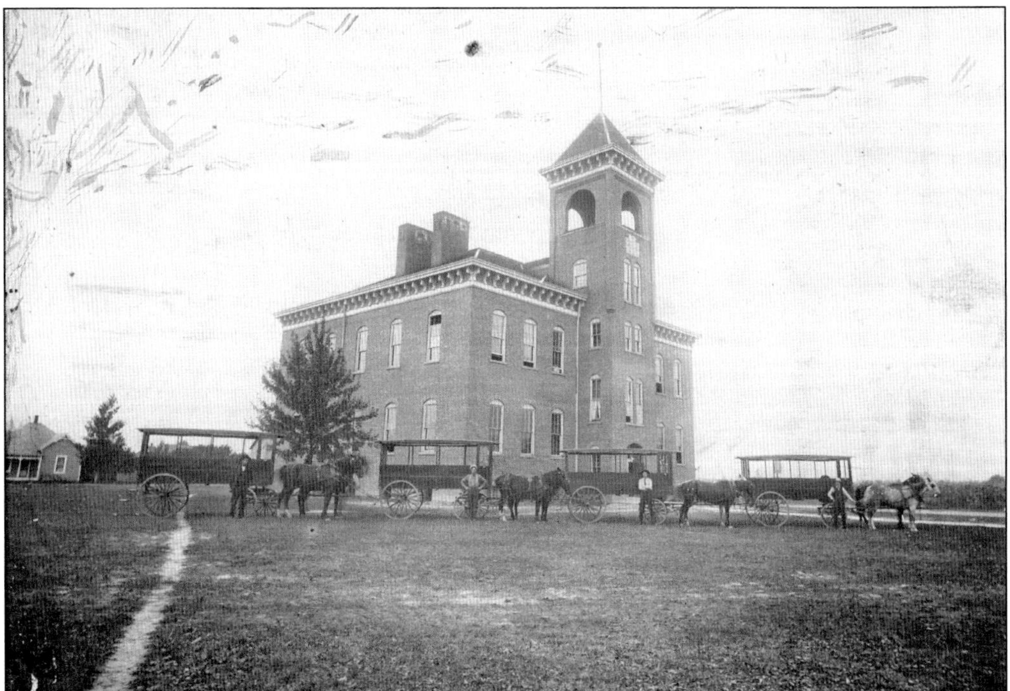

This Gaston school was consolidated, with the various district school students bused by horse and hack. The hacks have their window covers down and are probably lined up to load the students and return them home. (Jeffrey Koenker.)

This Harrison Township school was built in 1901. It was the District School 4 and was supervised by L.A. Johnson, school trustee. The new brick buildings were the pride of their communities and replaced the old frame schoolhouses, which were less sturdy and more vulnerable to fire. (Jeffrey Koenker.)

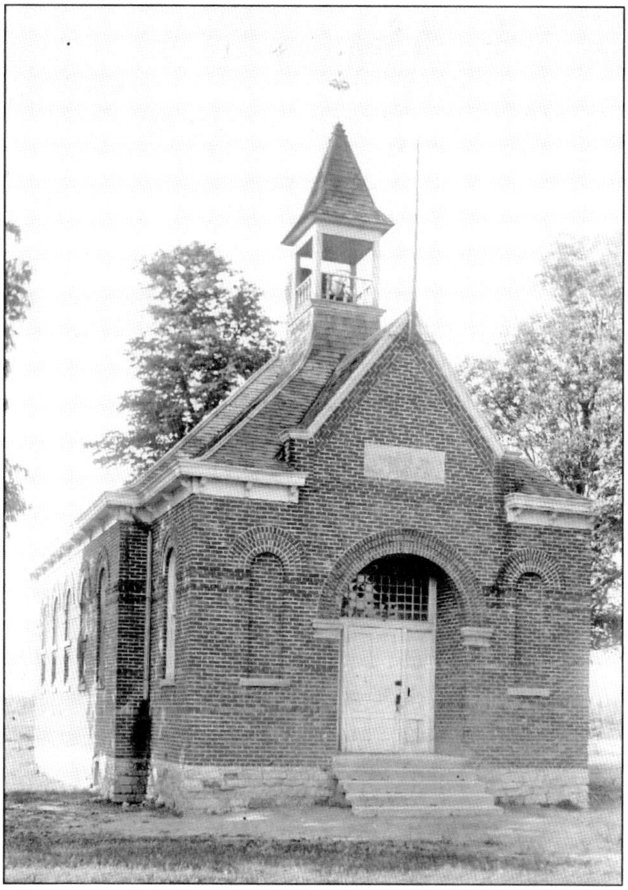

The Guinnup Dairy barn was built around 1900 and still stands in good condition. This butter box was found by the current property owners, Lee and Kathy Miller, and sits on a shelf in their kitchen. The carton shows a Gaston telephone number. The Gaston Home Telephone Company was organized in 1908, which helps provide an approximate date of the dairy. (Lee and Kathy Miller; photograph by Thomas R. Tomlinson.)

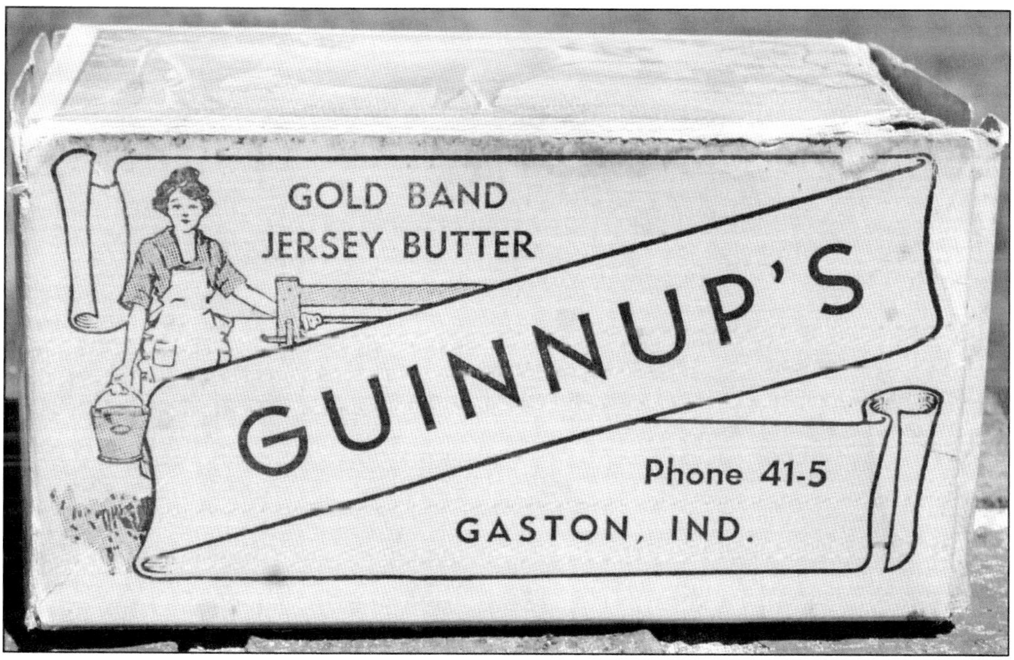

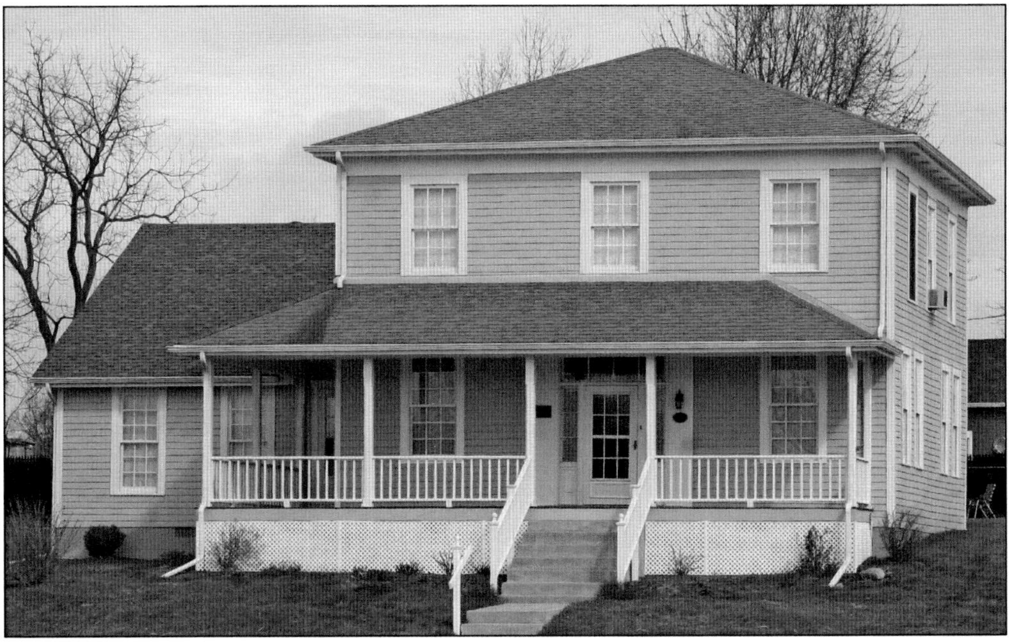

Sometimes known as the Job Garner house, this home was built by Jacob W. Miller, who bought the land from Job Garner in 1851. An engraving in the 1881 history of the county shows it much the same as today with its distinctive porch railing and roofline. It is listed on the Historic American Buildings Survey. (DCHS; photograph by Thomas R. Tomlinson.)

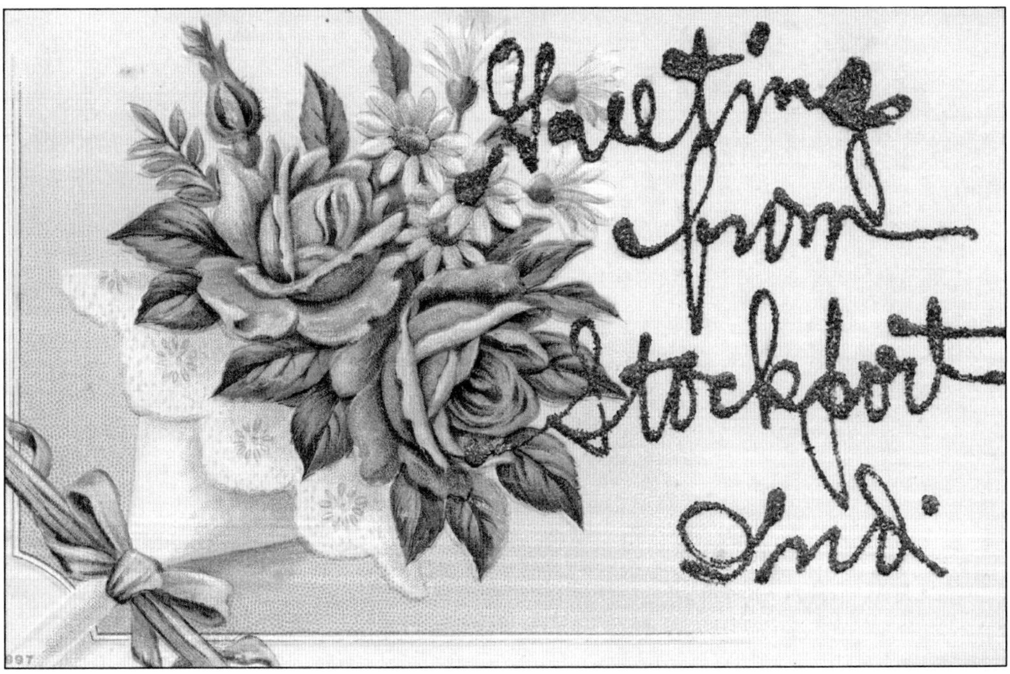

This generic postcard is reminiscent of the little village of Stockport, located on Wheeling Pike to the east and north of Gaston. Although nothing remains of the village today but a small cluster of houses, it had a post office from 1892 to 1914. Stockport had 25 residences listed in the 1907–1908 *Emerson's Muncie Directory*. (Jeffrey Koenker.)

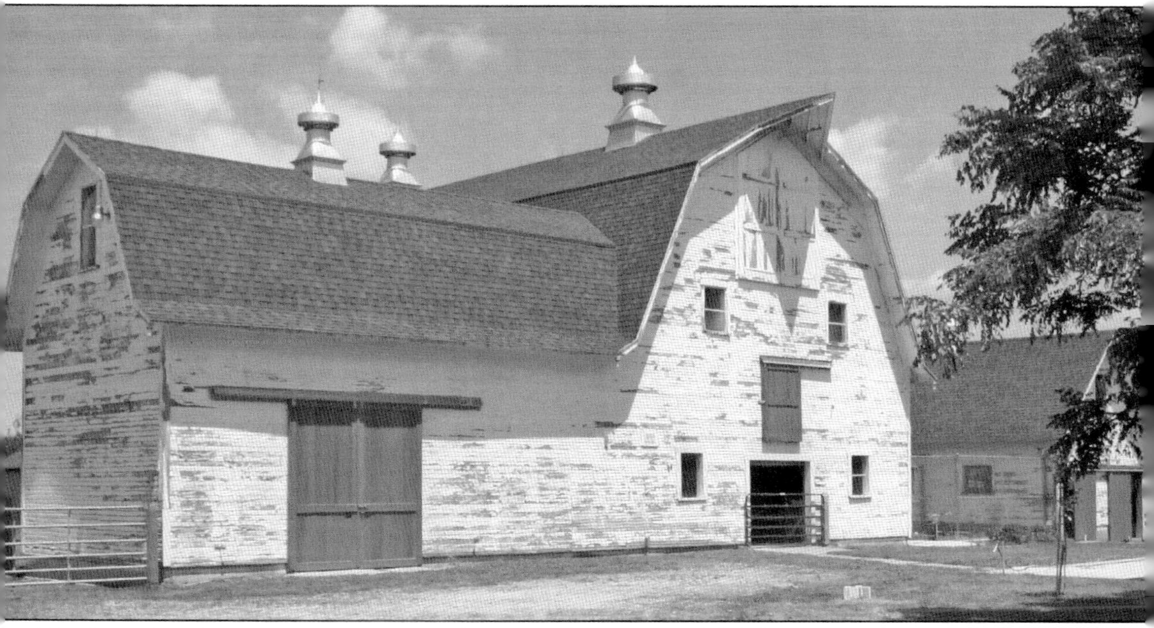

This large dairy barn was state of the art when it was built around 1930. In addition to a milking area and calving area, there was space to unload grains and make custom mixes. The most outstanding visual features are in the main loft, which has a magnificent rafter and support structure with heavy beams to support the large roof. In this central loft is a well-preserved basketball floor. The 2011 owner, Daniel MacBeth, has found that men stop by from time to time to tell him, "When I was a kid, I used to play basketball in that barn." The basketball hoop is still there in the loft, which has plenty of space for practice. MacBeth plans to continue restoration and preservation work on the barn. (DCHS; photograph by Thomas R. Tomlinson.)

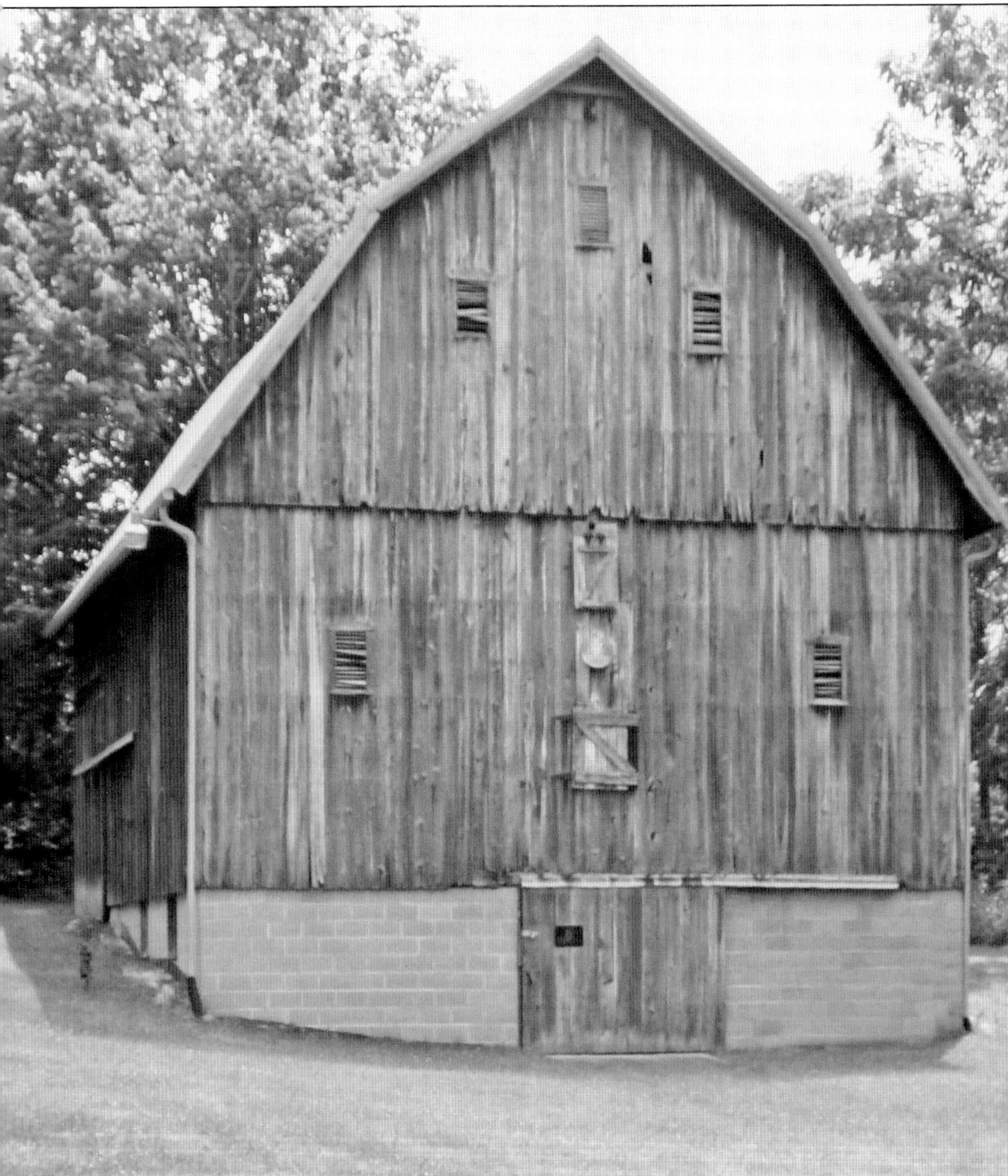

This barn, said to have been built about 1880, has the roof style variously called humpback, gambrel, or horsehip, after its shape. In the 1990s, it became the site of the Humpback Barn Festival of Poetry and Art. Local poet Mildred Trivers owned the barn at the time and strongly supported the festival, which was established in 1990, incorporated in 1992, and held annually in October until 1999. Groups such as the 401 Poetry Group and the Muncie Artists' Guild, as well as devoted individuals, worked to showcase local artists and poets. At one time, the festival attracted over 200 people and 30 poets. (DCHS; photograph by Thomas R. Tomlinson.)

Five

MUNCIE

Muncie was established as the county seat shortly after the county was formed in 1827. An early settler described the townsite as a "vast hazel thicket" and said there was only one road leading to it—the road from Richmond. Roads to the north and to Indianapolis were established. The little town on the river grew slowly and was still just a village when the railroad came through in 1852.

The gas boom began in the late 1880s, and free gas was offered as an inducement to bring factories to the town. The Ball Bros. brought their glass manufacturing to Muncie, and other glass factories and industries came. With the new factories, Muncie increased rapidly in population, as did other parts of the county. After the gas began to fail in the first decade of the 20th century, automotive components such as gears and batteries became basic industries.

In the 1920s and 1930s, the "Muncie as Middletown" books were researched and written. The KKK was active in Muncie during the 1920s. The 1925 capture of infamous criminal Gerald Chapman produced some good publicity. Fred W. Puckett, a police captain active in the Chapman capture, was elected sheriff in 1928. However, by the early 1930s, Muncie was sometimes referred to as "Little Chicago," not only because of its speakeasies, but also because of John Dillinger and others with fast cars and fast guns. Some of these characters visited Muncie from time to time.

During World War II, the local factories produced land mines, ammunition, and furnishings for submarine interiors, among other products, for the defense effort. Durham Manufacturing Company won honors for its part in the war effort and sent a delegation to the launching and christening of the SS *Muncie* victory ship.

There has long been a strong level of activity and support for cultural events, music, and the visual arts. Such groups as Matinee Musicale (established in 1889), Civic Theatre, the Muncie Symphony Orchestra, Masterworks Chorale, and today's Cornerstone Center for the Arts are representative of this aspect of Muncie. There are well-known local artists, from J. Otis Adams in the 1890s to the present day.

The Eastern Division of the Indiana State Normal School became Ball State Teachers College and then Ball State University. The health sector also expanded during the last decades of the 20th century, with Ball Memorial Hospital expanding services, along with the development of various medical specialties.

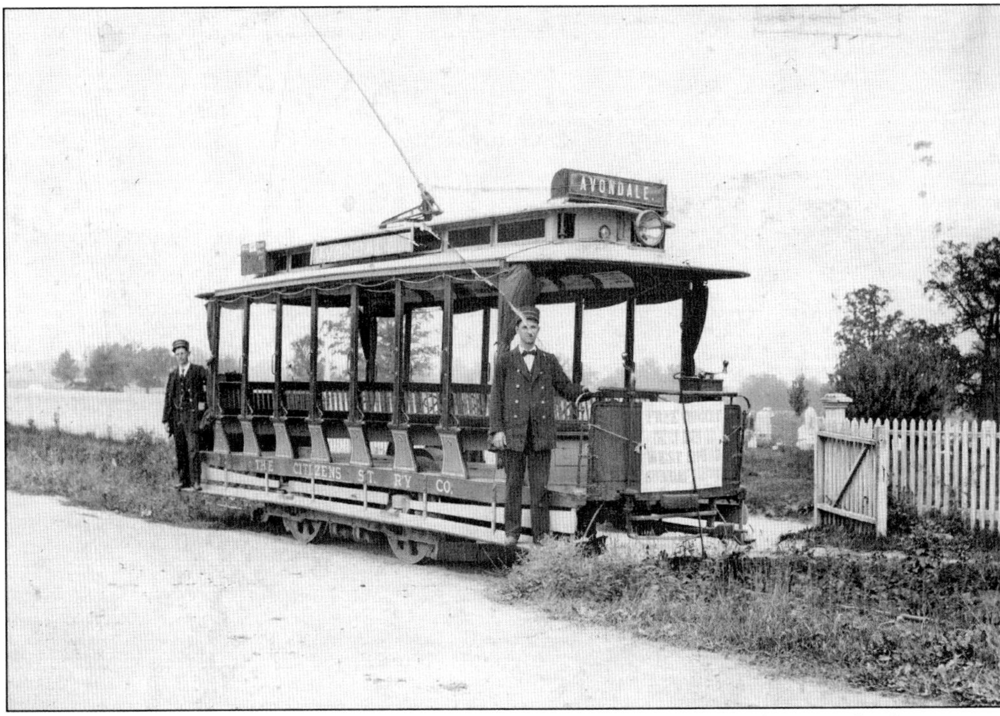

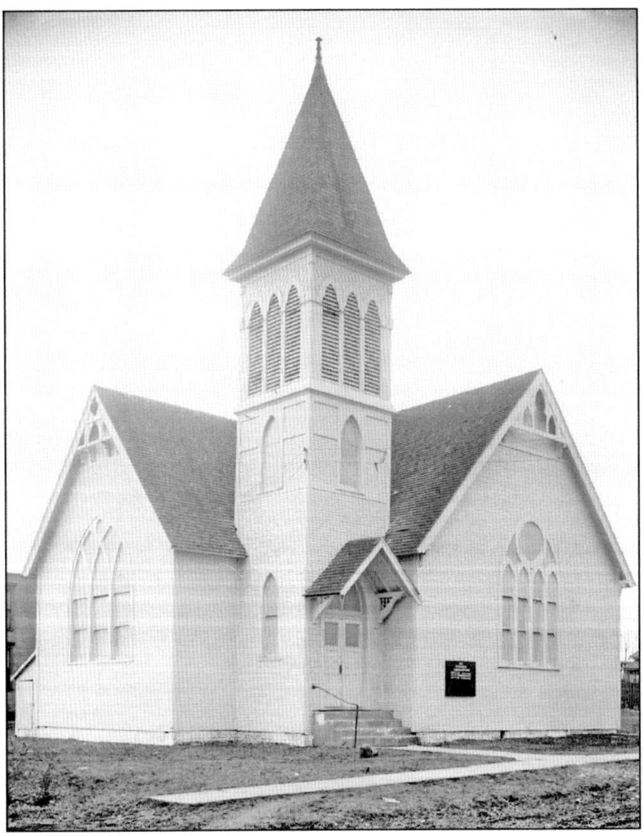

In this photograph, the Avondale trolley car was stopped at the Beech Grove Cemetery near the northern end. The Avondale addition was developed near the industries south of the railroad tracks in the 1880s. In 1889, it was said to have grown to 100 houses, with improved transportation by way of Ohmer Avenue, known today as Memorial Drive, or Twelfth Street. (Larry Campbell.)

This Congerville church appears to be newly constructed in this photograph. Congerville was named for its developer, the Conger Realty Company. Located east and south from the corner of Memorial Drive (Twelfth Street) and Walnut Street, it was developed from about 1890 to 1910. The name is also associated with the Congerville Flyers, a well-known football team in the 1920s. (DCHS.)

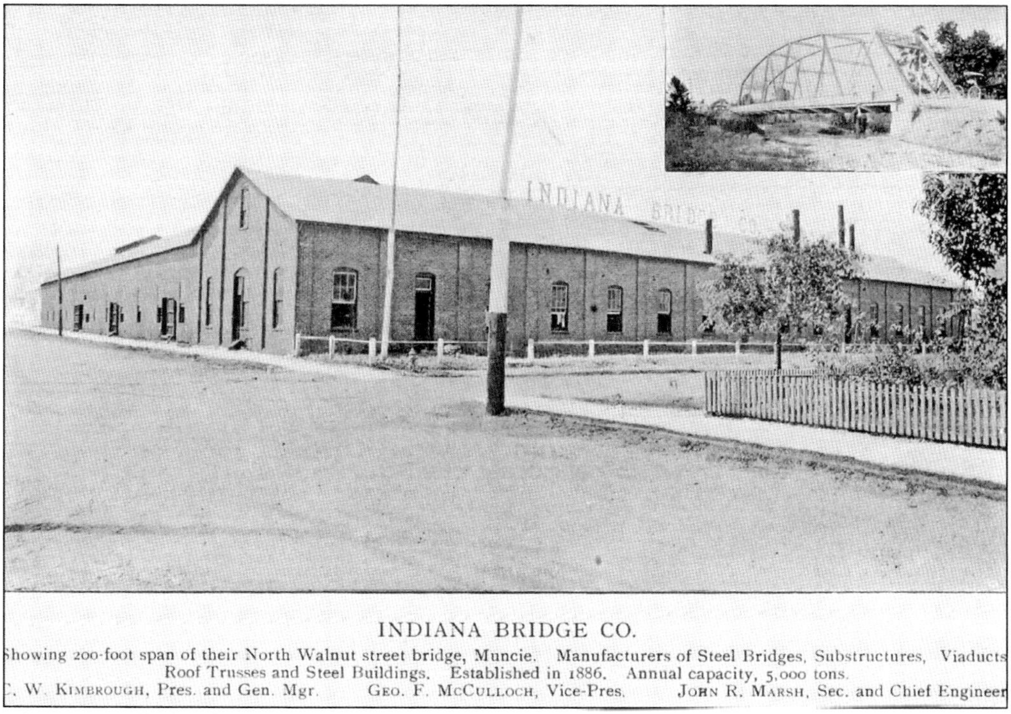

The Indiana Bridge Company built bridges all across the United States and manufactured structural steel for all kinds of buildings. This photograph, which appeared in *Our County* by John S. Ellis, includes an inset showing the Walnut Street bridge built by the Indiana Bridge Company in the late 1890s when the old wooden covered bridge was replaced. (DCHS.)

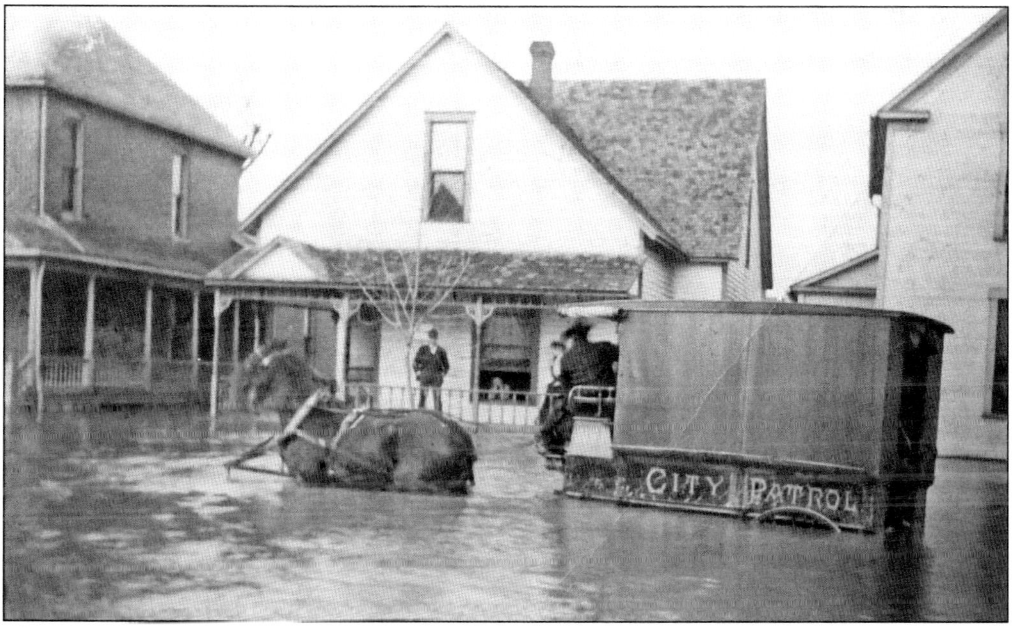

The flood of 1903 was one of the area's most notable floods. Much of Muncie was low and subject to flooding during heavy rains. The horse and "City Patrol" wagon provided a means to rescue stranded residents. (Michael Mavis.)

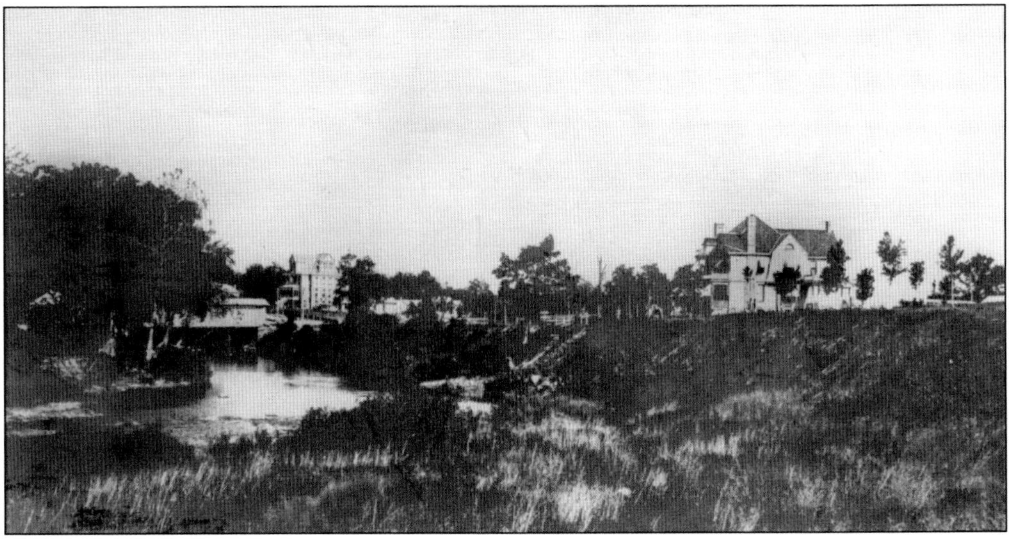

This 1890s photograph shows the old covered wooden bridge on north Walnut Street at left. At the north (right) end of the bridge is the first Children's Home, or Orphans' Home, as it was called in that era. White River is in the foreground with McCullough Boulevard on the right. (Minnetrista Heritage Collection, Muncie, Indiana.)

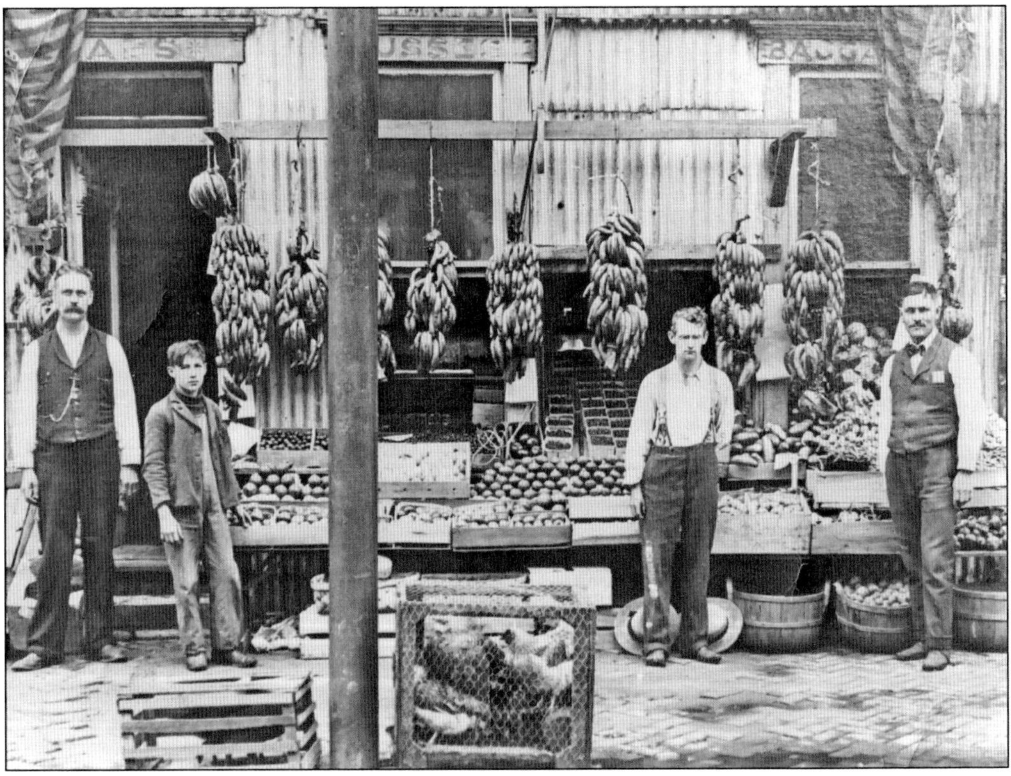

The fruit market at the southeast corner of Walnut and Charles Streets, where the Ball Stores building was later erected, is seen in a late-1890s photograph. The bananas are prominent among the produce on display. In the foreground is a cage of live poultry. (Minnetrista Heritage Collection, Muncie, Indiana.)

Close examination of this photograph shows that the calendars are turned to October 1918. The spindle below the large calendar holds receipts headed "Kimbrough Hardware." This bookkeeper appears to be recording sales for the day, or perhaps the previous day, in her ledger. (DCHS, Glass Negative Collection.)

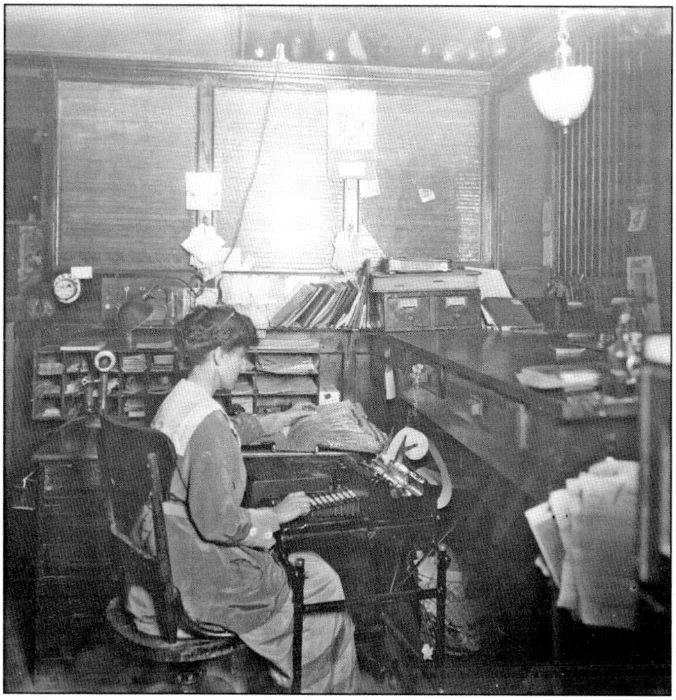

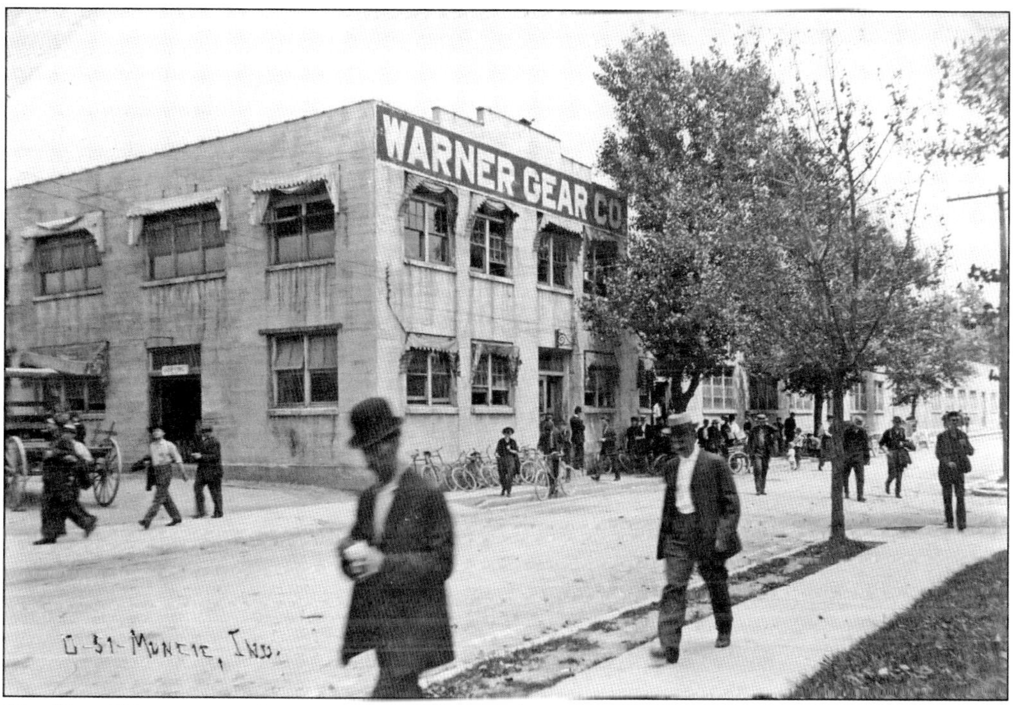

The Borg Warner story began with a differential invented by Hugh Warner, which he took to a show in New York in 1903. There he received an order from R.E. Olds for 5,000 differentials, which led to the partnership of Hugh Warner, Thomas Warner, and Abbott L. Johnson. The Warner Gear Co. building shown here was at an early location on Seymour Street. (Muncie Public Library.)

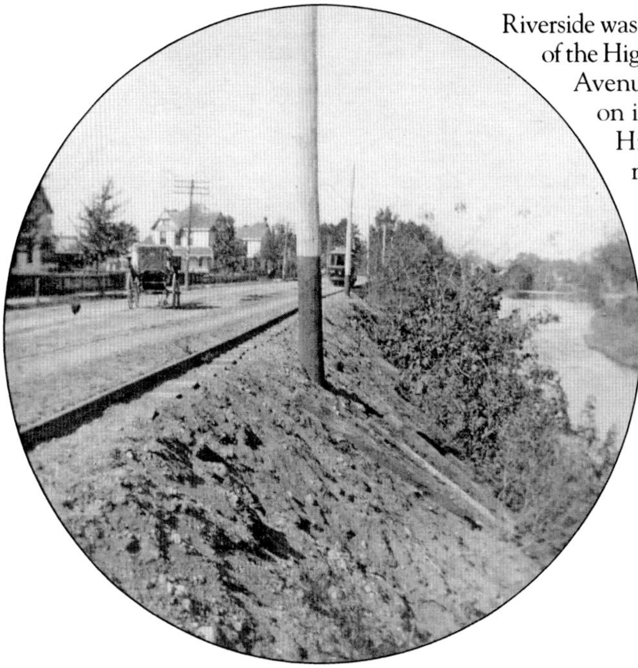

Riverside was a residential suburb of Muncie north of the High Street Bridge and west of Wheeling Avenue. The streetcar at left center was on its route from points east, including Highland Avenue and Woods Park, now McCulloch Park. It continued down Wheeling Avenue, giving Riverside residents ready access to Muncie. This view shows the high-banked levee side of White River before the concrete wall was in place. (Michael Mavis.)

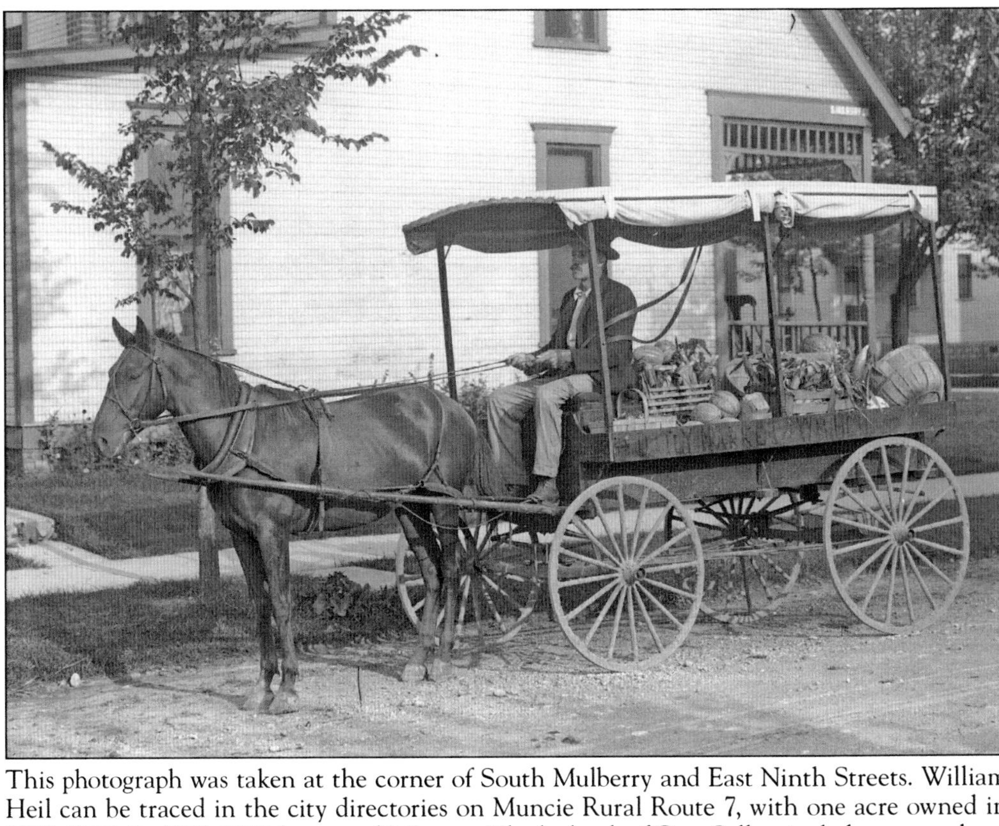

This photograph was taken at the corner of South Mulberry and East Ninth Streets. William Heil can be traced in the city directories on Muncie Rural Route 7, with one acre owned in 1907–1908. By 1915–1916, he owned 2.5 acres. The logbook of Otto Sellers includes a note about a photograph taken in August 1912. (DCHS.)

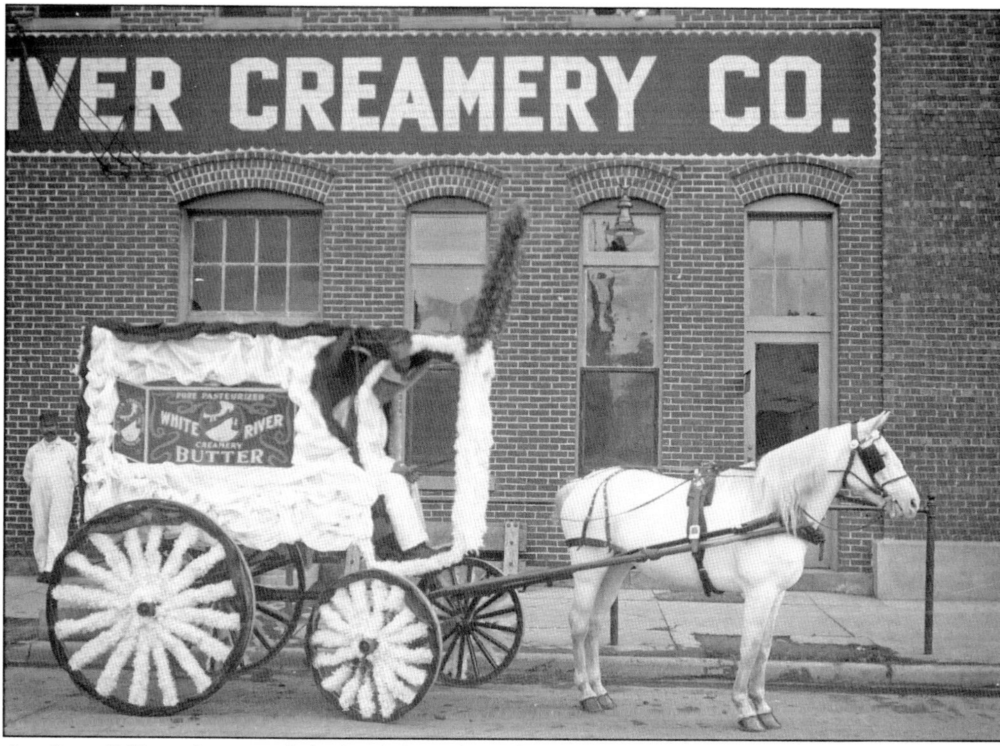

An Otto Sellers photograph logbook lists the following for White River Creamery on October 8, 1914: "horse and wagon trimmed for parade." And here it is, in front of the creamery on West Seymour Street, ready to go into the parade. The White River Creamery was bought by Fox River Butter Company by 1919–1920 and later by Beatrice Creamery. (DCHS.)

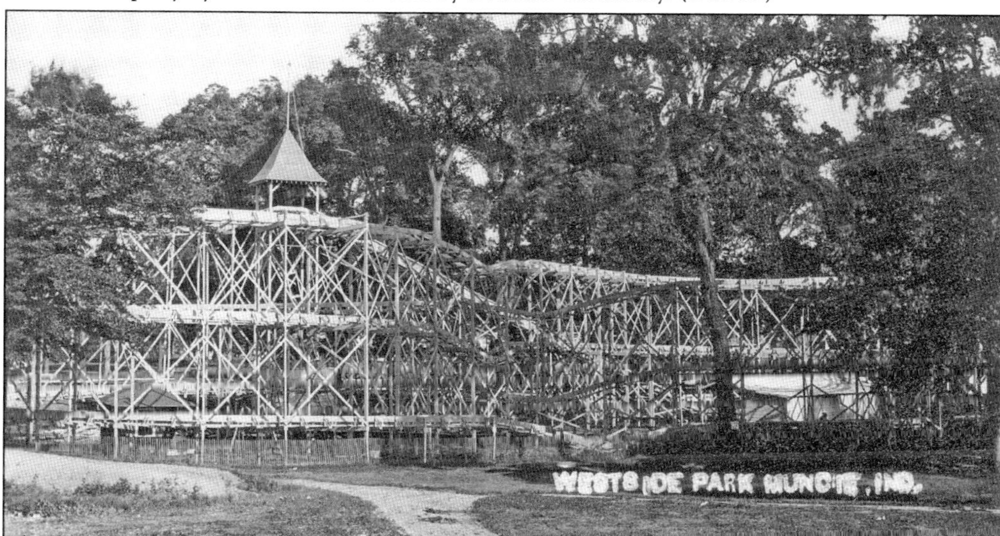

Westside Park was a large interurban park, a destination for those seeking family entertainment, from plays and recitals to roller coasters, baseball games, and balloon ascensions. The indoor roller-skating rink there was said to be the largest in the nation. A new triple-eight roller coaster was built in 1908 at Westside. (DCHS, Moore Youse Home Museum collections.)

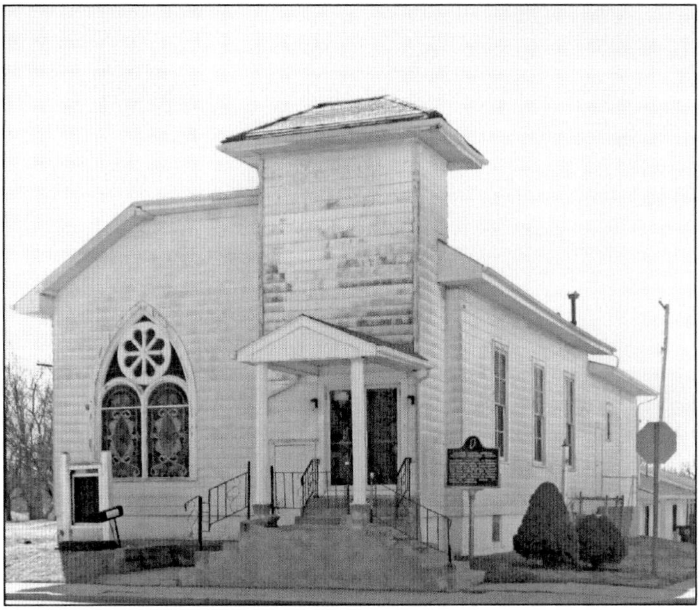

Shaffer Chapel African Methodist Episcopal Church is a designated state historical site with a marker. Built as the Whitely schoolhouse about 1893, it was purchased by the congregation by 1929. Church pastor J.E. Johnson was also a mortician. He brought to Muncie for embalming the bodies of two black men hanged by a mob in Marion on August 7, 1930. The bodies were returned to Marion for burial. (Photograph by Thomas R. Tomlinson.)

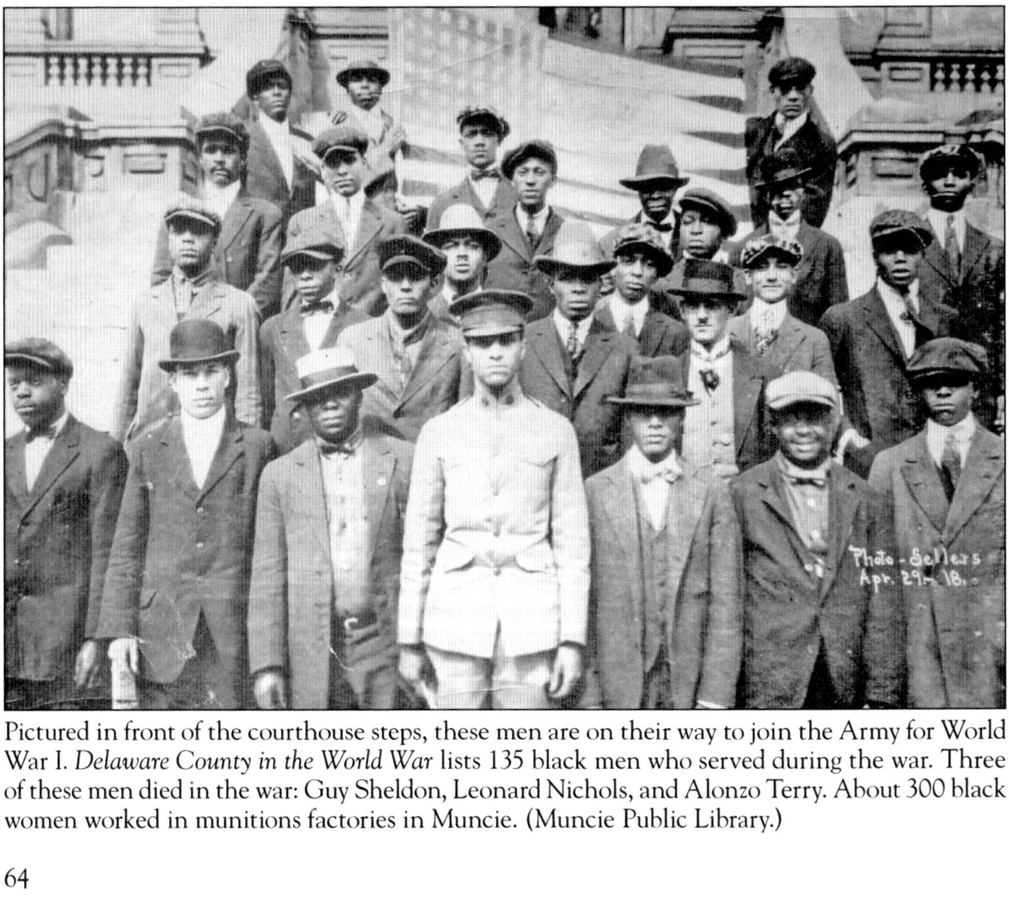

Pictured in front of the courthouse steps, these men are on their way to join the Army for World War I. *Delaware County in the World War* lists 135 black men who served during the war. Three of these men died in the war: Guy Sheldon, Leonard Nichols, and Alonzo Terry. About 300 black women worked in munitions factories in Muncie. (Muncie Public Library.)

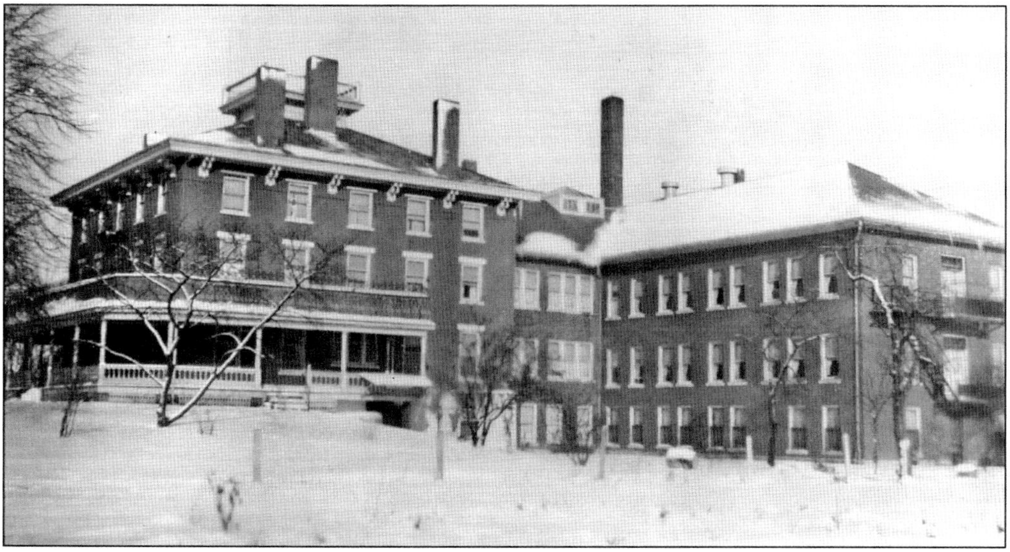

A house belonging to Dr. Anthony was built onto and became the Home Hospital in 1913 under the supervision of Dr. George R. Andrews and with the material aid of Amos and Burt Whitely. In 1920, Andrews became ill and could not continue. Ball Memorial Hospital was opened in 1929 as a public hospital. (DCHS, gift of Barbara Murray.)

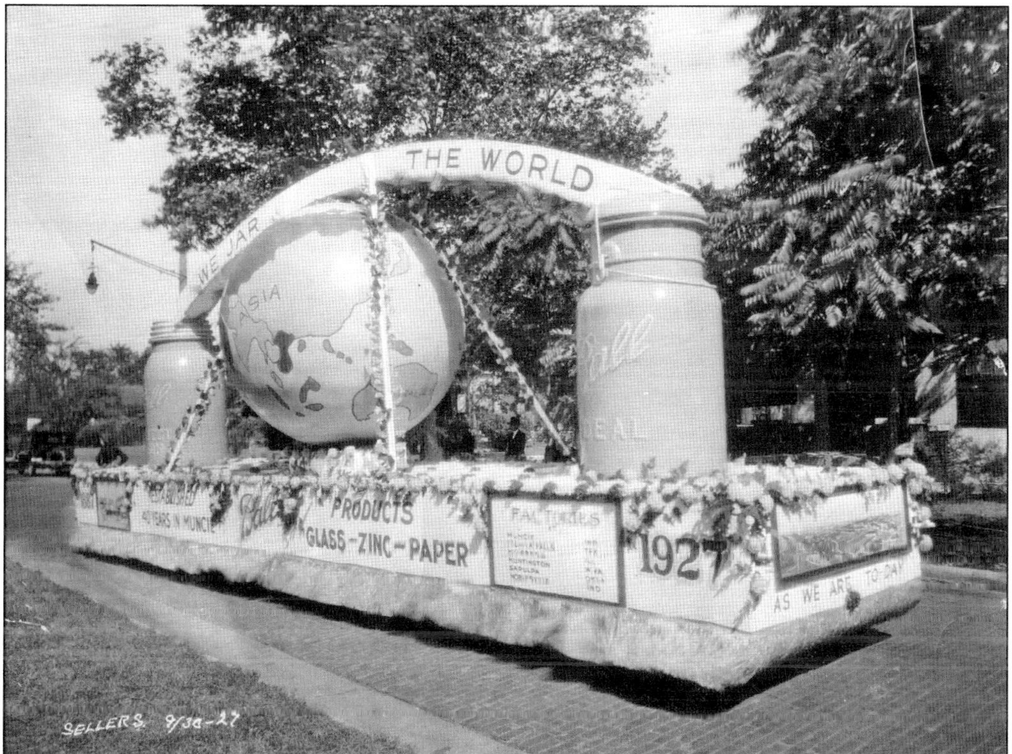

The float reveals that Ball Bros. was established in 1887 and had been in Muncie for 40 years, with the products of glass, zinc, and paper. Listed are factories in Wichita Falls, Texas; Hillsboro, Illinois; Huntington, West Virginia; Sapulpa, Oklahoma; and Noblesville, Indiana. (DCHS.)

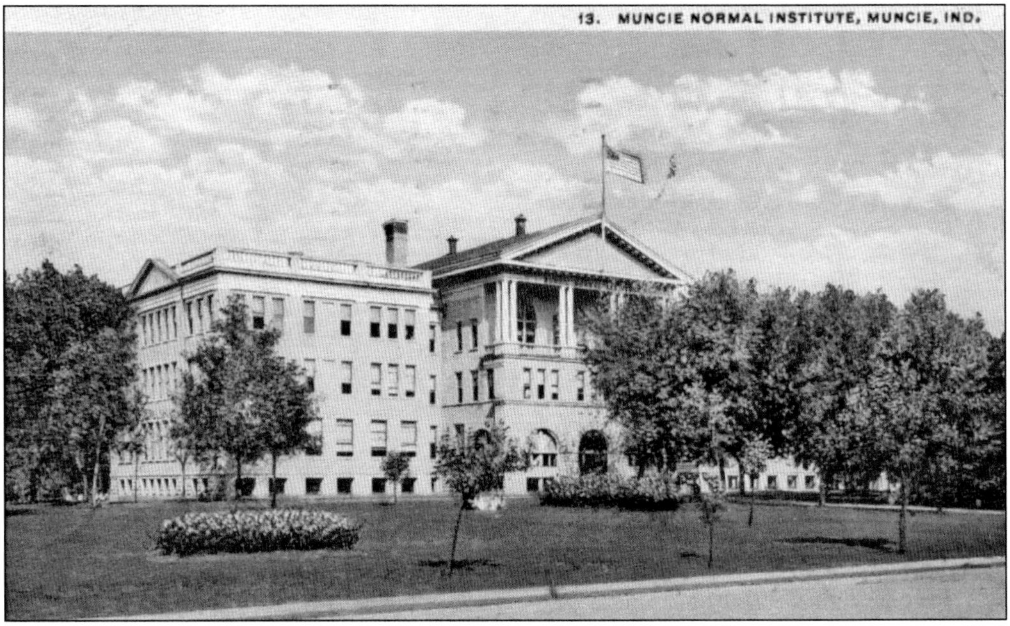

The term normal school or normal institute was used to describe teacher education as a standard or pattern as it developed in the late 1800s. Normal City was the name of the suburb where the proceeds from the lots were used for the structure shown in the photograph, now part of the administration building at Ball State University, formerly Ball State Teachers College. (Muncie Public Library.)

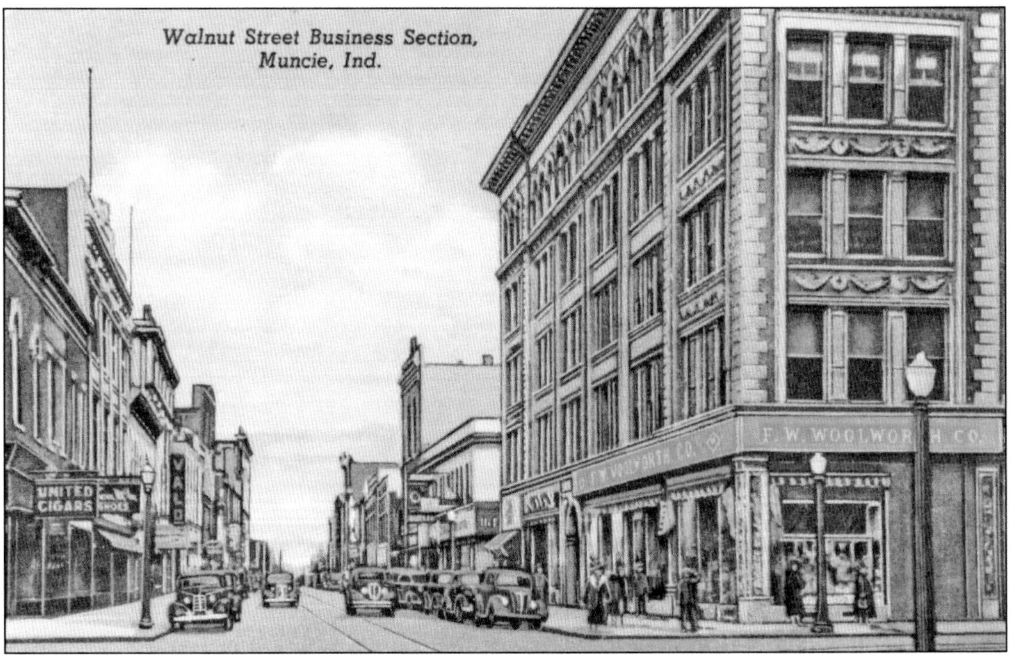

This 1930s postcard shows the Woolworth store on the corner of Walnut and Charles Streets. The building was the Johnson Block, now long gone. Among other businesses, it housed the Murray Jewelry Store on one of its floors and Dr. Jean Morris, an ophthalmologist, on another floor. (Muncie Public Library.)

In this photograph, two employees of the Owens-Illinois Glass Company are displaying a land mine made by the Muncie factory during World War II. A newspaper article from December 1941 announces new war contracts giving Durham and Glasscock orders to produce land mines. Also announced was a contract to Superior Steel Products Company for ammunition. (Minnetrista Heritage Collection, Muncie, Indiana.)

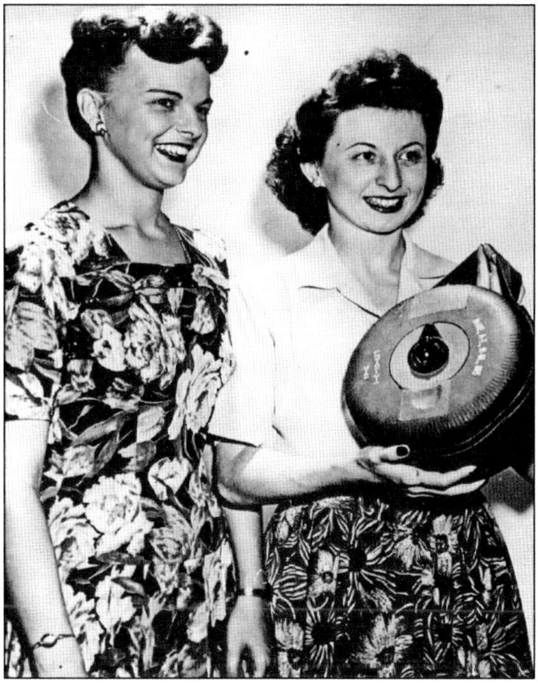

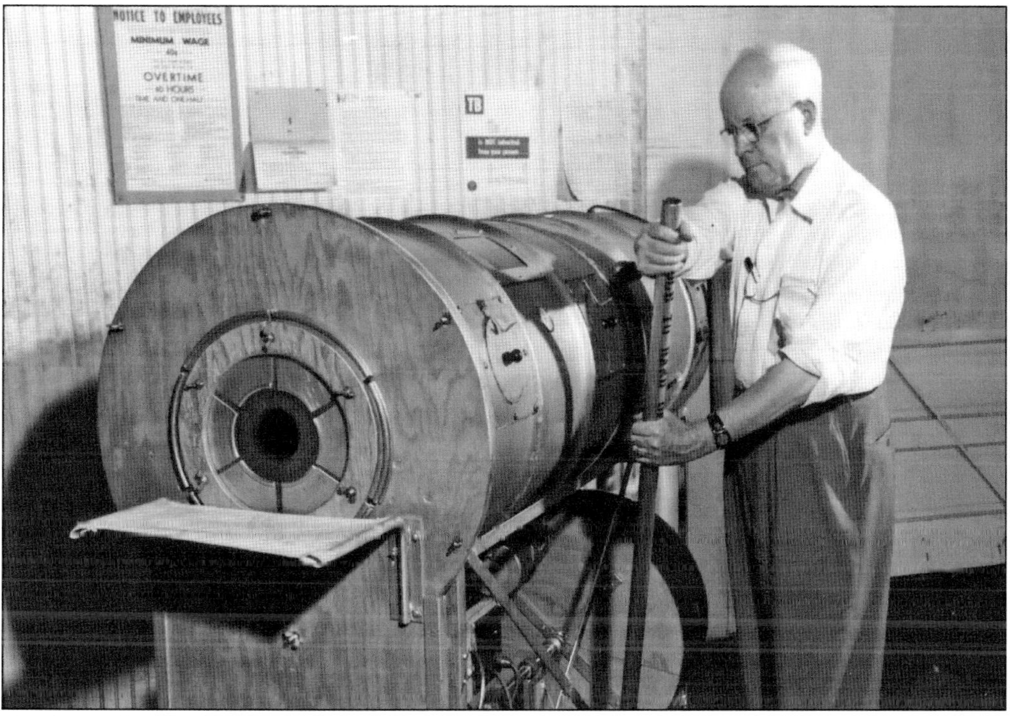

A poliomyelitis epidemic struck the Muncie area in 1949. Treatment involved the use of iron lungs to assist in breathing, with no cure or preventative available at that time. The available supply of iron lungs was soon exhausted. Local inventor James "Jack" Reichart designed an iron lung that could be assembled from locally made components, and his Excel Manufacturing Company employees built several of the machines. (Minnetrista Heritage Collection, Muncie, Indiana.)

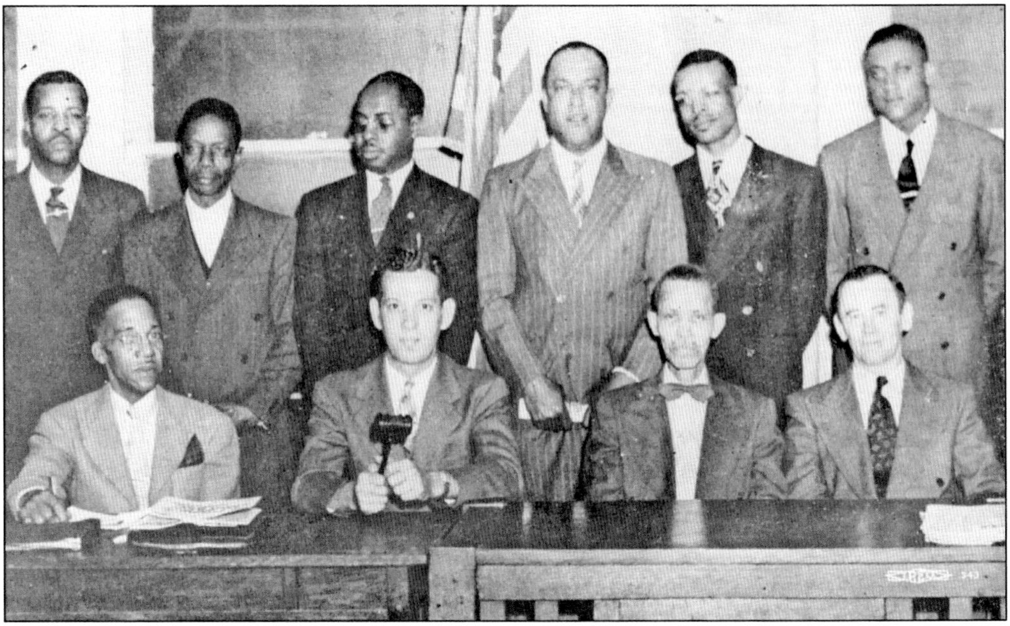

This meeting at Franks Foundry in the late 1940s shows union officers meeting to discuss union business and working conditions. This was a period in which the unions were very strong, not only in Muncie and East Central Indiana, but across the nation as well. (Muncie Public Library.)

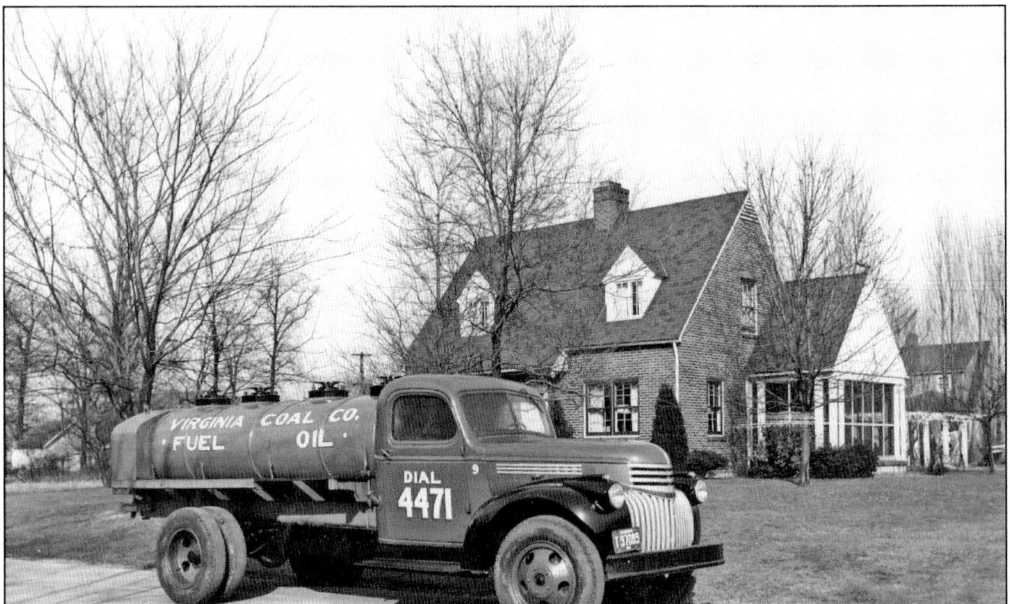

Joseph Darlington brought his family to Delaware County about 1929 and took a job at the Elevator Cash Coal Company. He continued working there when it became the Virginia Coal Company and then the Virginia Coal and Oil Company. Their trucks delivered coal and heating oil to homes. Darlington became the owner of the company and ran it until his death in 1952. (Margaret Darlington Montano.)

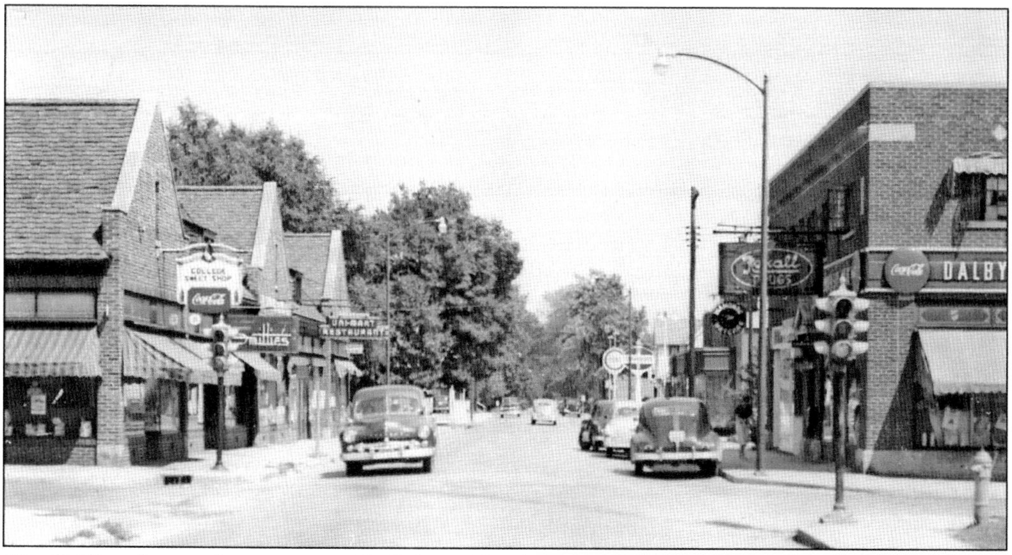

The "Village" near the campus of Ball State Teachers College, later Ball State University, was a favorite area for students and residents alike. On the left are Smittie's, the College Sweet Shop, and the Uni-Mart Restaurant. Kerney Wilson's Standard Service Station is at center right. On the right in the foreground, the University Drug Store was run by Maynel Dalby for about 30 years, beginning in the 1920s. (Muncie Public Library.)

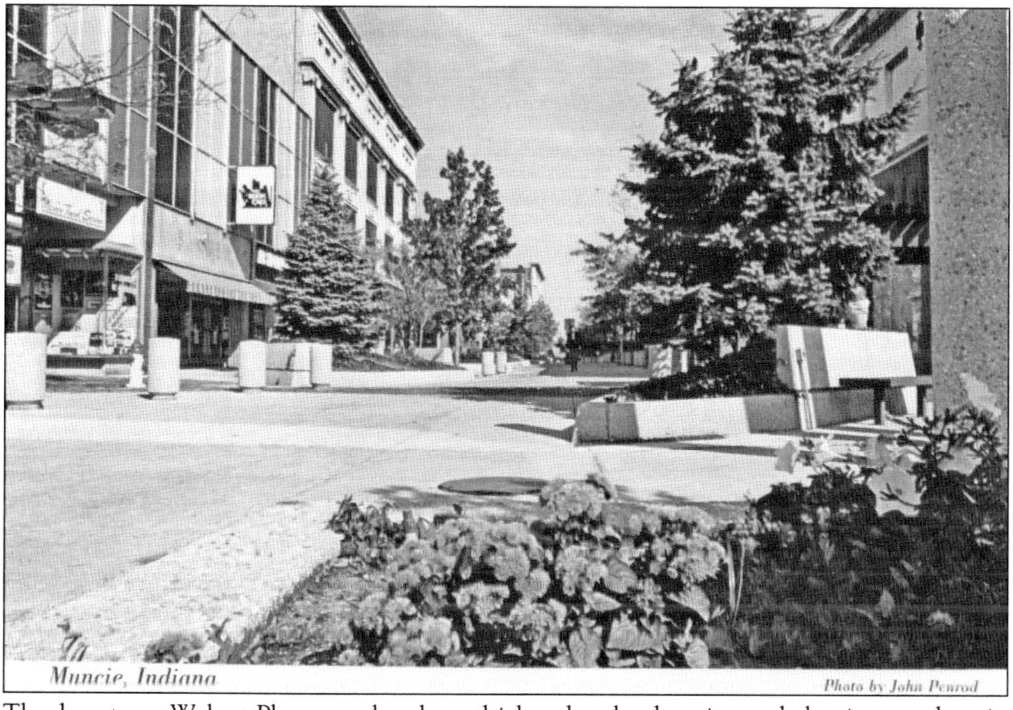

The downtown Walnut Plaza was closed to vehicles when landscaping and planting was done in 1975. During its time as a pedestrian area, traffic was lost to areas along McGalliard Road. The change to allow vehicles, along with the restoration of the original fronts of the buildings in recent years, has made a much more attractive downtown area. Various downtown events have been arranged to attract people to the area. (Muncie Public Library.)

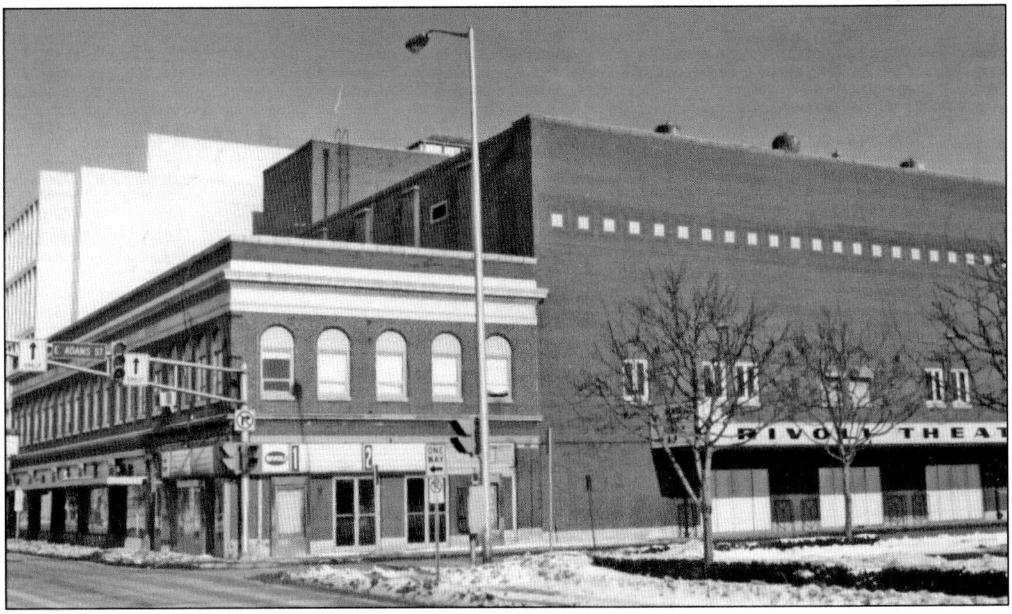

The Rivoli Theater was a favorite movie theater for many years. Many longtime residents remember fondly various popular movies viewed on the Rivoli screens. This photograph shows it on a slushy, sunny day after it closed. Changing lifestyles, technology, and economics were involved in its closure and eventual removal from the scene. (DCHS.)

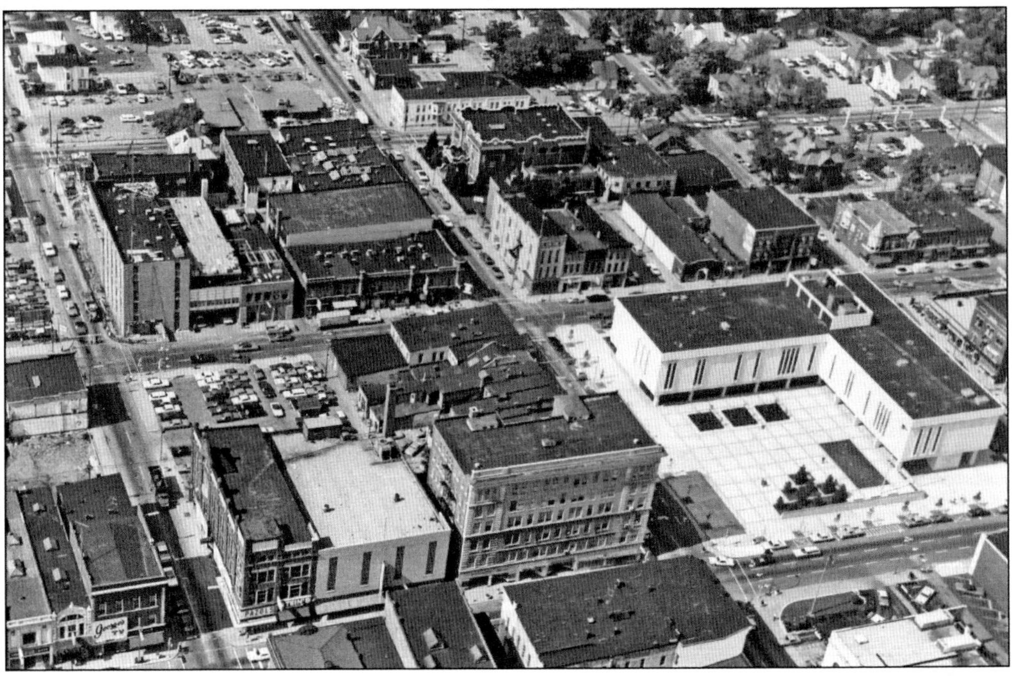

This aerial view of the courthouse and downtown Muncie is from 1969, after the new courthouse was built. Many buildings have been removed, with three-quarters of the block south (to the left) of the courthouse changed completely and three-quarters of the block to the southwest (upper left) of the courthouse demolished. Newer buildings include the MITS bus station and the downtown post office. (DCHS.)

Six

Selma

The origin of Selma was quite different from the other principal towns in Delaware County. It was not on a river, nor was it on a road or path frequently used by travelers. It was platted in 1852 after the railroad surveys were made and was laid out along the line of the railroad. The east half of the plat was owned by Joseph Greenwalt, the west half by Francis M. Dowler. Railroad Street was 80 feet wide and thus split the town into a northern part and a southern part. The plat was laid out with Muncie Street as the divider between east and west.

As it turned out, Albany Street was where the merchants settled. The business district was thus settled along North Albany Street, north of the railroad. The roads south to Smithfield and north to Albany provided good access to the town for the township inhabitants.

Smithfield, a little town along the river to the south of Selma, had been the principal settlement in the area. This was changed with the new town along the railroad, which was also on State Road 32 when it was built through. One of the most prominent physical features of the county, located west of Selma, is the "Selma Sink." This boggy area has required extra railroad maintenance and special highway construction.

Selma and Liberty Township had gas wells, and the town experienced growth due to the gas boom. In 1904, a fire started in the DeLong Hotel and destroyed many buildings in the business center. By this time, the gas era had largely ended. New buildings were erected, and the town became incorporated in 1907.

The interurban was welcomed in the new 20th century and provided inexpensive travel to other parts of the county and state. In the late 1930s, a fox farm was established at the eastern edge of the town. After World War II, the businesses of Selma continued to prosper as the surrounding area made it a trading center for many years. Then, as transportation and economics changed, the town suffered the same kind of decline as did other such county centers.

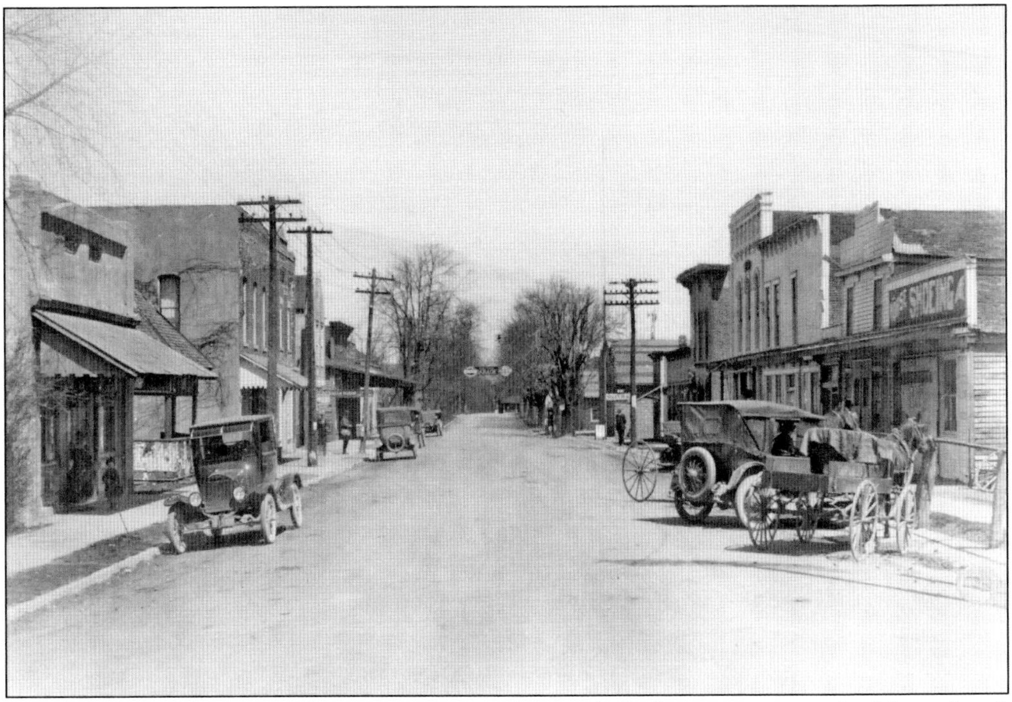

Albany Street has long been the main street in Selma, with the business area north of the railroad. This photograph, probably from the first decade of the 20th century, was taken after the fire of 1904. A vacant lot can be glimpsed at the left edge of the photograph. (Michael Mavis.)

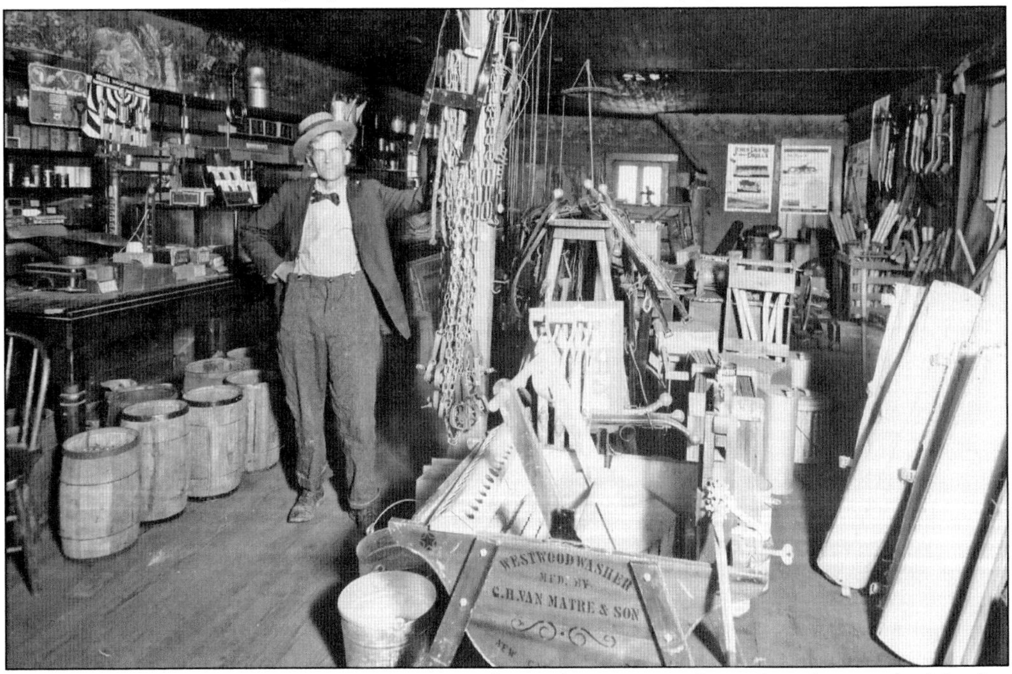

This photograph of J.O. Murray in his store shows the variety of merchandise stocked for his customers. From the wooden washer in the foreground, to barrels of dried foodstuffs and other items, plus shelves of cans and boxes, he had a little of everything needed. (Larry Campbell.)

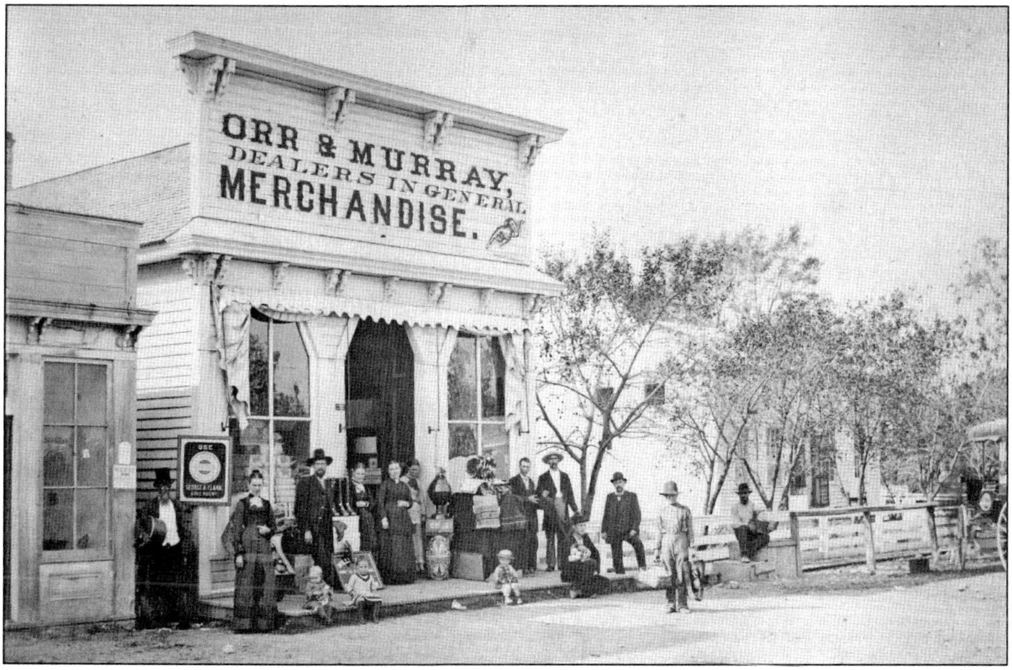

Everyone turned out for this c. 1880 photograph of a popular store and gathering place. The building survived many years and was used as a canning factory, a lumber company, and a garage. After World War II, it became Swingley's Farm Equipment store. (Jeffrey Koenker.)

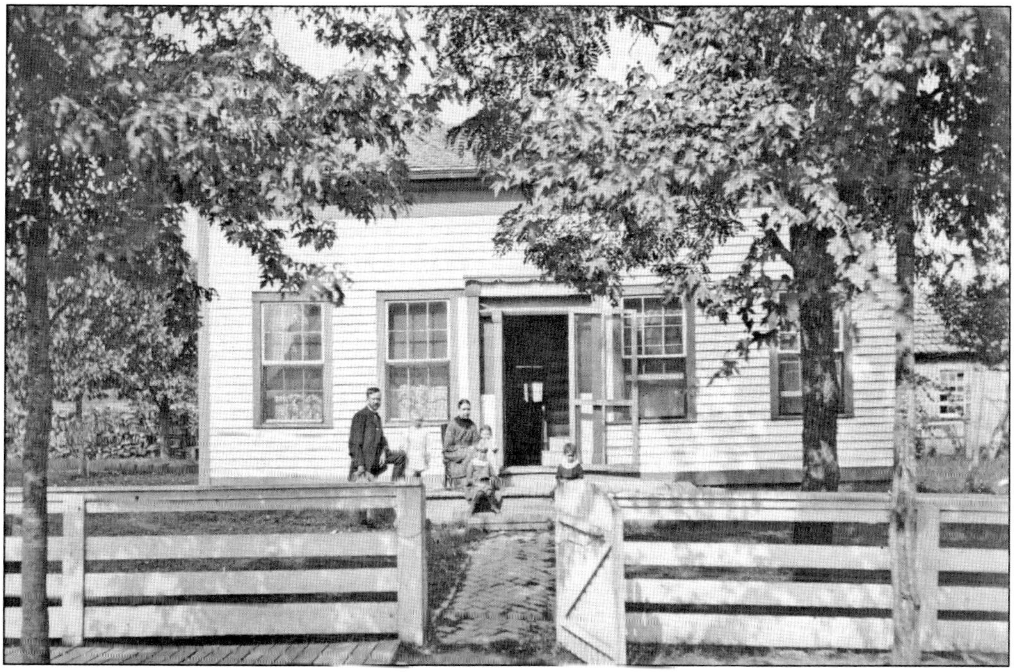

This photograph of the Orr homestead shows, from left to right, J.N. Orr, James "Jim" Orr, Artemissa Lewellen (housekeeper), Blanche Lewellen, Bertha Orr (who later married a Pittenger), and Daisy Fertich. Orr family members were pioneers in Liberty Township. (Minnetrista Heritage Collection, Muncie, Indiana.)

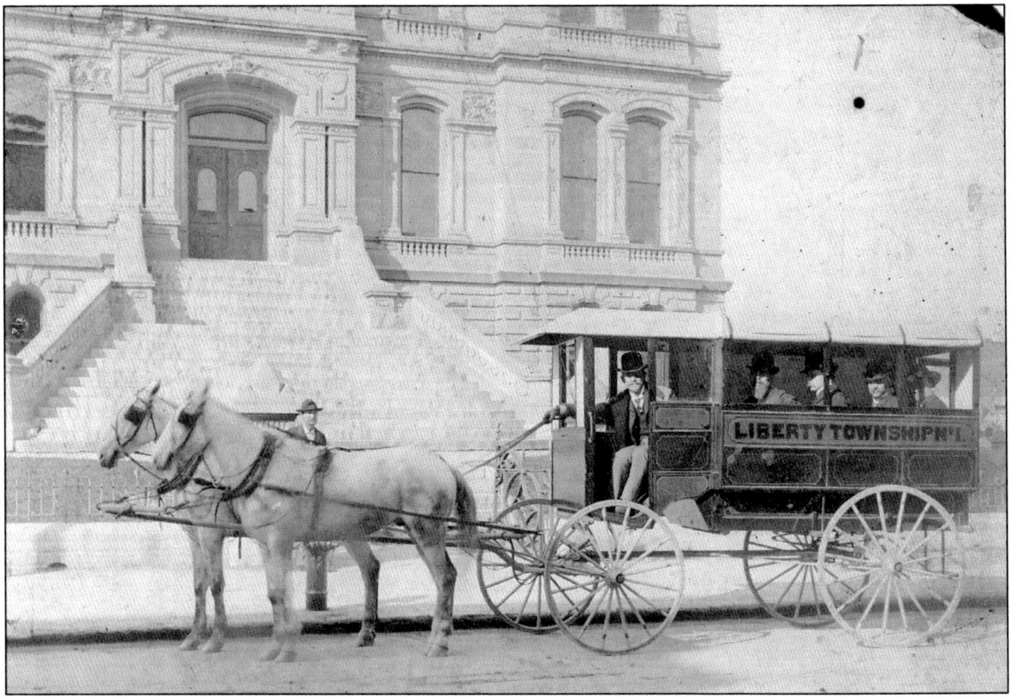

During the 1901–1902 school year, Arlin J. Bailey drove his school hack, carrying the local school officials to a trustee meeting at Eaton. He stopped at the county courthouse before continuing on the journey with, from left to right, Charles Van Mater, county superintendent; ? Howell, trustee of Perry Township; W. Henry Williams, trustee of Liberty Township; and an unidentified man. (David Bailey.)

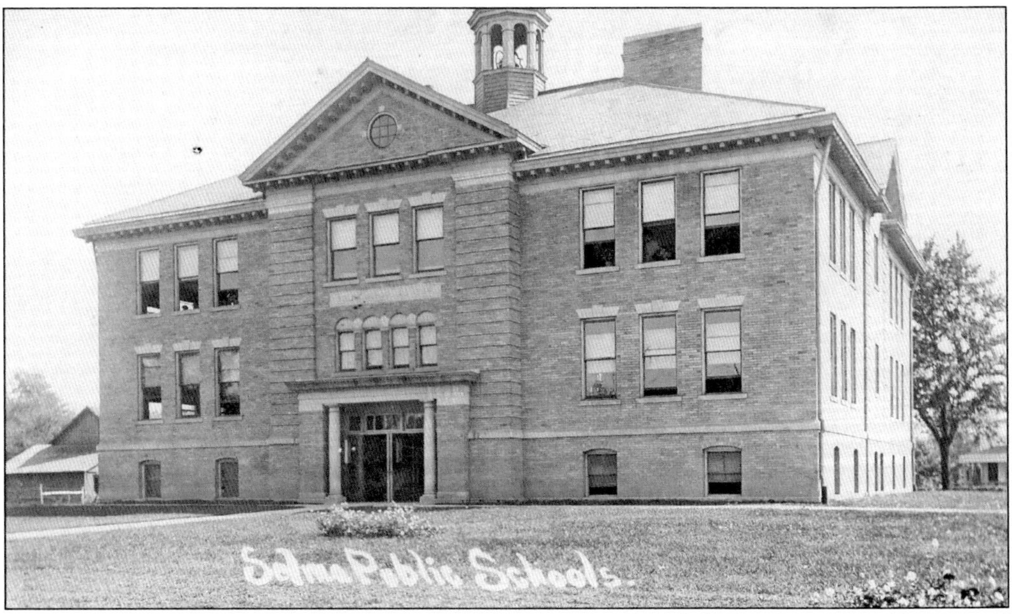

This facility was built in 1904 as one of the newly consolidated graded schools. Many additions and changes were made over the years as the community grew and changed. The building continued until it was torn down in 1980. (Jeffrey Koenker.)

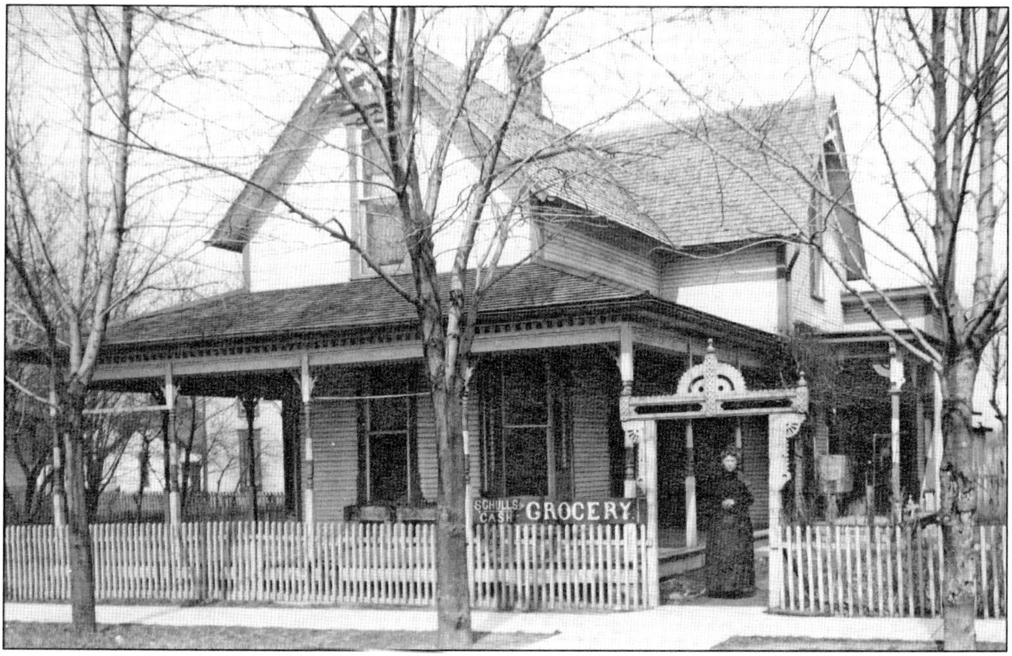

"Schull's Cash Grocery" proclaims the sign on the picket fence next to a rather elaborate gate. A room or two on the side of the house were probably used to stock popular items. Edward Schull was listed as a grocer in the 1900 census. His son John H. Schull was listed as a baker in the same census. (Jeffrey Koenker.)

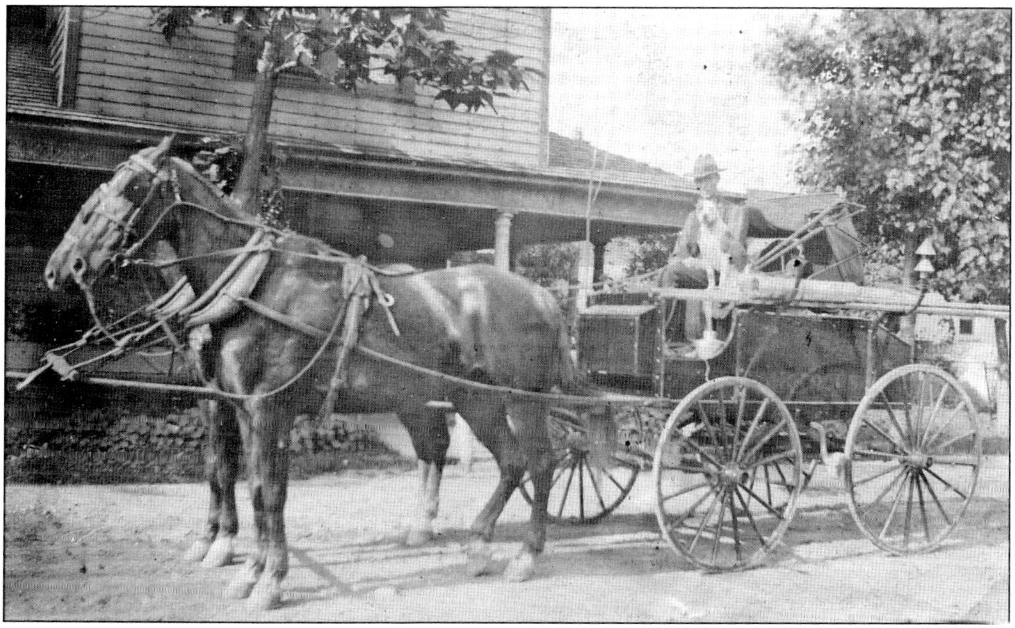

This photograph of a wagon hauling nitroglycerin is from the years of oil and gas drilling in the area. Nitroglycerin, handled carefully without exposure to pressure, was used in gas drilling. After a well reached a sufficient depth without pressure strong enough, 80–100 pounds of nitroglycerin would be lowered and a solid piece of iron, the "go-devil," was dropped on the nitroglycerin, causing it to explode. (David Bailey.)

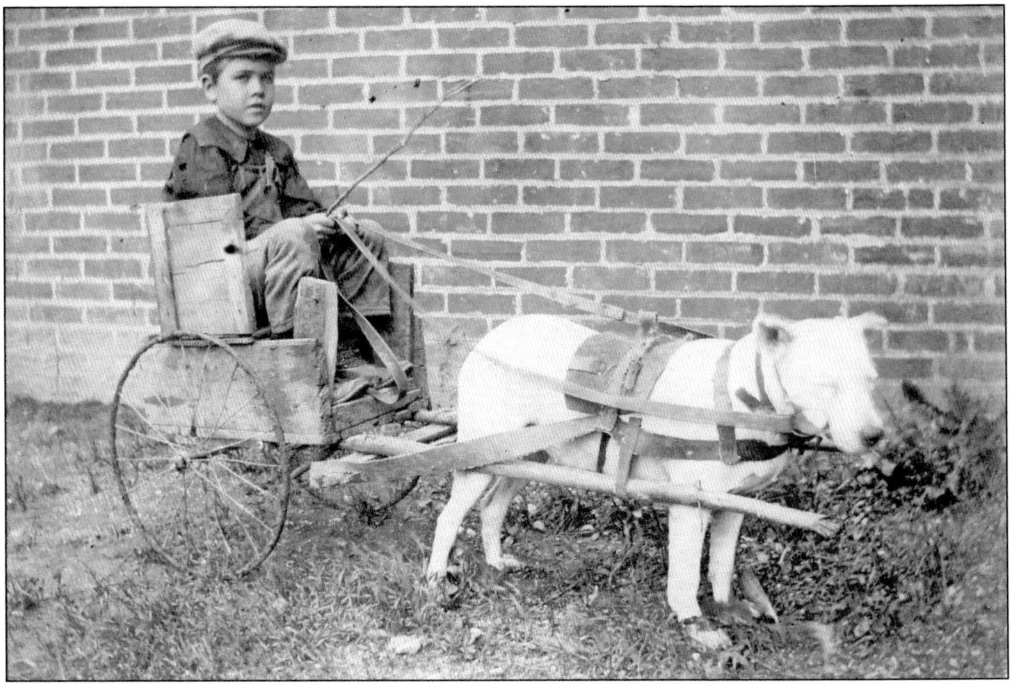

This photograph is labeled simply "John White and his dog cart." It may date from the 1890s. The construction of the cart shows considerable ingenuity, with an old cupboard door on the side, stout sticks for the shafts, and leather straps perhaps salvaged from the local livery. (David Bailey.)

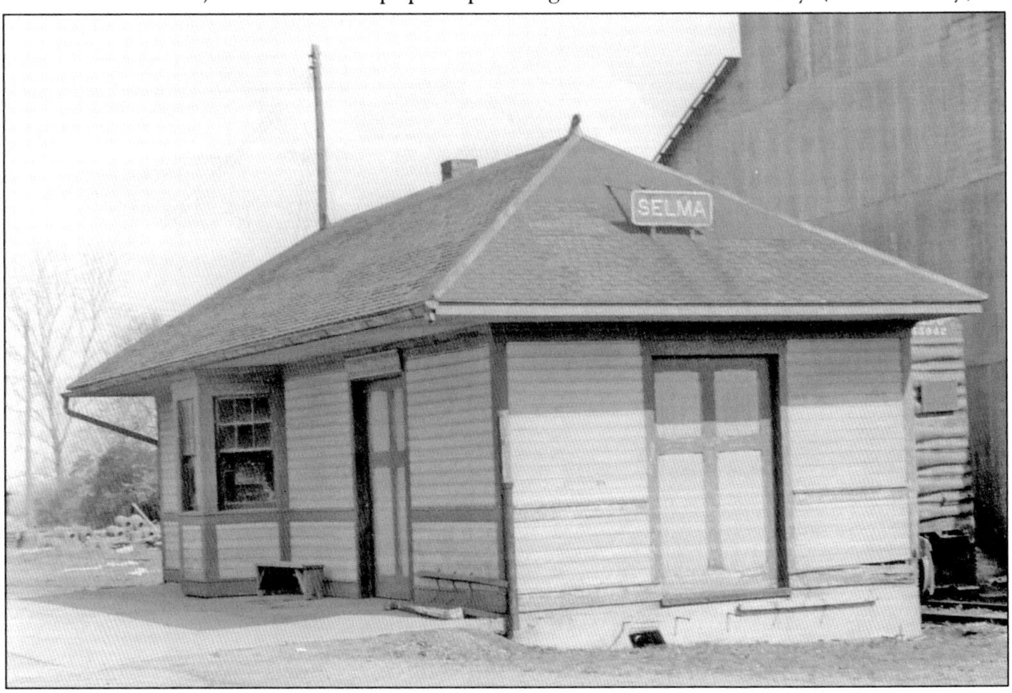

This station house sits with its back to the rails next to the grain elevator in the background. A railroad car, possibly loaded with grain, is just visible between the station house and the elevator. (Jeffrey Koenker.)

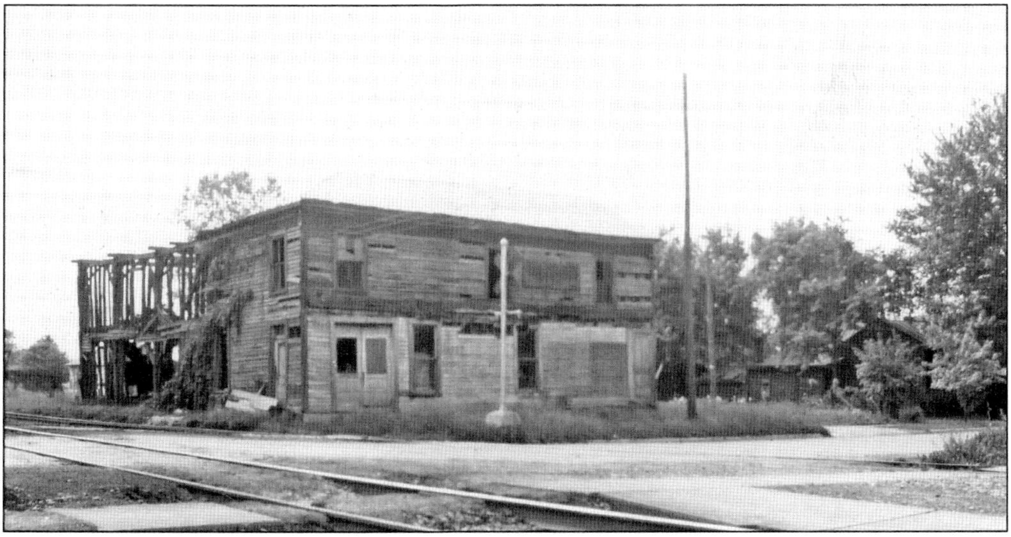

"Thunder Castle" was the popular name for this structure built in 1854 by William Lewis, a warehouse merchant. It was on the east side of Albany Street and on the south side of the railroad tracks. It had several different uses over the years. (Larry Campbell.)

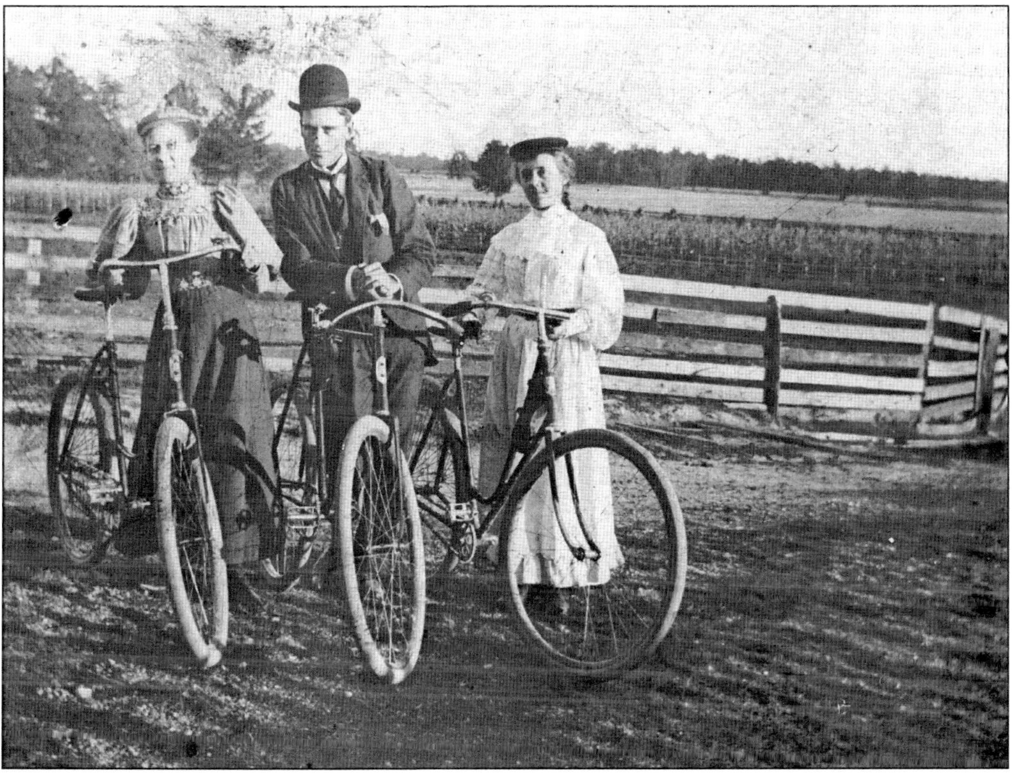

On bicycles in the countryside sometime during 1897–1898 are, from left to right, Edna Clark, Lemuel Arthur Pittenger, and Nell Orr. L.A. Pittenger, as he was later known, was born in Desoto and grew up on a farm near Selma. From 1927 to 1942, he served as president of the Muncie Normal School, which became Ball State Teachers College and then Ball State University. (David Bailey.)

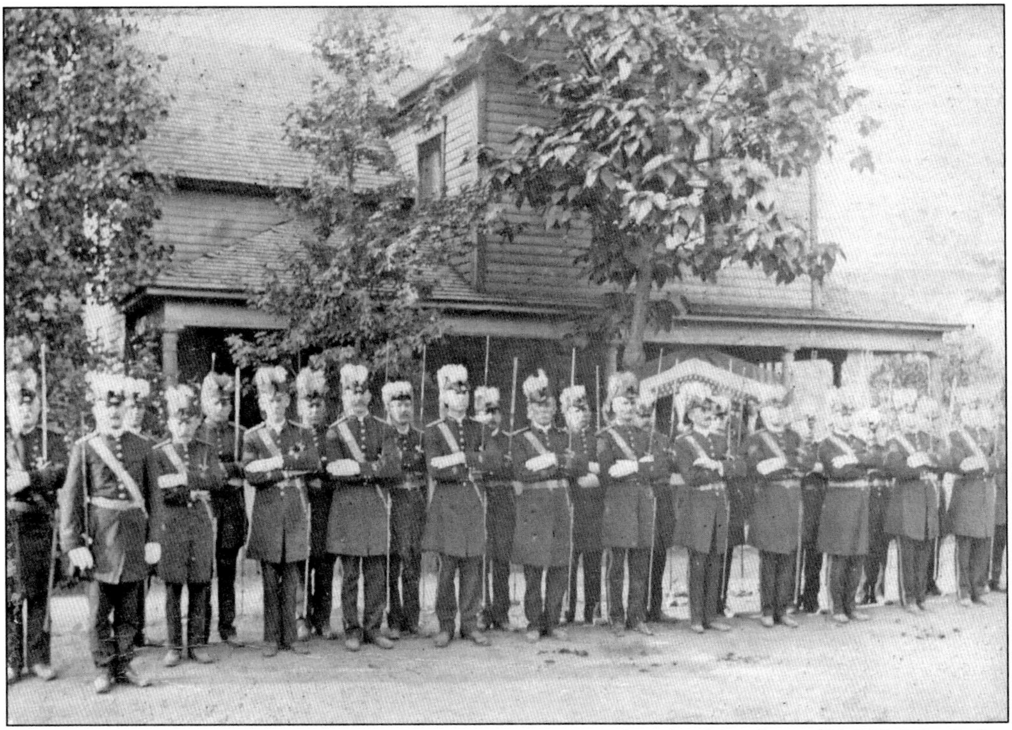

Most of the small towns had a lodge of the Independent Order of Odd Fellows (IOOF). The lodge in Selma was organized in 1857. By 1880, they had a membership of 54. This photograph of their military unit was taken as they assembled along Railroad Street. (David Bailey.)

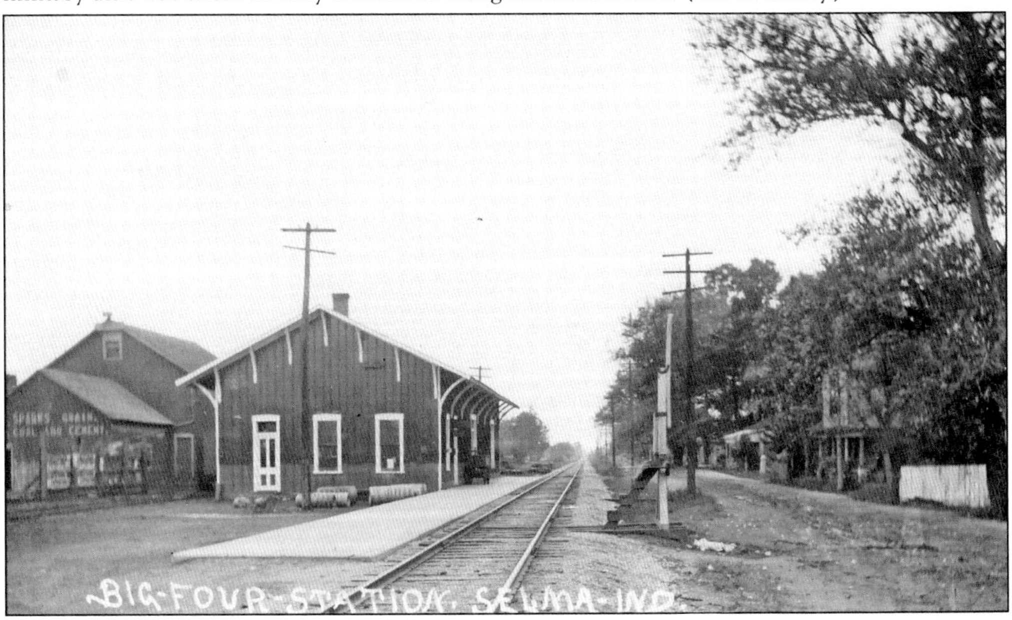

This c. 1910 photographic postcard shows the Big Four Railroad Station nicely painted and trimmed. A hand truck sits at the side of the little building, and old railroad ties are stacked in piles in the distance by the side of the track. The Big Four was the Cleveland, Cincinnati, Chicago & St. Louis Railway. (Jeffrey Koenker.)

This photograph of William and Margaret Swingley, from about 1935, was probably taken in the spring, as that is the usual time new lambs need a helping hand. The Swingleys lived at Eaton when they were first married but later moved to Selma. They were the parents of Jane Swingley Racer of Selma. (Jane Swingley Racer.)

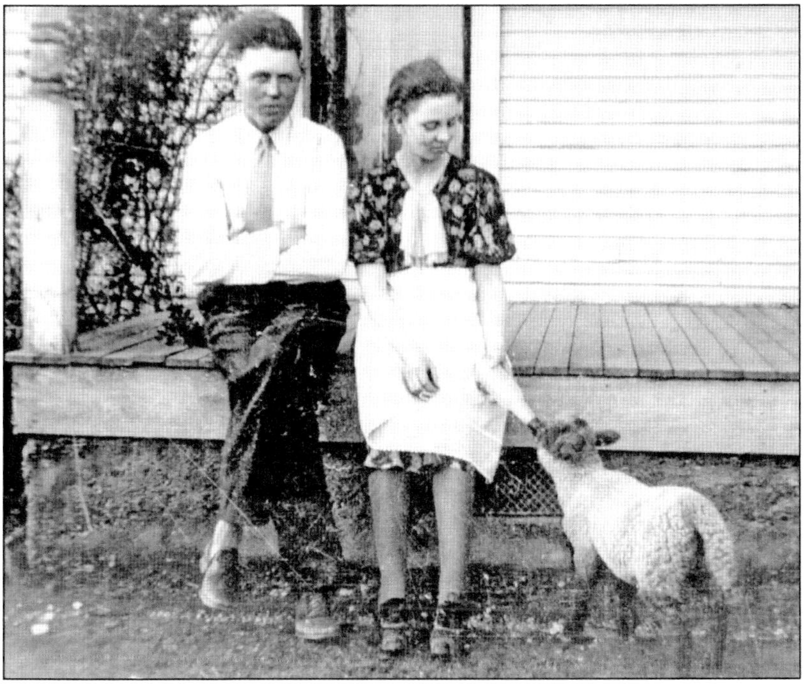

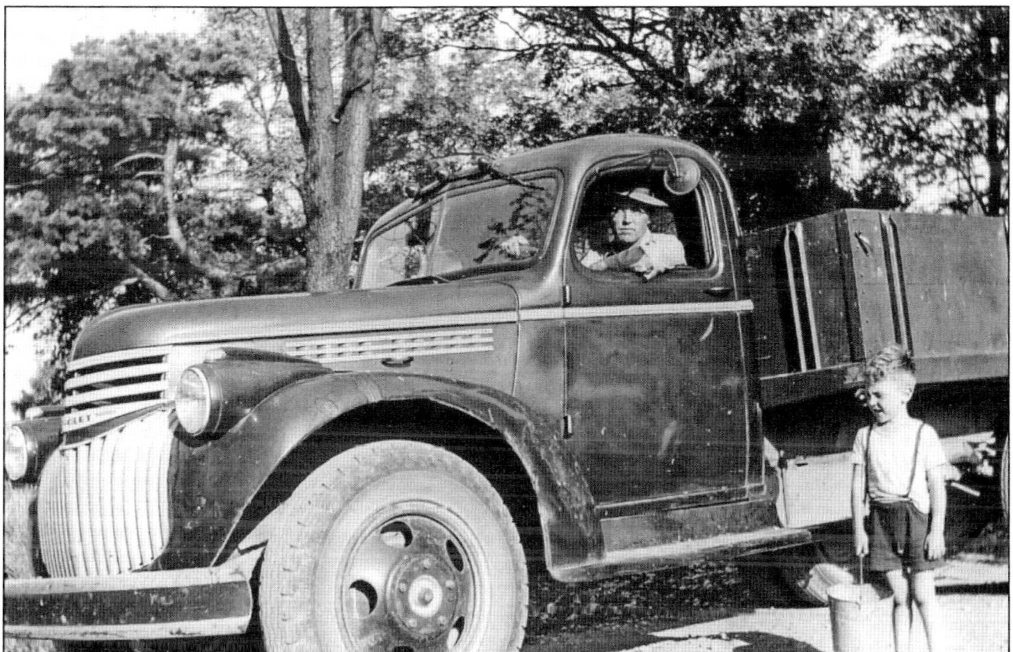

William Swingley's crops were his contribution to the war effort, as American agriculture was a primary support to the nation during the demanding times of World War II. This c. 1944 photograph shows Swingley in his truck. His son James stands nearby with a bucket. (Jane Swingley Racer.)

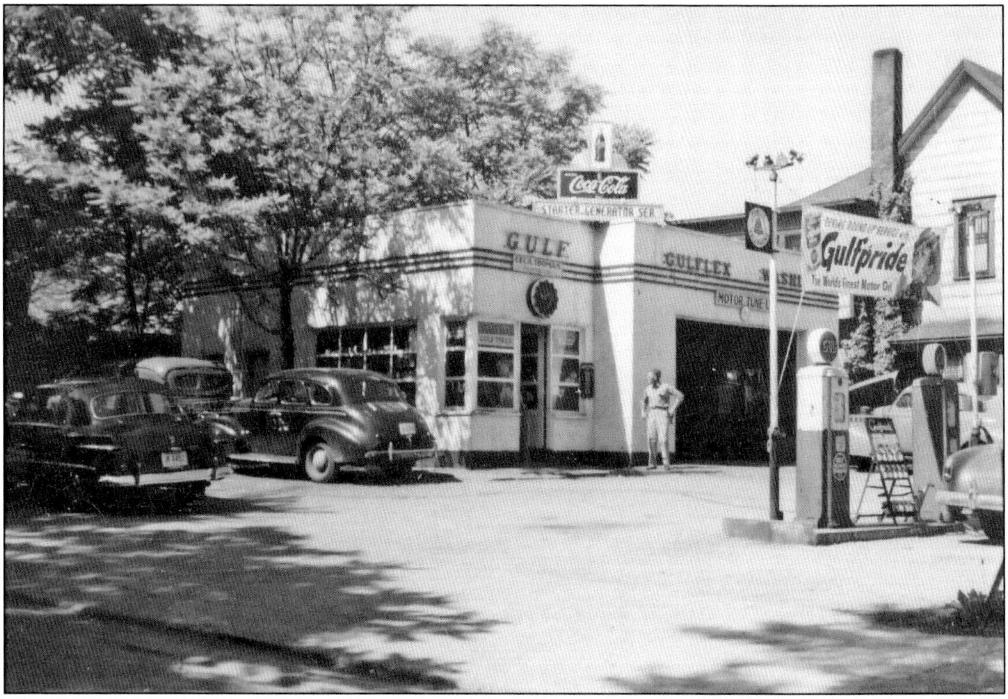

This Gulf station was at Cherry and Jackson Streets in Selma. It was owned by Cecil Thomas. The sign atop the front wall indicates that starter and generator services were offered. (Larry Campbell.)

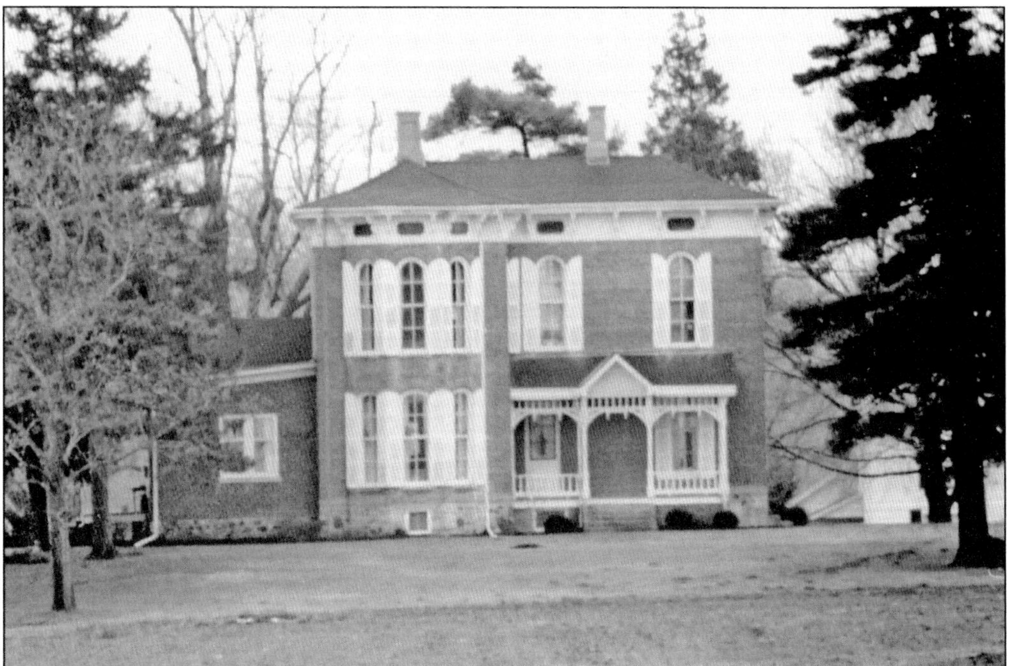

This Italianate-style house was built about 1885. It has been listed as an outstanding building on Indiana's state historic sites and structures inventory. A few of these stately brick structures are still dotted around the county, being kept up and lived in by their owners. (DCHS.)

Seven

Yorktown

In 1836, Yorktown was platted by Oliver H. Smith as 104 lots on land he had purchased from Goldsmith Gilbert, a first settler in the area. Being located on the road from Muncie to Indianapolis, Smith saw it as in a position to grow and prosper. Canals were the popular transportation idea in this era, and one was planned to come to Yorktown. This never developed, as railroads came to the fore as a cheaper and more quickly built alternative. Smith lived in Indianapolis and was politically active. Thus he was able to influence the path of the railroad so that it passed through Yorktown. The railroad was built out from Indianapolis to Belle Fountaine, Ohio, in the 1850s.

Yorktown also had its own gas company, but drilling for gas was much more successful in the north and east parts of the county than in the south and west parts. Although not as affected by the gas boom as some towns in Delaware County were, Yorktown gained industries that produced goods in demand and made for a much more manageable growth in the first decades of the 20th century.

Smith Street has always been and continues to be the main street in Yorktown. The business district developed from Broadway to Walnut Street at an early date and continued to be centered there. These businesses provided the expected services and goods to the community with a blacksmith shop, a livery and boarding stable, groceries, pharmacy, barbershop, and later a telephone office, among others.

Growth continued after World War II, and the establishment of the Marsh warehouse on the west side provided impetus to further development. The school system grew rapidly to accommodate new residents to the area and built new facilities for its many students. The town adopted a town manager government. The incorporated area expanded to the east and north to include new housing developments in the area. Easy access to Interstate 69 made Yorktown an attractive site for newcomers to the area.

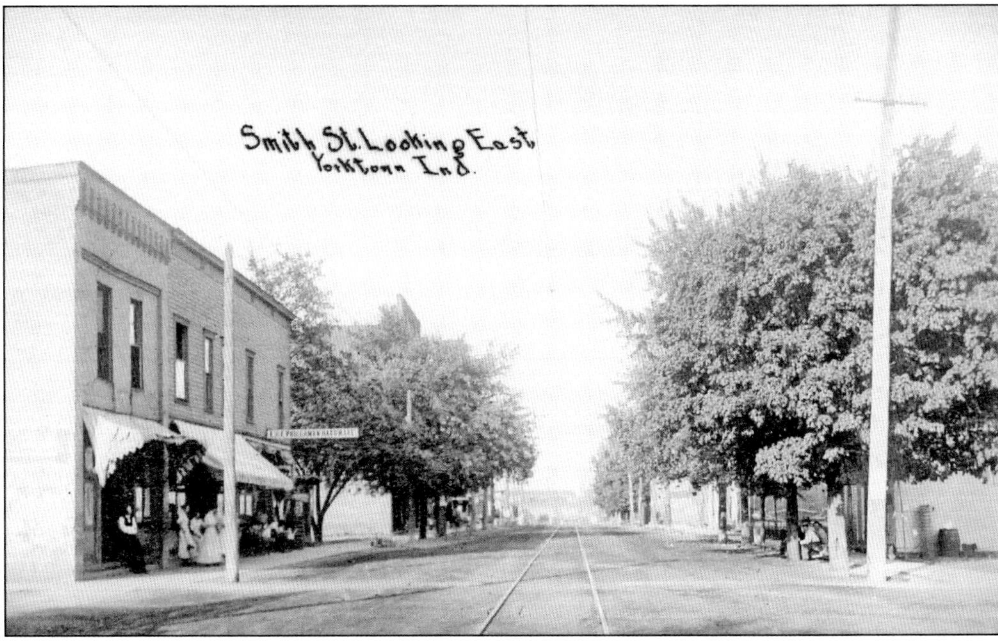

This photograph was taken after 1909, as that was when Elmer and Fred Prillaman are said to have opened their hardware store (sign at left). In this scene, the angle of the street to the northeast becomes more obvious in the shadows cast by a late afternoon sun. In the center distance can be seen the factory building, which is also in the background of the IUT Bridge photograph. (Jeffrey Koenker.)

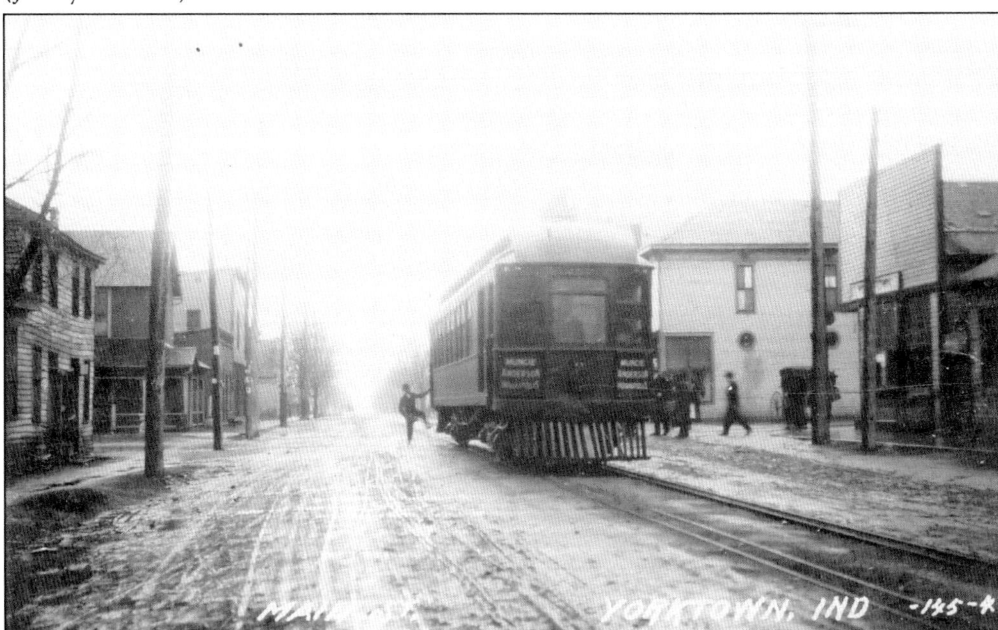

The main street in Yorktown was and is Smith Street. This photograph is probably from the 1890s, as it clearly shows the mud street next to the interurban track. The Yorktown interurban station is at the far right. The car sign lists the destinations Muncie, Anderson, and Indianapolis. (Jeffrey Koenker.)

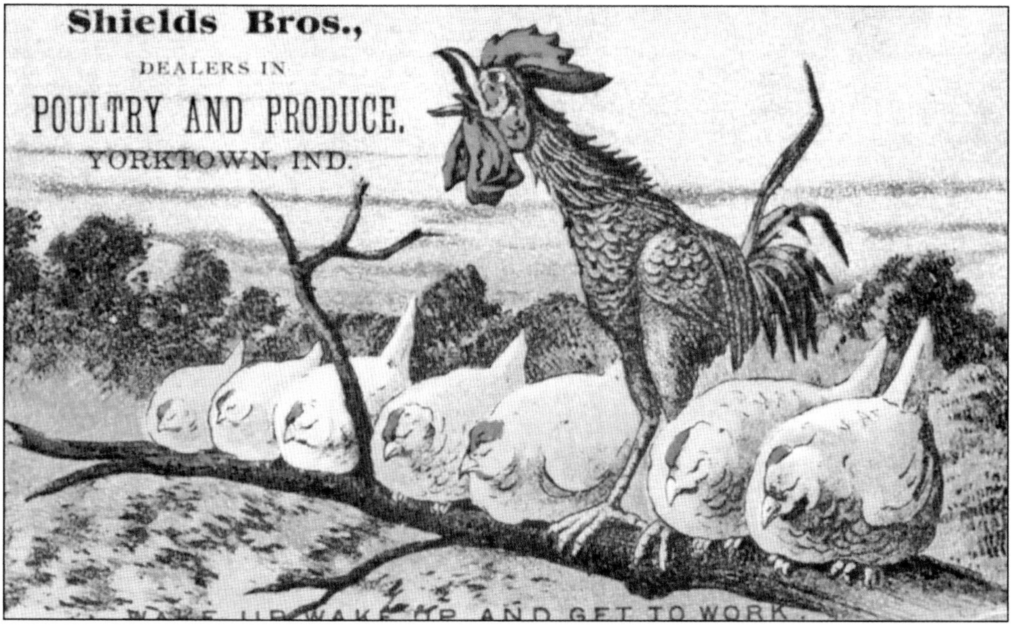

This amusing advertising postcard is very appropriate for a dealer in poultry and produce. Several members of the Shields family are listed with Yorktown addresses in the 1905–1906 *Emerson's Muncie Directory*, and this is probably the approximate date of the postcard. (Jeffrey Koenker.)

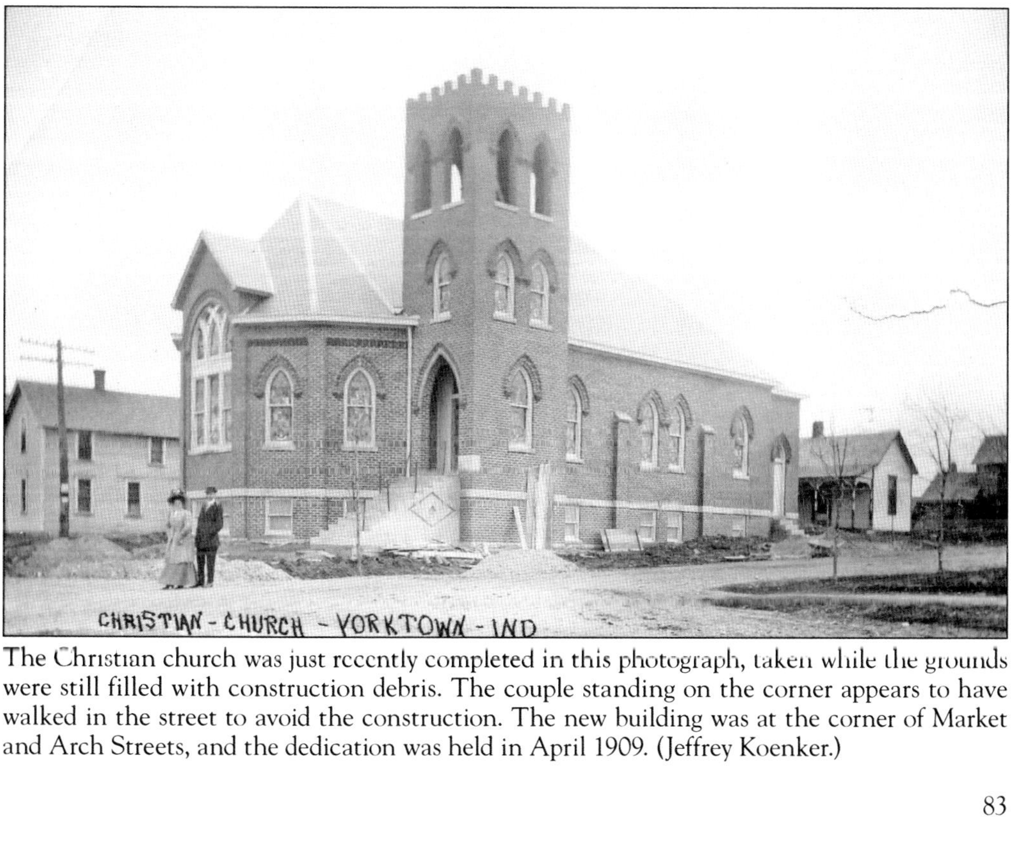

The Christian church was just recently completed in this photograph, taken while the grounds were still filled with construction debris. The couple standing on the corner appears to have walked in the street to avoid the construction. The new building was at the corner of Market and Arch Streets, and the dedication was held in April 1909. (Jeffrey Koenker.)

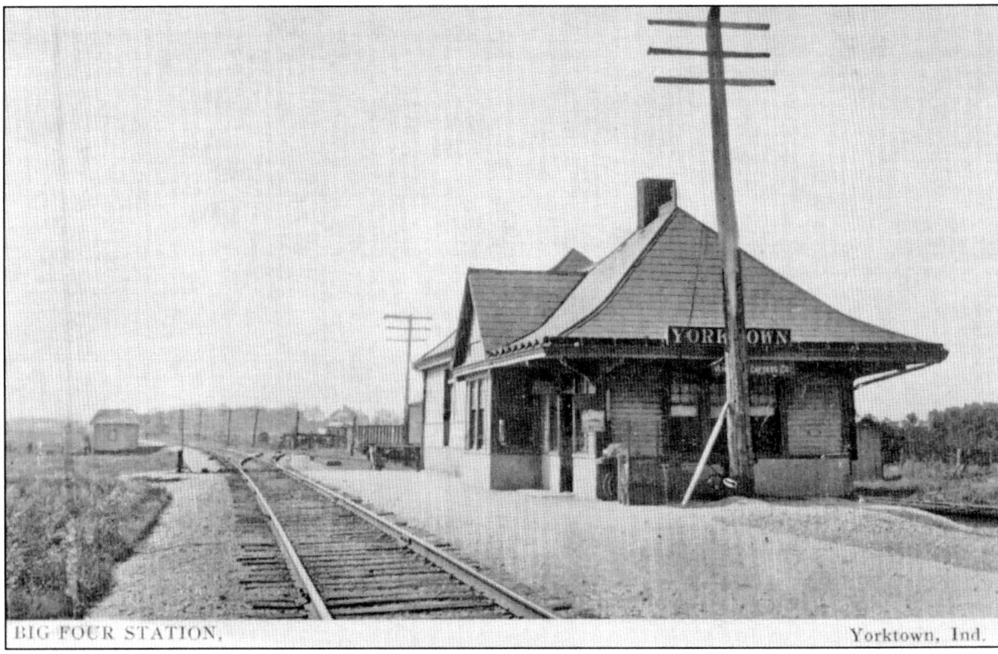

The Cleveland, Columbus, Cincinnati & Indianapolis came into being in 1868, with that station depot shown on the 1887 atlas. In 1889, the railroad became the Cleveland, Cincinnati, Chicago & St. Louis line and was best known as "The Big Four." (Jeffrey Koenker.)

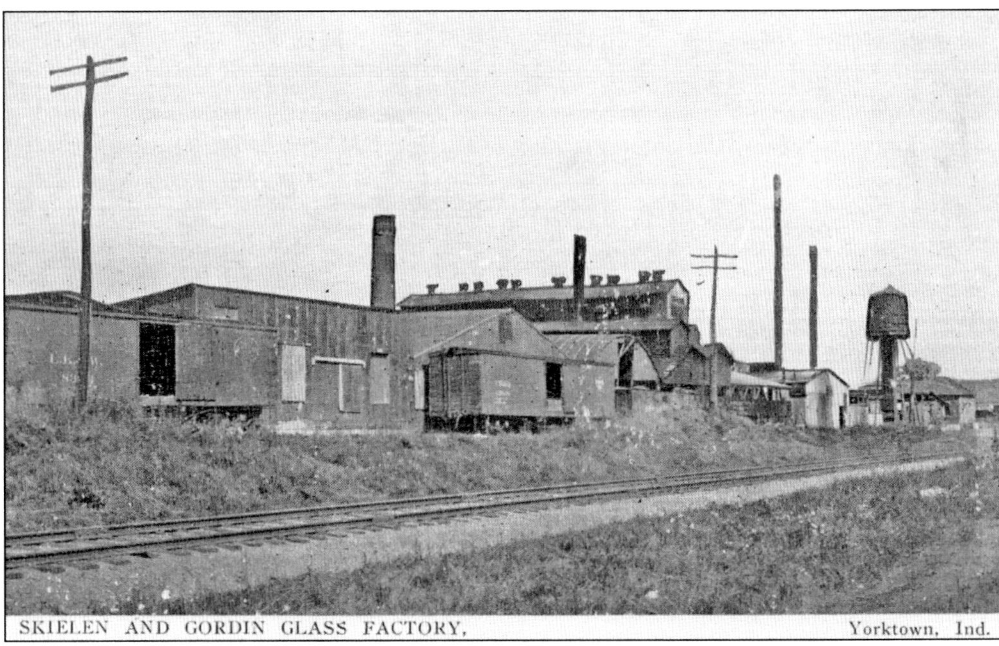

This postcard managed to misspell or misidentify both names, as the glass factory was actually the Skillen and Goodin Factory, owned by Dee Orla Skillen and Earl Goodin. The glass factory came to Yorktown during the same period that other glass manufacturers came to Albany, Eaton, and Muncie—during the gas boom. (Jeffrey Koenker.)

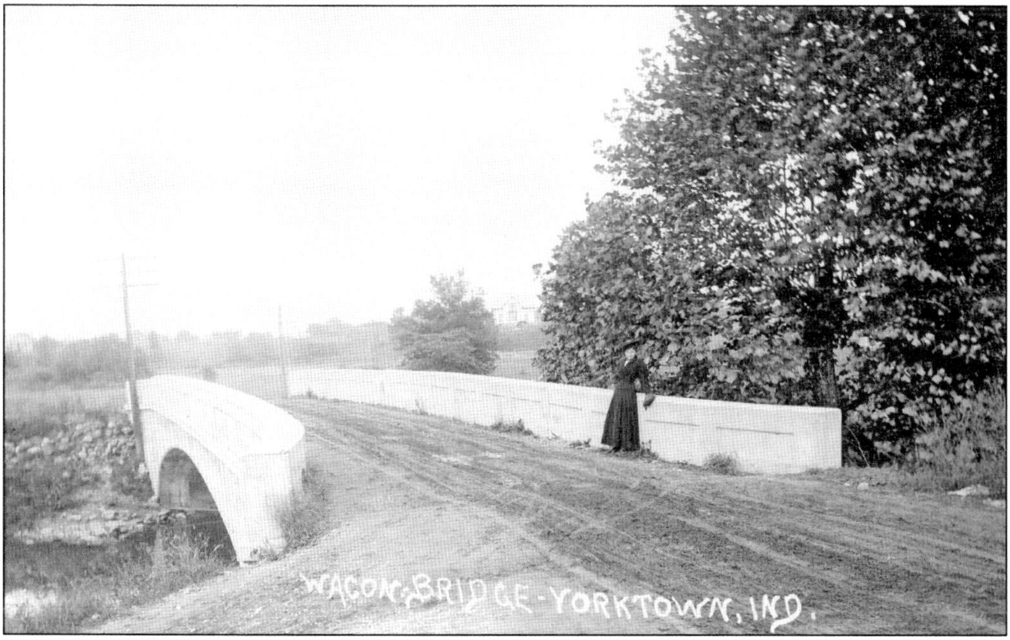

This concrete bridge illustrates the change from iron bridges to less expensive concrete structures. The iron bridges lasted much longer but cost more and required upkeep, which included plank flooring that had to be replaced or paved over. Delaware County still had six of the iron bridges left in the first decade of the 21st century. The woman pictured is unidentified. (Jeffrey Koenker.)

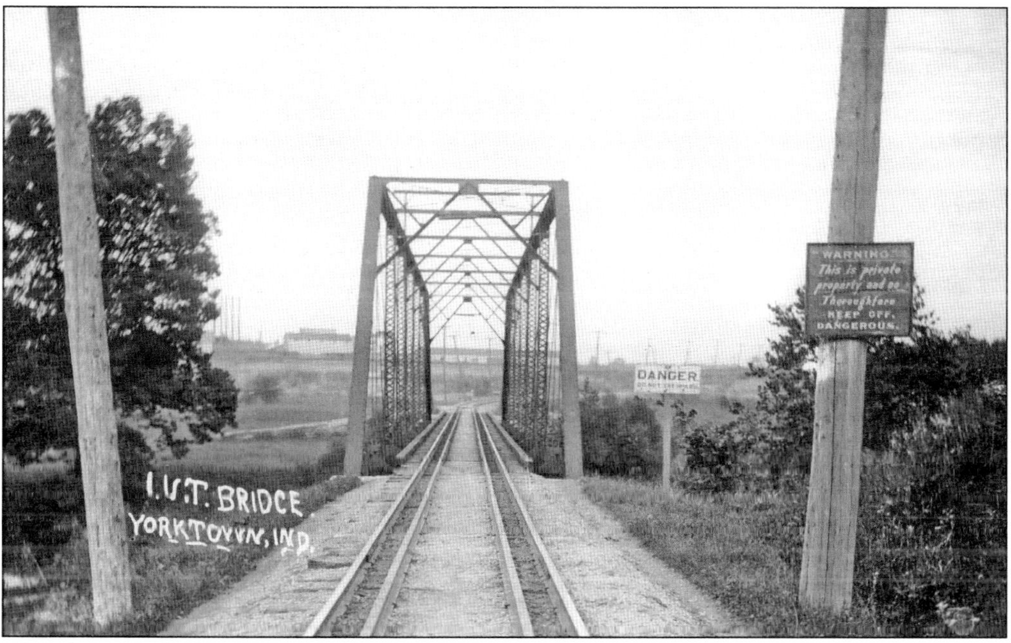

The photograph shows the Indiana Union Traction Company's bridge over Buck Creek, with factory buildings in the far background. The IUT had an extensive network of rails all over central Indiana, east and west. Extending to Fort Wayne in the north, to the south the network approximately followed US 40 across the state, with extensions to Sullivan and Martinsville. (Jeffrey Koenker.)

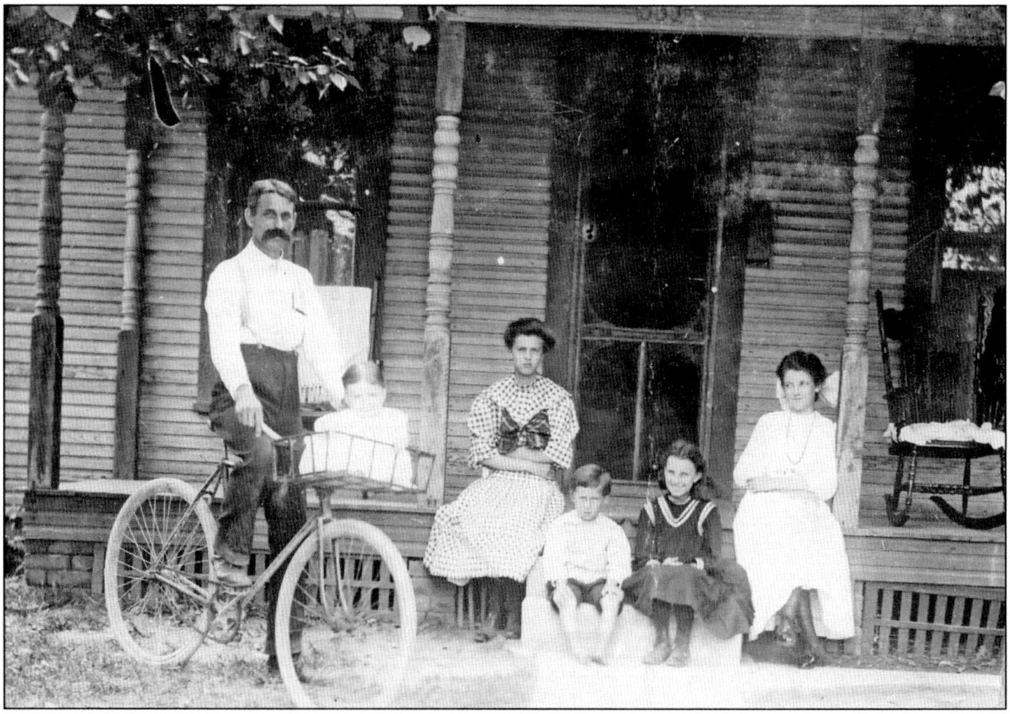

The Neff family is pictured around 1908 in their front yard. From left to right are Lewis Neff (father), Fay Neff (in basket on bicycle), Lila, Clyde, Lena, and Amanda (mother). Fay Neff married Allen Ross, who had a grocery store in Yorktown. (Jeffrey Koenker.)

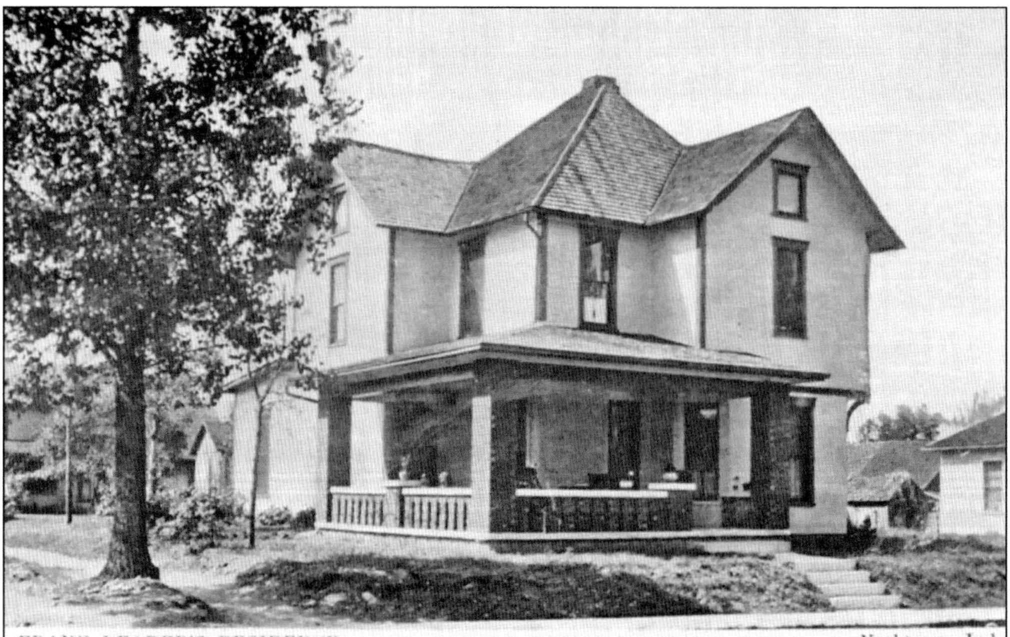

FRANK LEADER'S RESIDENCE, Yorktown, Ind.

Frank Leader may have resided in Yorktown for only a few years. The Leader Glass Works was shown in the 1896 fire maps along with the Yorktown (West Muncie) Roller Mill in the Muncie section. Leader was listed as a glass blower in the Muncie directories in the early 1900s. (Jeffrey Koenker.)

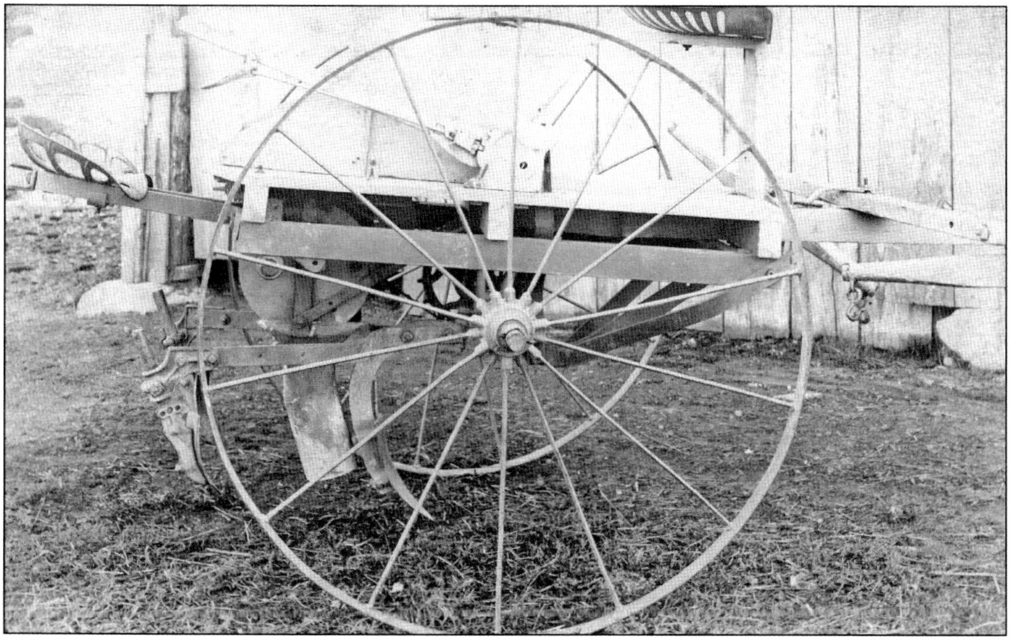

Oliver Hawk invented the potato planter shown in this undated photograph, probably from the early 1900s. Oliver was the son of Sylvanus O. Hawk, a farmer in Mount Pleasant Township. Oliver married Clara Jester, also a native of the same township. He was living in Muncie with his wife when he died in 1941. (Jeffrey Koenker.)

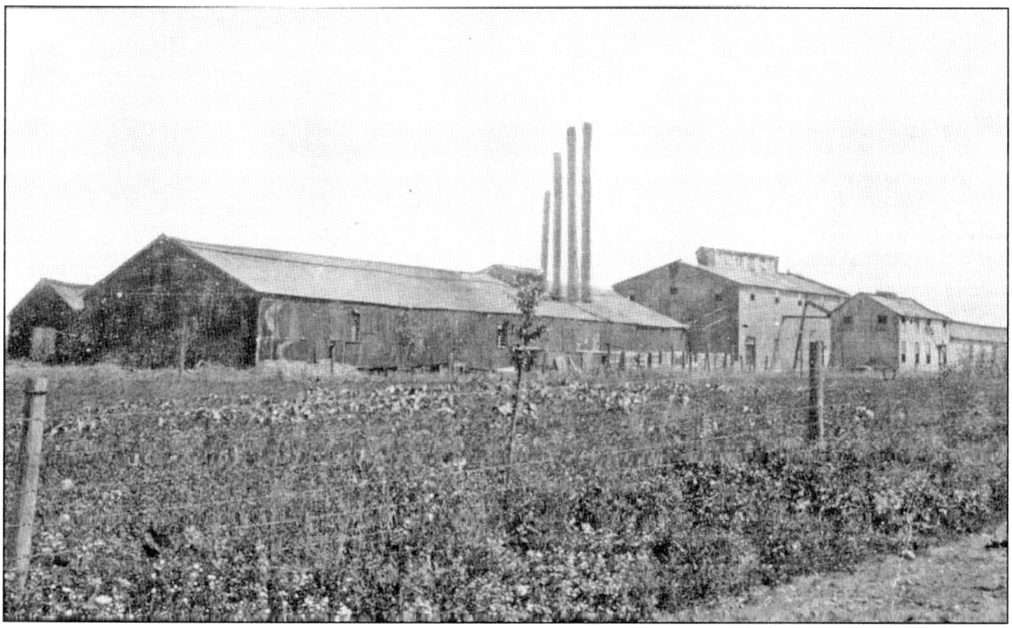

Mineral wool is described as a stone wool or rock wool produced from high temperature molten stone, with a stream of air or steam blown through it. It was first produced commercially in 1871. Modern production uses a process that has been likened to the production of cotton candy. A corner of this factory can be seen in the left background of the IUT Bridge photograph above. (Jeffrey Koenker.)

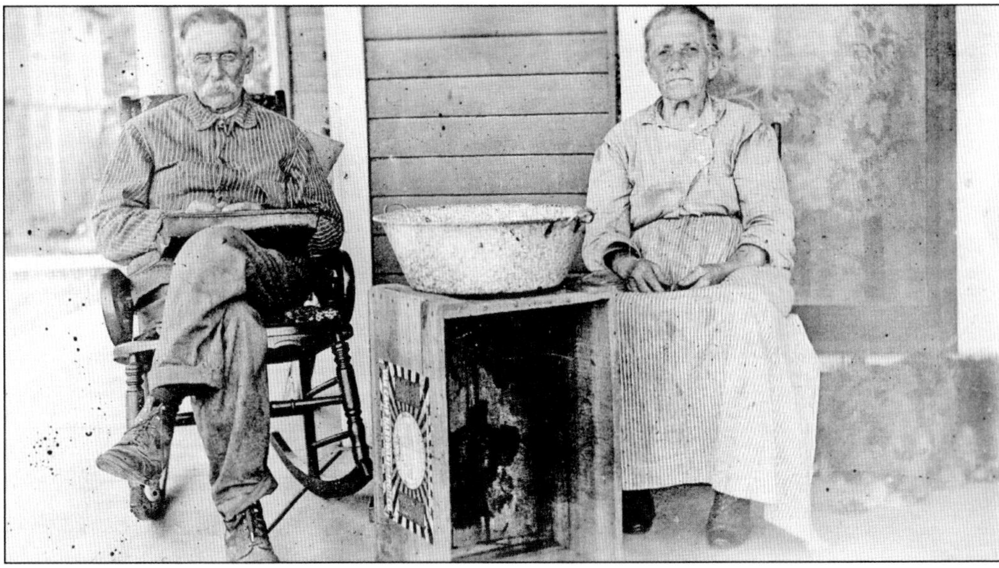

This photograph is labeled as follows: "Granpa Jester and Jane cleaning gooseberries, about 1919, at the Jester Home in Yorktown." Joshua Jester and his wife, Eliza Jane, were both members of Hofherr's Chapel. Eliza Jane died in 1920 after a serious illness that lasted 10 days. She was buried in Hawk Cemetery near Yorktown. (Jeffrey Koenker.)

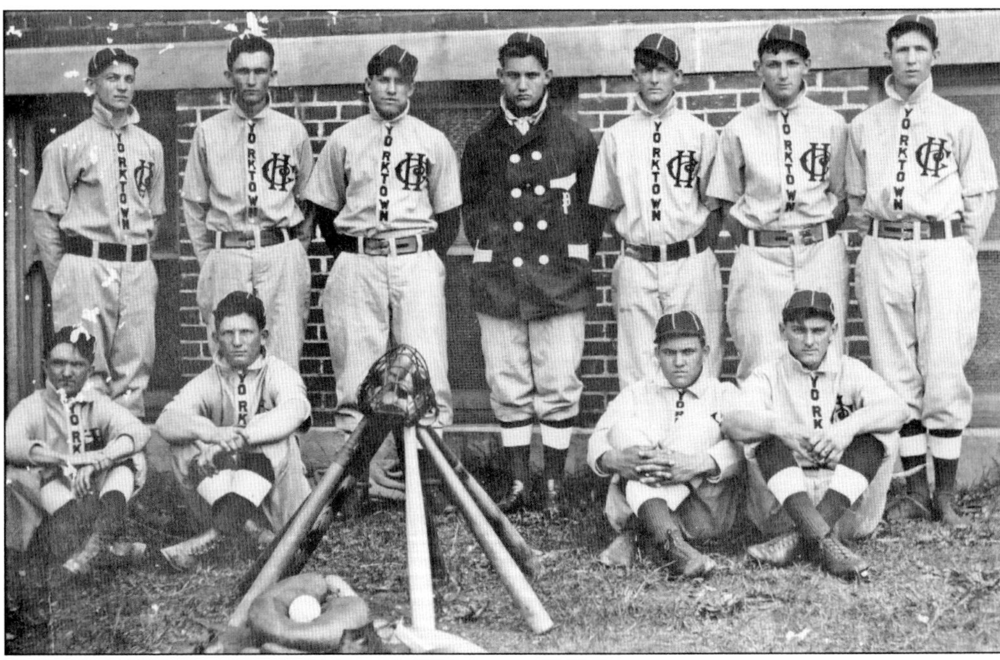

Members of the Yorktown baseball team are pictured in their uniforms about 1908. The vertical letters and left side emblem were made popular by the Cubs in 1909. The undersweaters formed part of the color scheme, with white worn for the "home uniform." The collar folded up and pinned at the throat was part of the popular style at the time. (Minnetrista Heritage Collection, Muncie, Indiana.)

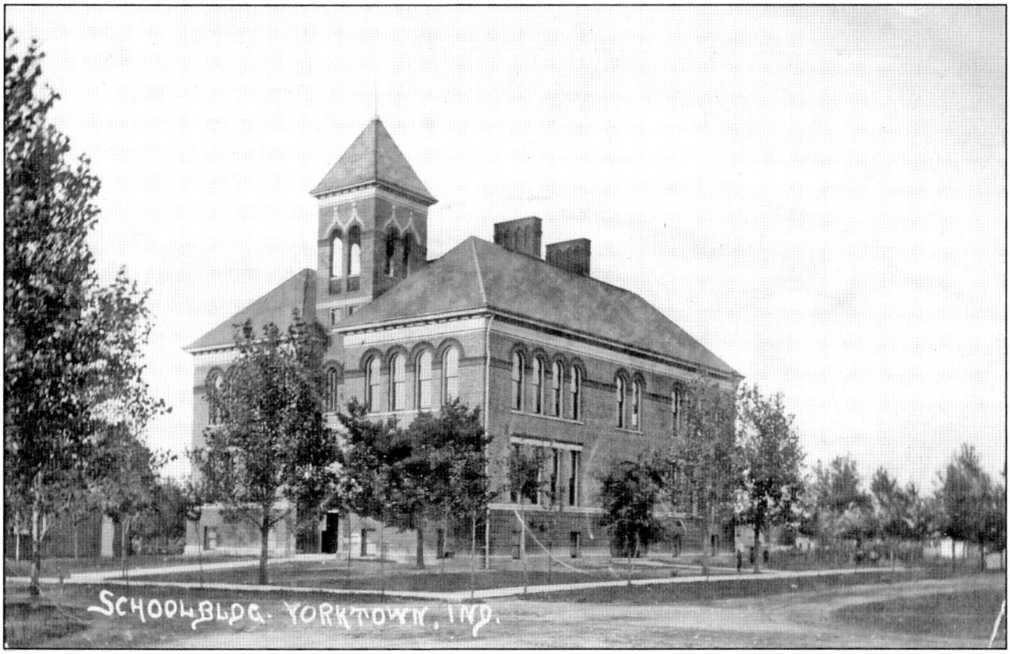

This school building served the Yorktown community for many years, before and after an extensive remodeling about 1926. A gymnasium had been added in 1910, allowing basketball games to be played in the school. The team was called the "Tigers" by the first coach, Merle Swanger. (Jeffrey Koenker.)

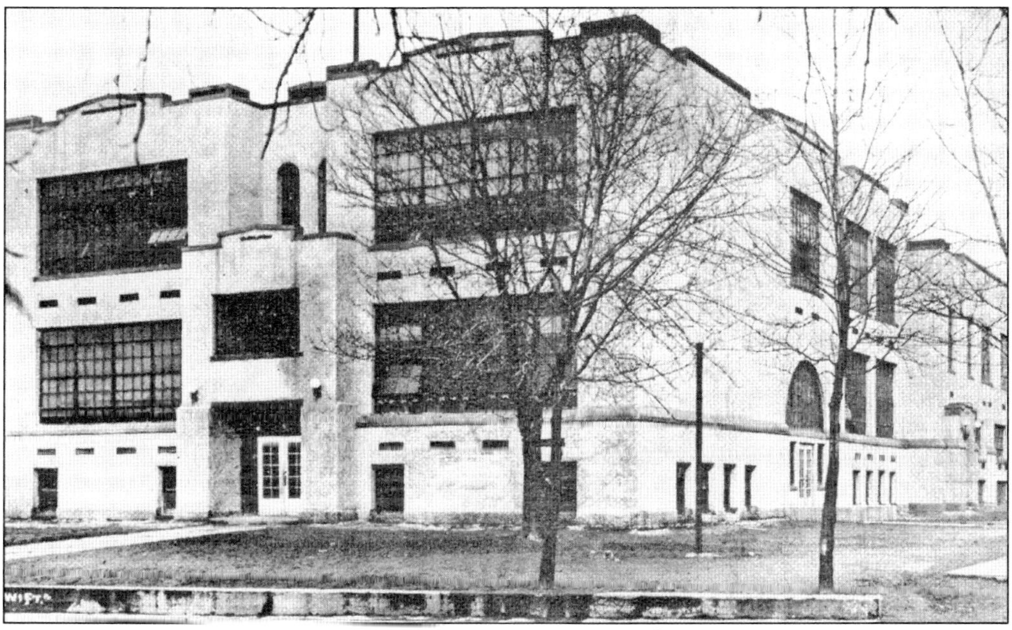

The school seen here appears to be a very modern structure, but it is the old building that was remodeled about 1926. Although it looks much different at first glance, a focus on the main entry shows it to be the same building seen above with a new facade. The remodeling was truly remarkable, as it appeared to be a new building. (Jeffrey Koenker.)

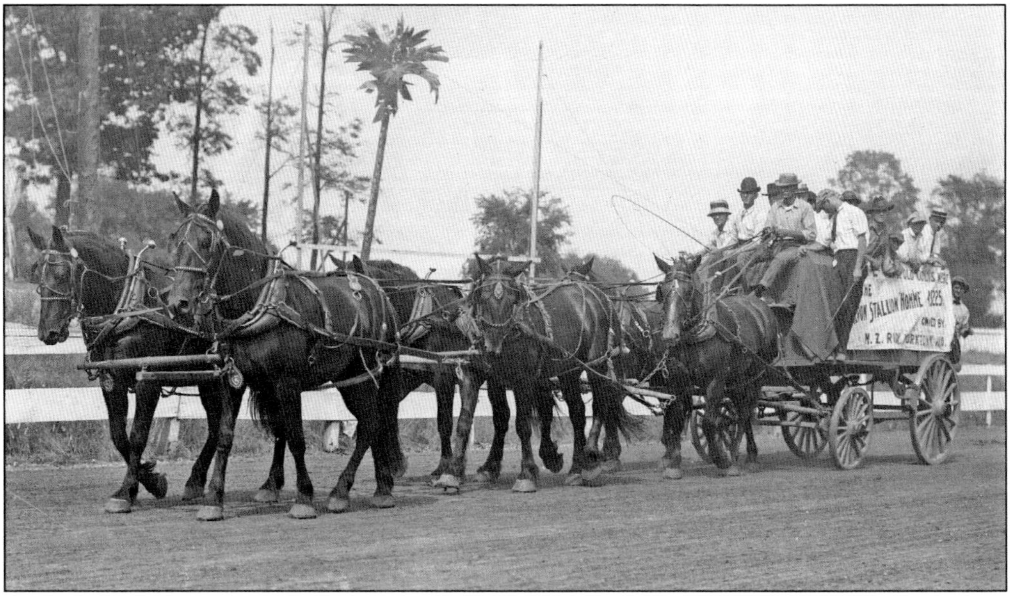

This photograph from a glass negative appeared in the *Muncie City Directory* of 1919–1920, with a caption describing the six-horse team of two-year-olds sired by a Percheron stallion, Homme. The advertisement for Rudy's Breeding Barn described this import from France as "a fine individual, weighs 2,250 lbs., with extra heavy bone of good quality." Monte Z. Rudy was the owner of this enterprise. (DCHS.)

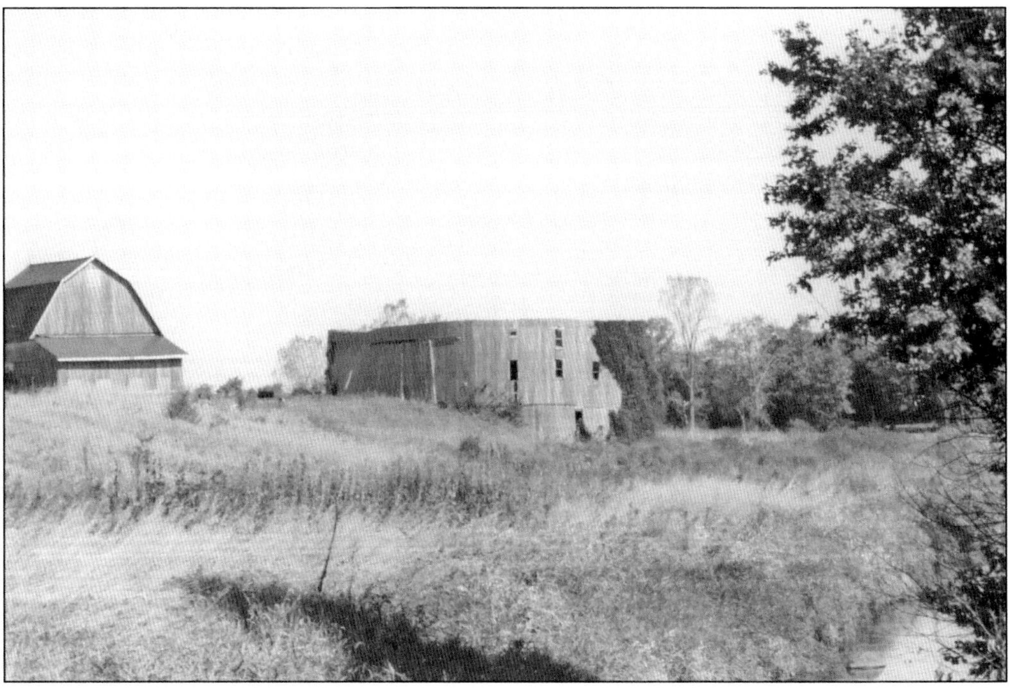

The Hofherr round barn, near Yorktown in Mount Pleasant Township, was on the Historic American Buildings Survey. Its structure allowed the roof to fall inward, and the barn fell into decay and collapsed. Then there were only two round barns left in the county. (DCHS, photograph by Norma Lasley.)

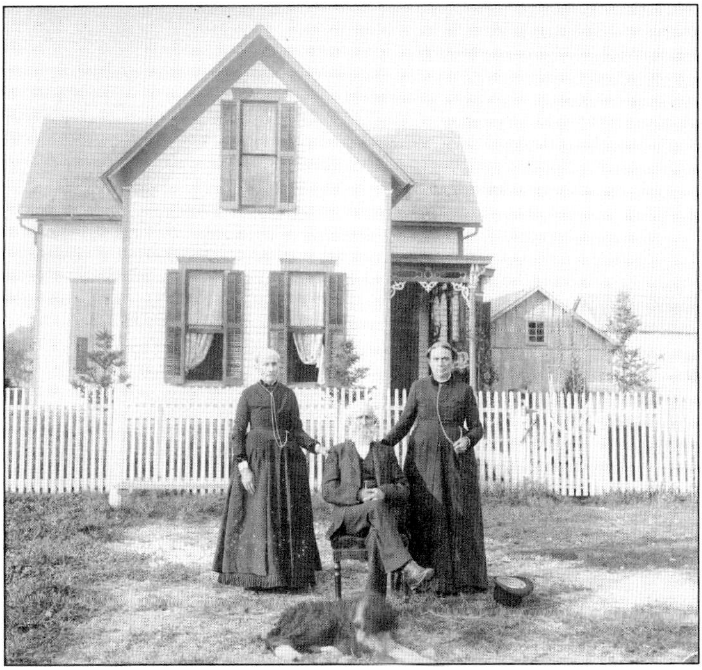

The Frederick Priest Home near Priest Ford is pictured here with Frederick Priest (1818–1894) and Leah Priest (1824–1892), who were both buried in Mount Tabor Cemetery, as well as Hannah Dowden, who died in 1899 at the age of 78. The Priest family owned the land where there was a ford over White River. The Priest Ford Road of today serves as a reminder of this early family. (DCHS.)

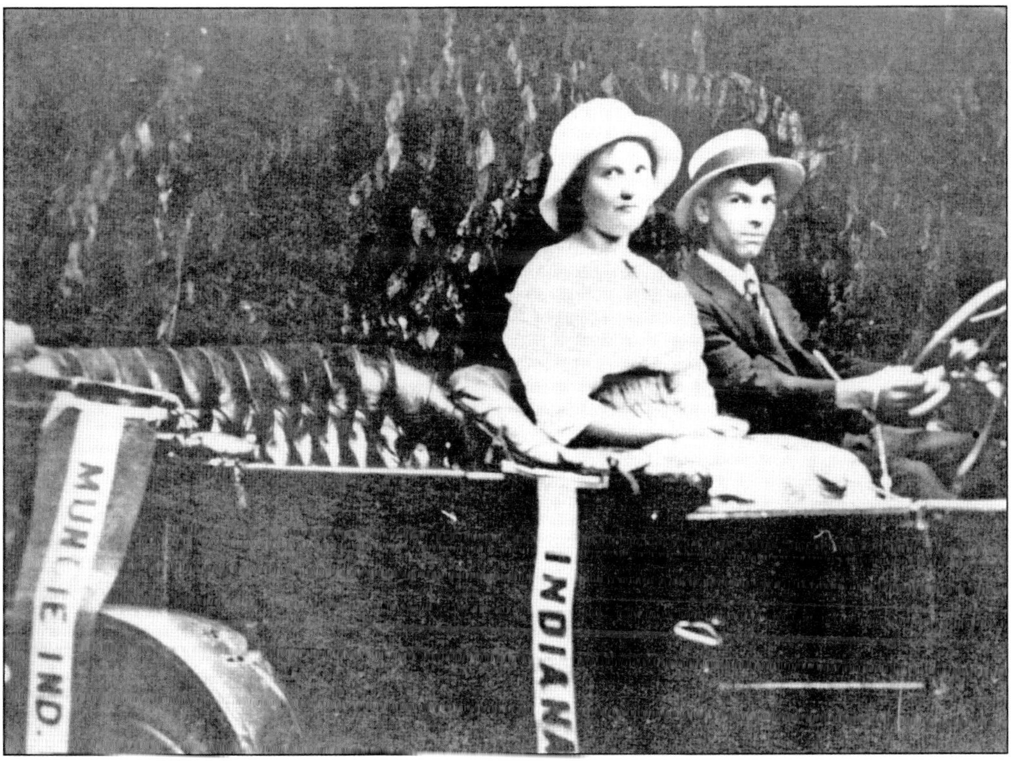

The photograph shows Freda and Herbert Jester at the Delaware County Fair, probably in the 1920s. The streamers seem to indicate they may have been part of a parade. The County Fair was a popular occasion for people throughout the county, including entertainment for both farm and city folk. (Jeffrey Koenker.)

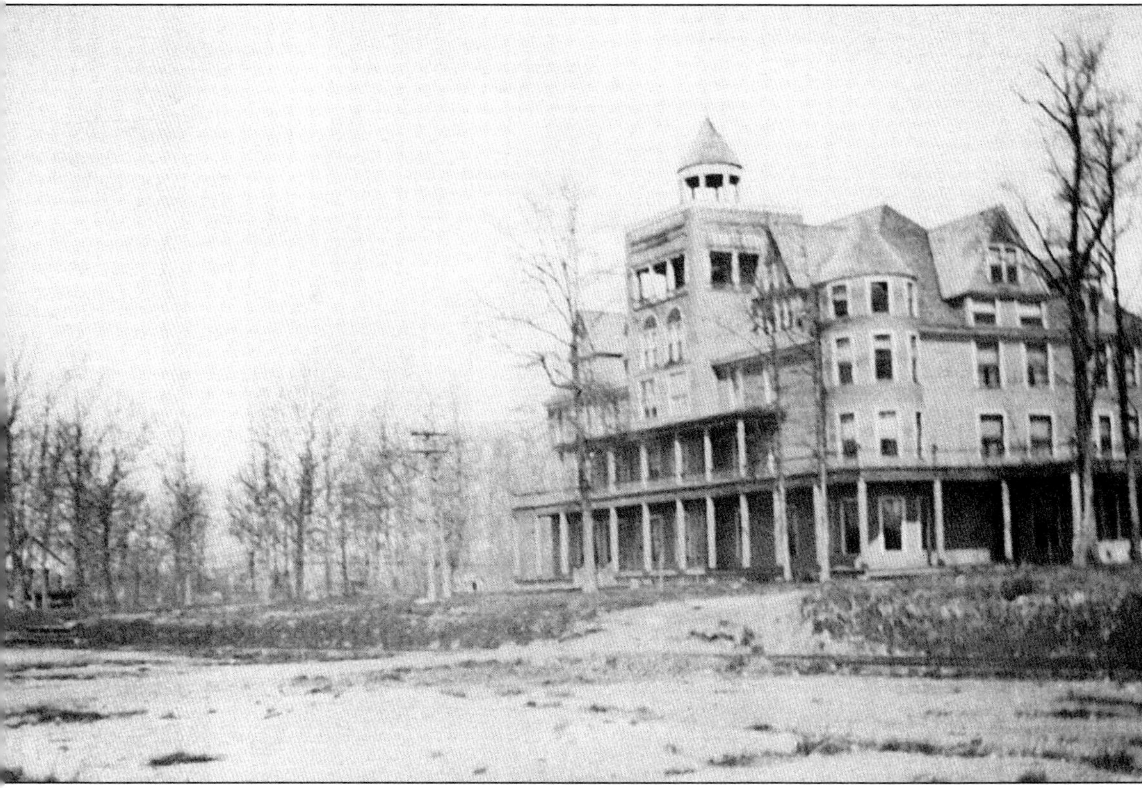

West Muncie was located west of Muncie, very near to Yorktown. It was planned in the early 1890s as a resort area, with a lake formed by a dam on Buck Creek, a hotel, and a post office, plus a housing development. The West Muncie hotel (shown above) had 70 rooms. At one time, there were special trains running from Muncie to carry visitors to the resort on weekends. A steamboat carried passengers around Lake Delaware. Then there was an economic downturn. The dam, constructed near the intersection of Corn Bread Road and Buck Creek, collapsed from flooding and was not rebuilt. The houses did not sell, and the hotel was occupied only by the owner's family. On March 24, 1898, the *Morning News* ran an article describing "a sad monument of a boom town, with empty houses crumbling into ruins." (Michael Mavis.)

Eight

VILLAGES AND FARMS

While driving through the county today, the traveler will see small clumps of older houses here and there without stopping to think about how those houses came to be in that place. The older county maps will usually show villages in those places. Many landowners through the late 1800s laid out a plat and took it to be recorded, under the chosen name, at the county courthouse. At least a few lots were usually sold, sometimes to older residents of the area who wished to retire from farming life to life in a village. In a few cases, no settlement ensued, and the land continued to be farmed. Some of these settlements lost their names over time, but many of the villages retained their names and are still found on today's maps. These villages each have their own histories, some of which are told in the pages of this chapter.

Many activities changed greatly in the period of 1890 to 1920. The village post offices disappeared after Rural Free Delivery was developed in the 1890s and was generally adopted in 1902. When travel was difficult, the village store and nearby post office were great conveniences. With travel by motor vehicle and better roads, larger trade centers became more convenient with more amenities.

Farming in the early days was on a small scale, which gradually increased with the years. Delaware County, among other Midwestern counties, saw industrialization become the economic force. The farms changed with the times and mechanization came in the form of reapers, first horse-pulled then later pulled by machines. Threshing operations further mechanized the farm tasks. Large dairy operations were needed near larger towns and cities in the first half of the 20th century. Farm operations are all on a large scale in the modern era. The farm scenes in this chapter are from an earlier, simpler time. Many of these activities will seem strange to the younger persons of the 21st century, but this is the way people lived in the not-so-distant past.

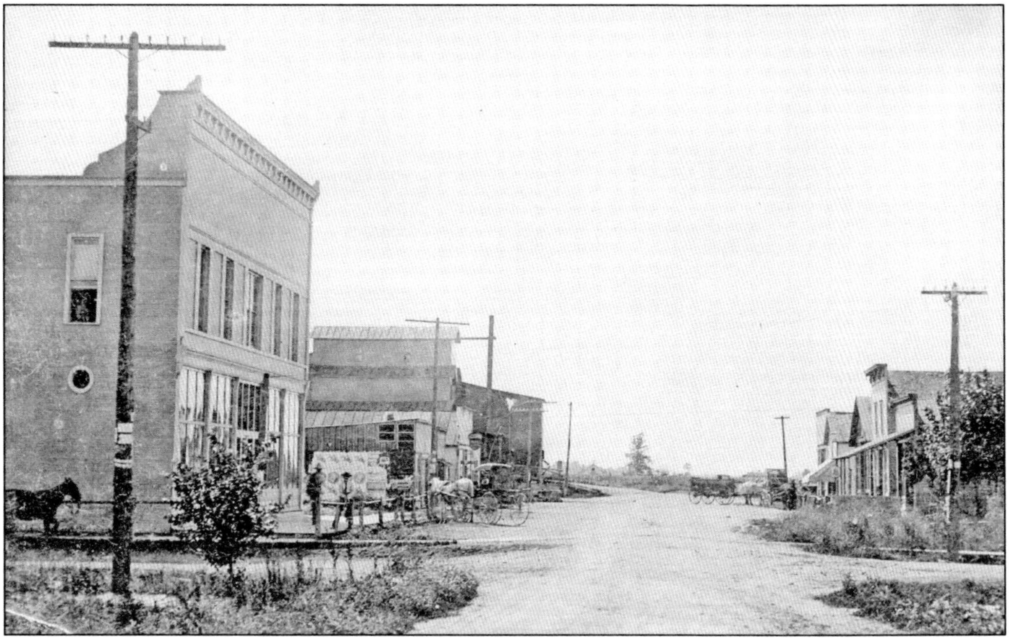

Cammack was laid out by David Cammack in 1882. He had a sawmill nearby, which meant the new residents could build with sawed wood instead of logs. The village was built at switch A of the Lake Erie & Western Railroad, which may already have attracted a few settlers in the 1870s. This view looks west on Jackson Street. (Jeffrey Koenker.)

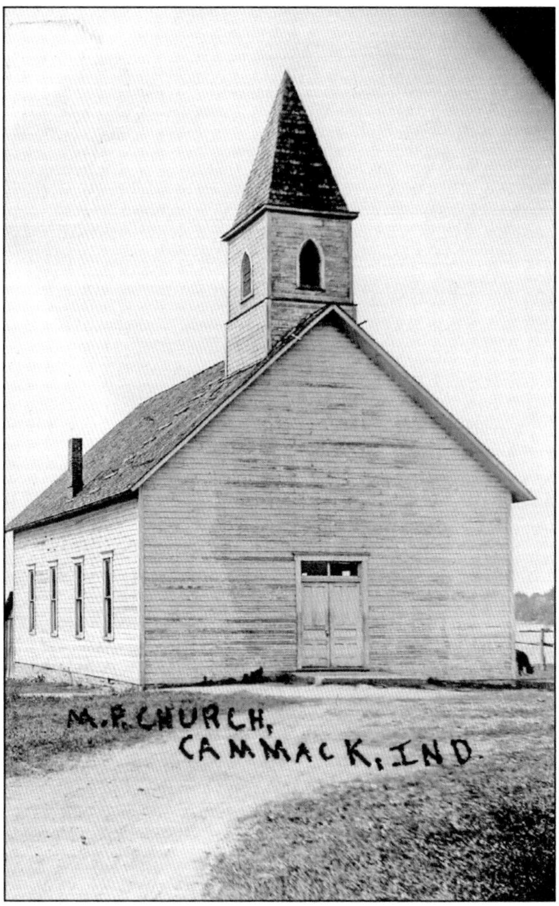

The Cammack Methodist Protestant Church was built in 1893 on land donated by Betty S. Dragoo and Sam H. Dragoo. The congregation had been meeting for several years prior to the decision to build the church, locating it in Cammack. Cammack United Methodist Church celebrated its 100th anniversary in August 1993. (Jeffrey Koenker.)

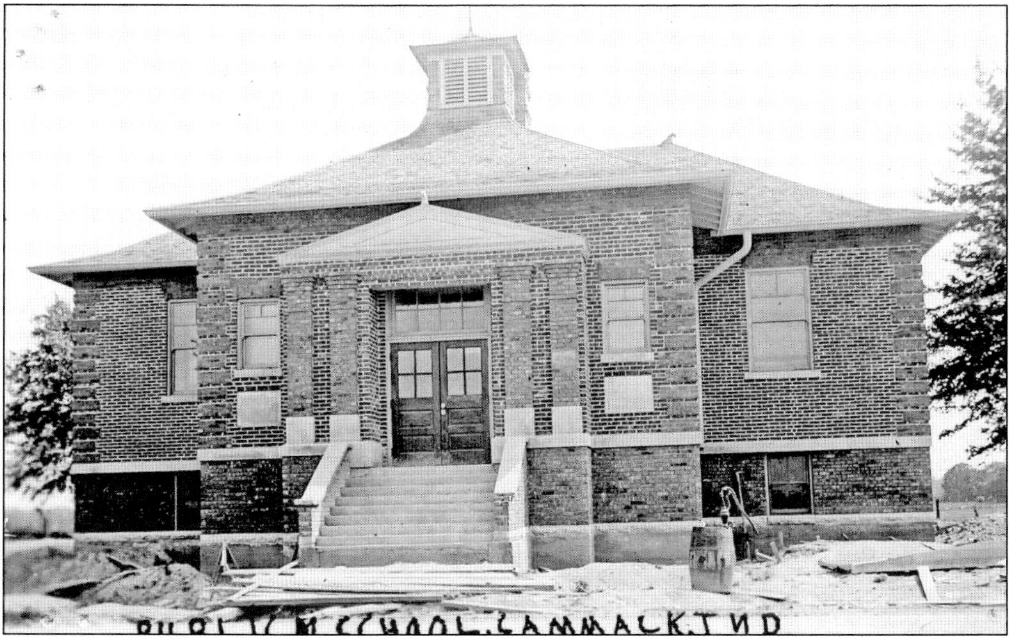

Cammack's old school, located at the corner of Jackson Street and the Yorktown-Gaston Road (600 West), was destroyed in a windstorm about 1910. While the new school was being built, classes were held in the Redmen's Lodge. The new brick two-room building with a full basement held classes for grades one through eight. (Jeffrey Koenker.)

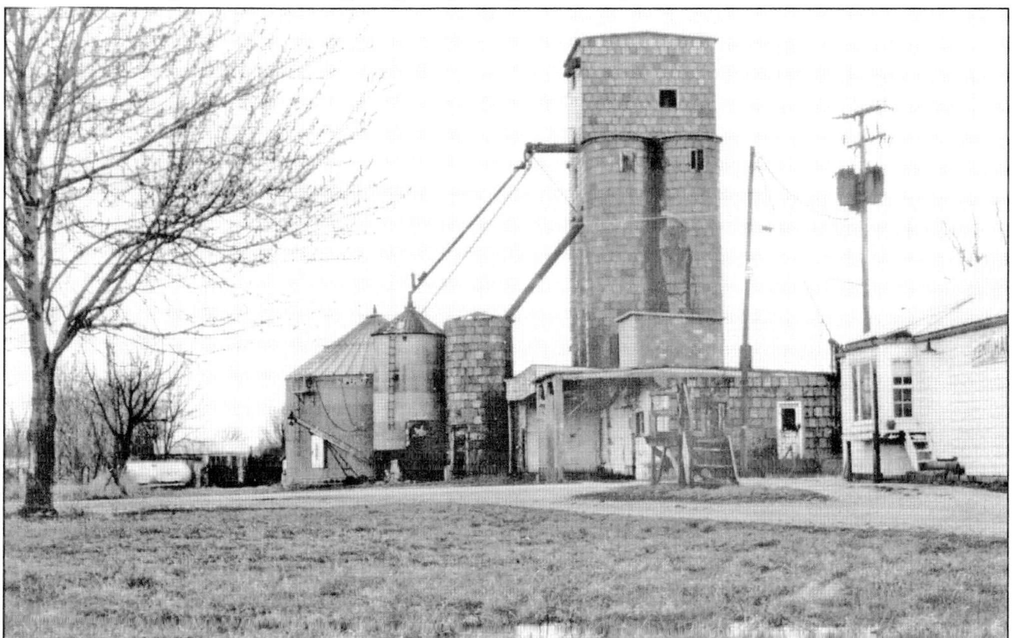

The elevator was said to be on the original sawmill site. The 1887 atlas shows the sawmill alongside the railroad, which made a good location for both businesses. The tallest part of the elevator and one of the silos appears to be constructed with ceramic tile. On pronouncing Cammack—local parlance has the accent on the second syllable as "Kuh mack." (Larry Campbell.)

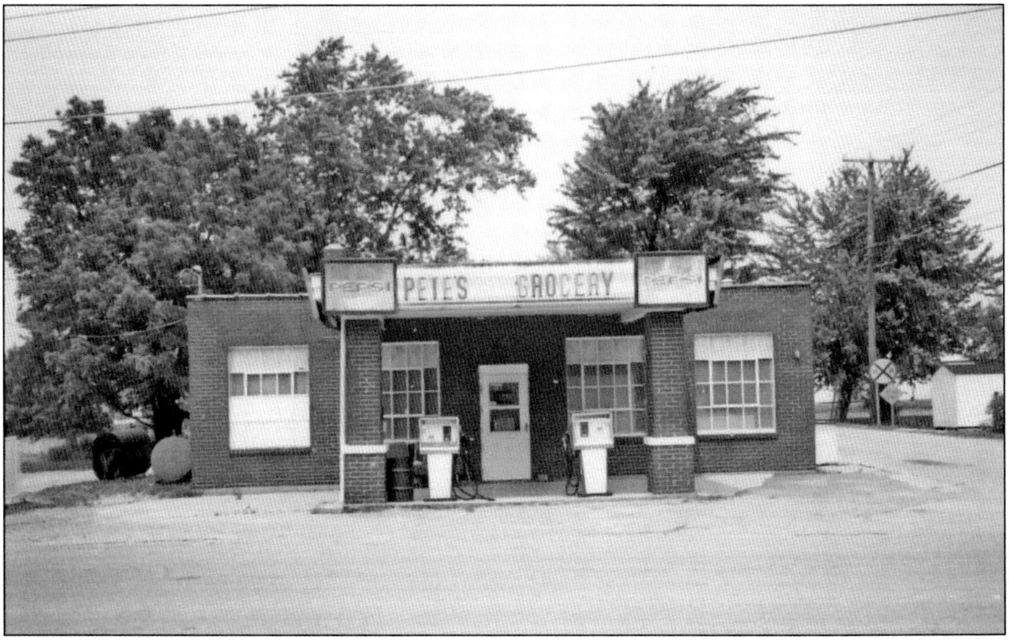

As businesses declined and left the village, the little corner grocery and filling station still served a local need, with Vernon "Pete" Davis carrying on after his father retired. At the corner of North Cammack Street and West Jackson Street, the building has been renovated and enlarged as a restaurant in recent years. (Jeffrey Koenker; photograph by Jeffrey Koenker.)

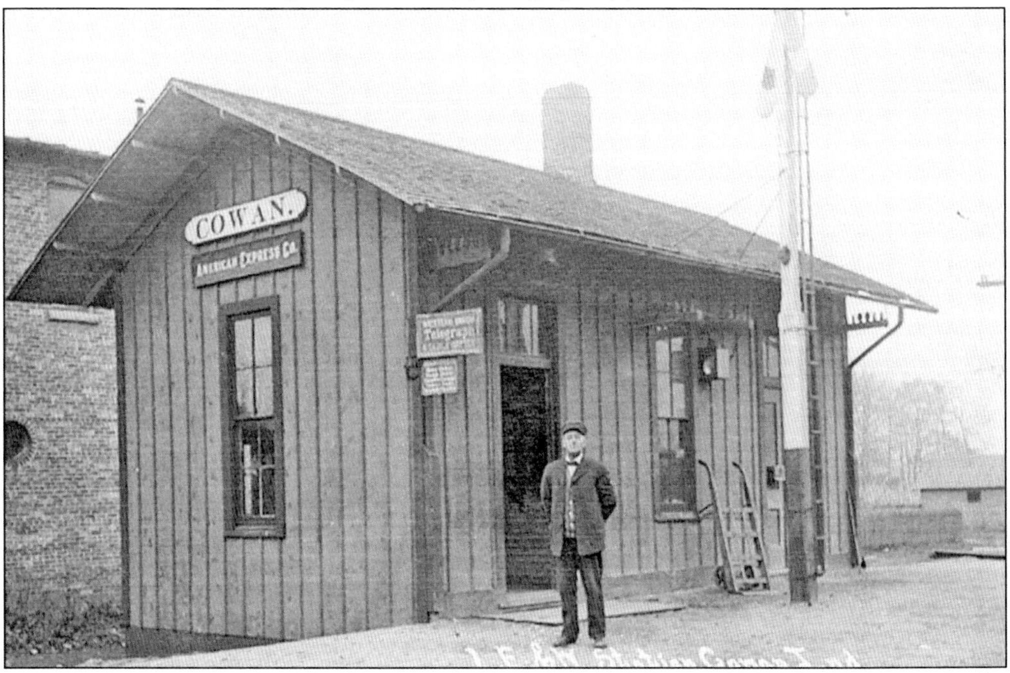

One of the reasons Charles McCowan located his village in this place was that it was on the Lake Erie & Western Railroad line. The "Mc" was later dropped, and the village became known simply as Cowan. There were two stores, two sawmills, and a tile factory in Cowan a few years after it was established. (Jeffrey Koenker.)

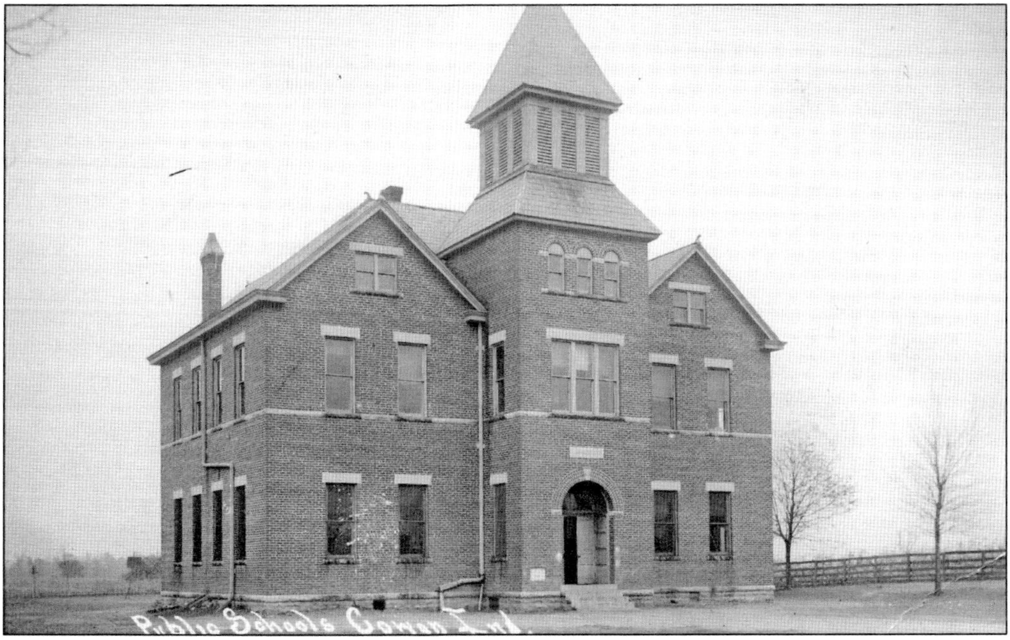

The new grade schools of the early 1900s separated the children into rooms of one or two grades for each teacher. Schools were planned for grades one through eight, with an eighth grade graduation being the rule during this period. (Jeffrey Koenker.)

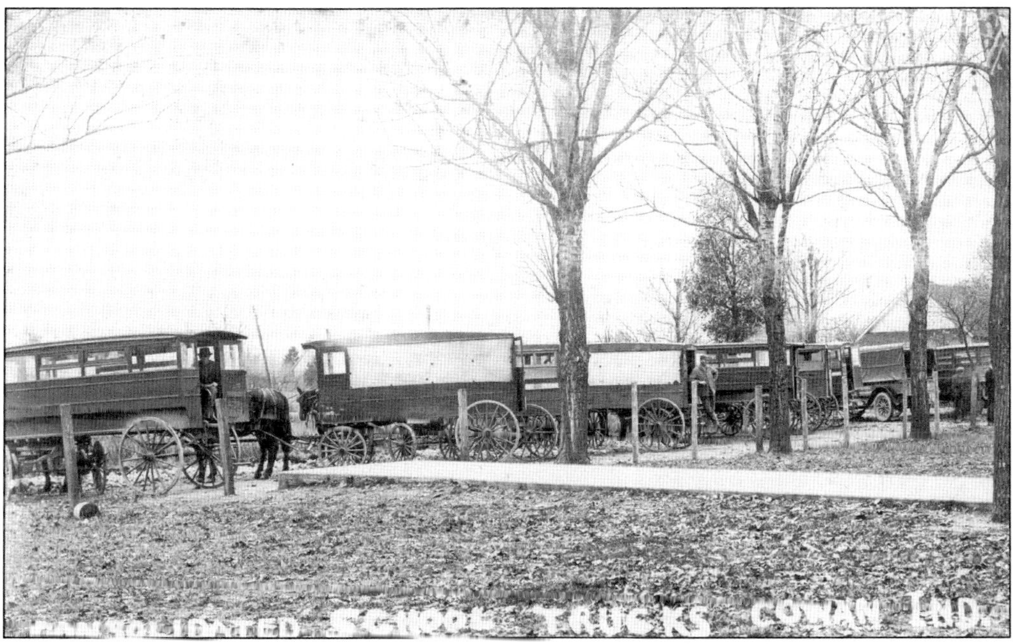

The new consolidated schools pulled together the old district schools in graded rooms. Supt. Charles VanMatre worked with the school patrons to form plans for their schools and vote on the plans. Transport of the children to the schools was provided by horse-drawn wagons or hacks. (Jeffrey Koenker.)

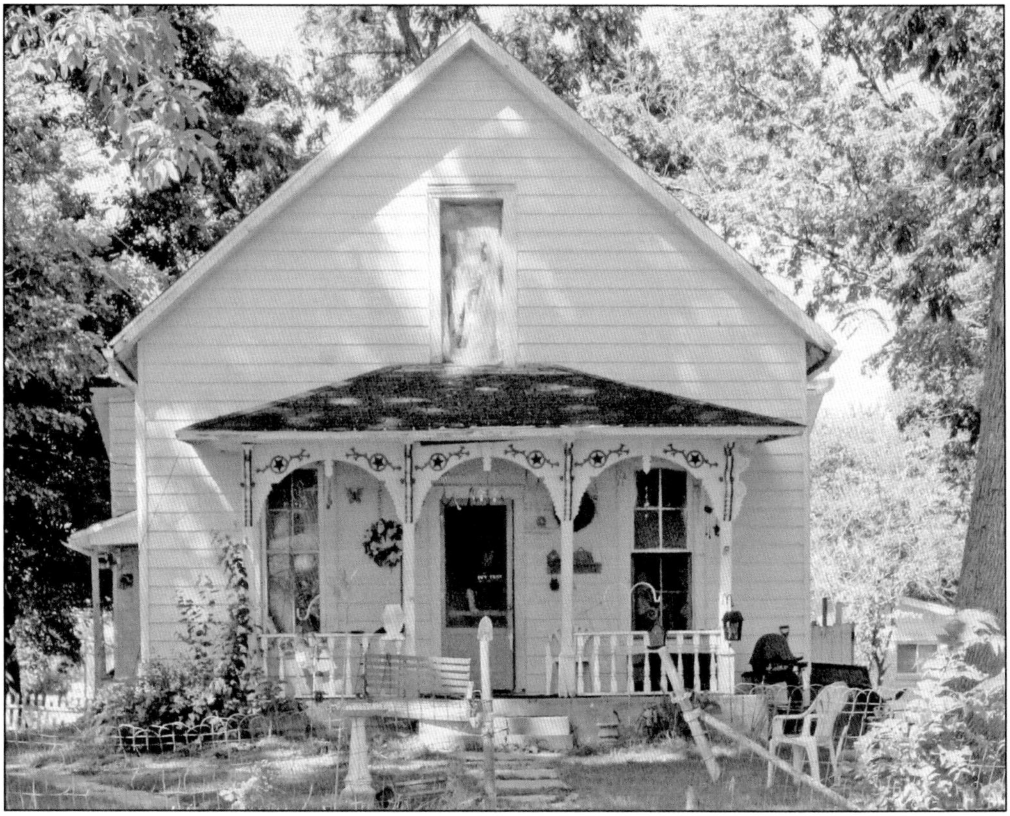

This little Victorian house, said to be the first house constructed in Cowan, surely was the first built of sawed lumber, as it dates to about 1880. McCowan's Station, as it was sometimes called, was on the Fort Wayne, Muncie & Cincinnati Railroad. (Jeffrey Koenker.)

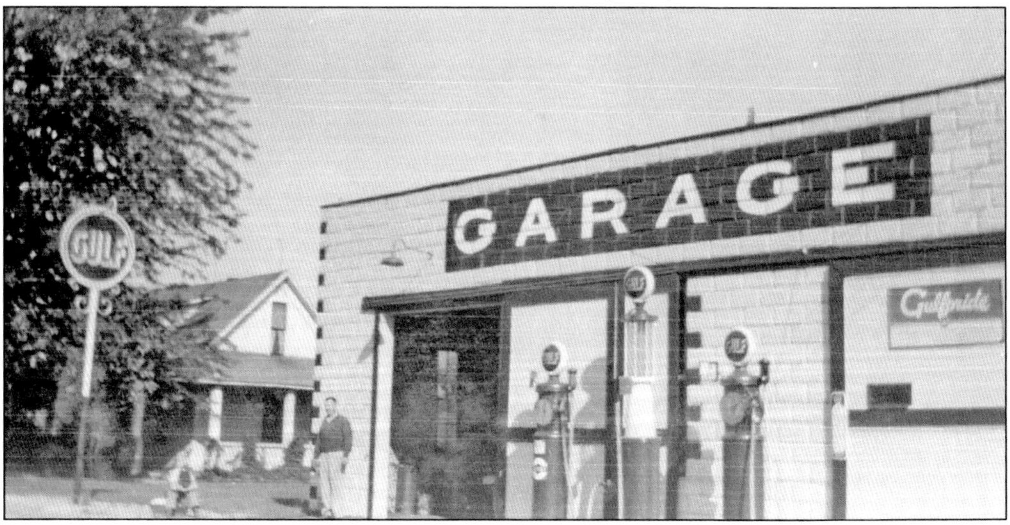

This Cowan garage is shown about 1935. It was owned by World War I veteran Norman Qualkinbush, father of Altabel and Norma Jean Qualkinbush. To join the service, Qualkinbush lied about his age to take his brother's place. He did not expect to survive his deployment, but he returned home, married, and had a family. (J. Paul and Norma Jean Reavis.)

Altabel Qualkinbush, about age three in this photograph, was born in 1924 to Norman E. and Ethel (Hutchison) Qualkinbush. The family moved to Cowan in 1935, where Altabel and her sister Norma Jean went to school. Altabel was the first certified professional secretary in the county and worked for Nickel Plate Railroad. (J. Paul and Norma Jean Reavis.)

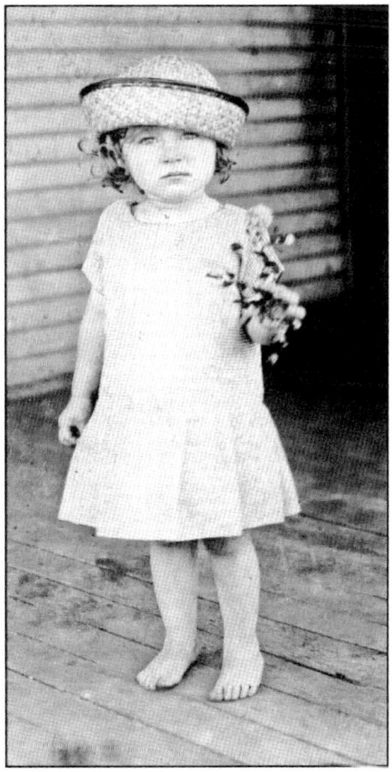

J. Paul Reavis, who married Norma Jean Qualkinbush, is pictured in the July 1946 image below. He enlisted in World War II in 1945 and served 15 months. His dog Skipper was trained in the Dogs for Defense program near the end of the war and returned home very well trained. (J. Paul and Norma Jean Reavis.)

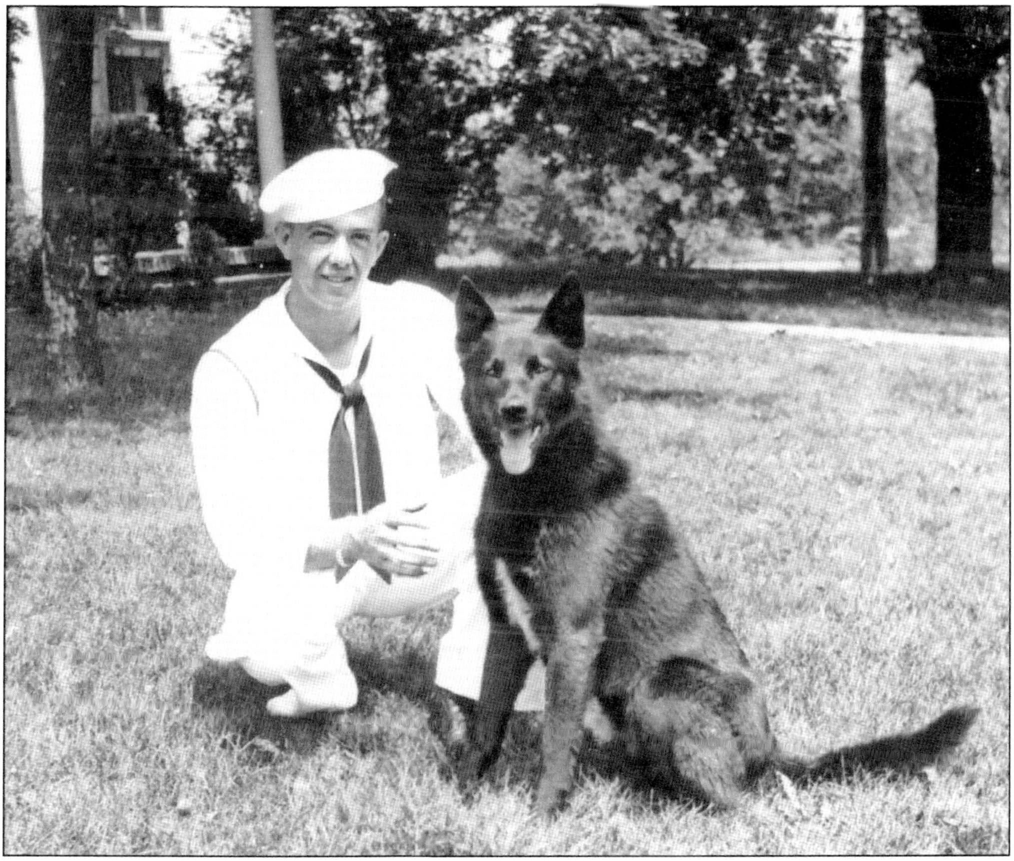

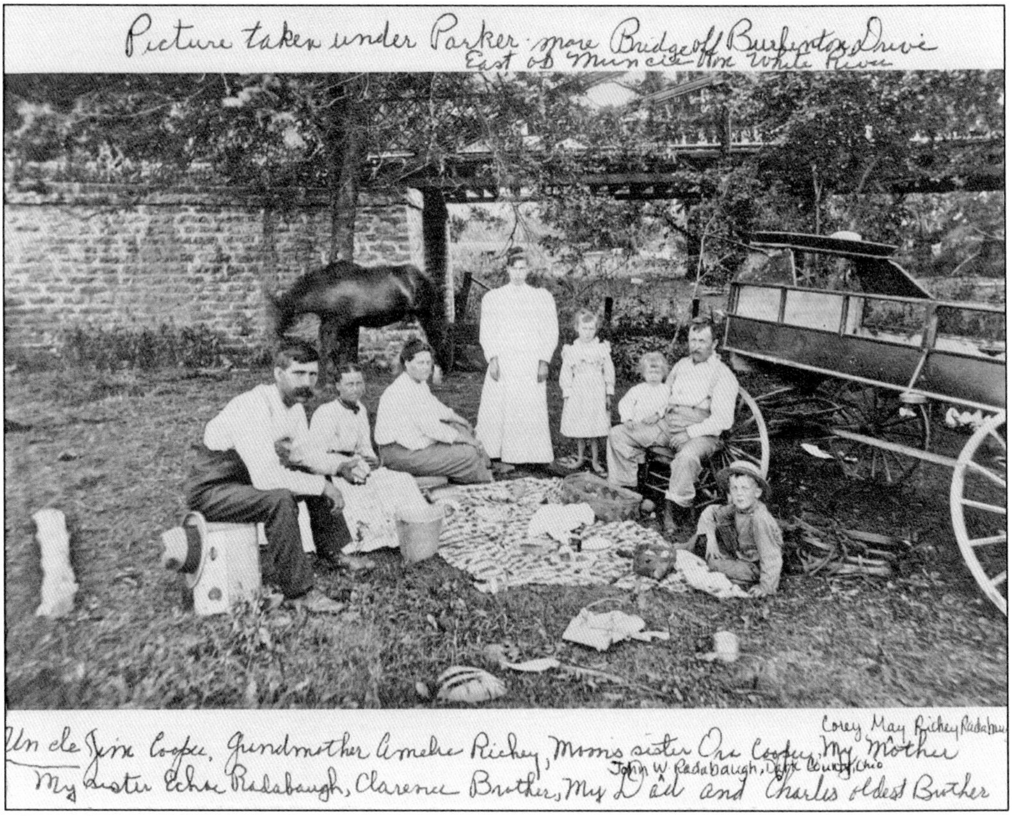

The Parker Moore Bridge was located east of Burlington Drive on White River, near land owned by Parker Moore. This picnicking family photograph is said to show, from left to right, the following: Uncle Jim Cooper, grandmother Amelia Richey, Mom's sister Ora Cooper, mother Corey May Richey Radabaugh, sister Echoe Radabaugh, brother Clarence Radabaugh, father John W. Radabaugh (from Darke County, Ohio), and oldest brother Charles. (Minnetrista Heritage Collection, Muncie, Indiana.)

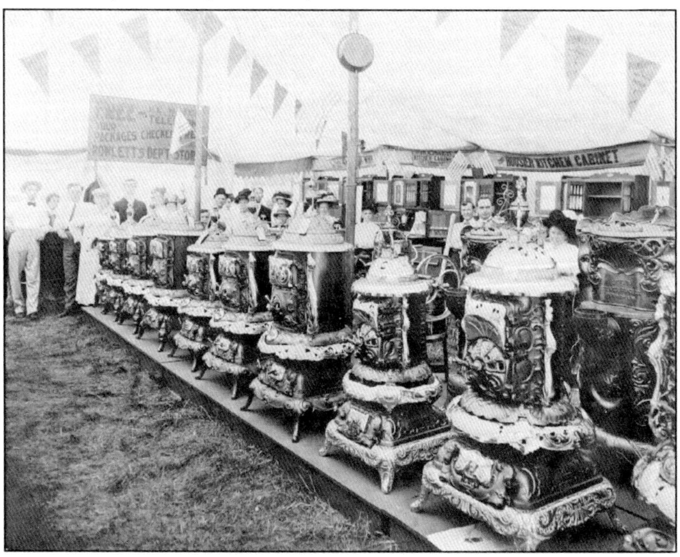

This county fair display is by the Rowlett Department Store, then located on Washington Street on the north side of the courthouse in Muncie. On the far right is a Hoosier Kitchen Cabinet display. That Albany factory burned in the early 1900s, and the company relocated to New Castle. The stoves in the foreground have isinglass (thin sheets of mica) in the doors to allow the fire inside to be seen. (Michael Mavis.)

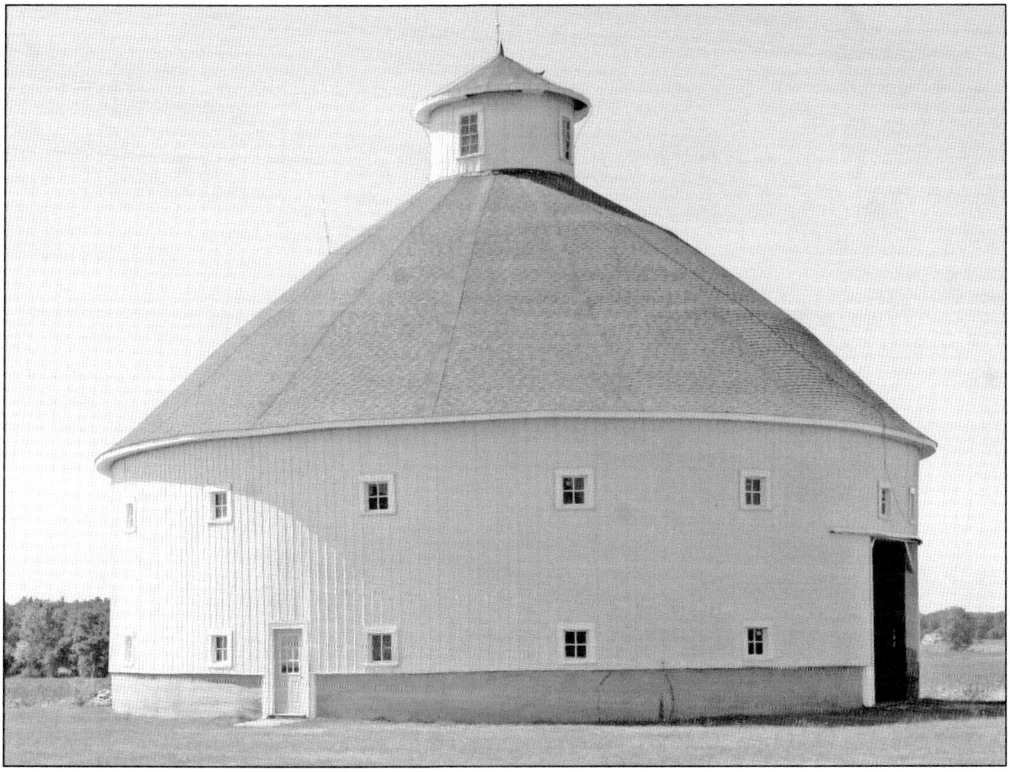

This round barn on the Selma-Albany Road is said to have been built about 1908. The barn has concrete lower walls and partitions, including a partition apparently inscribed in the wet concrete with "Ethel Nov 1913." The barn has been in the Grove family since 1949 and has been extensively renovated in order to preserve the roof and the structure. (Photograph by Thomas R. Tomlinson.)

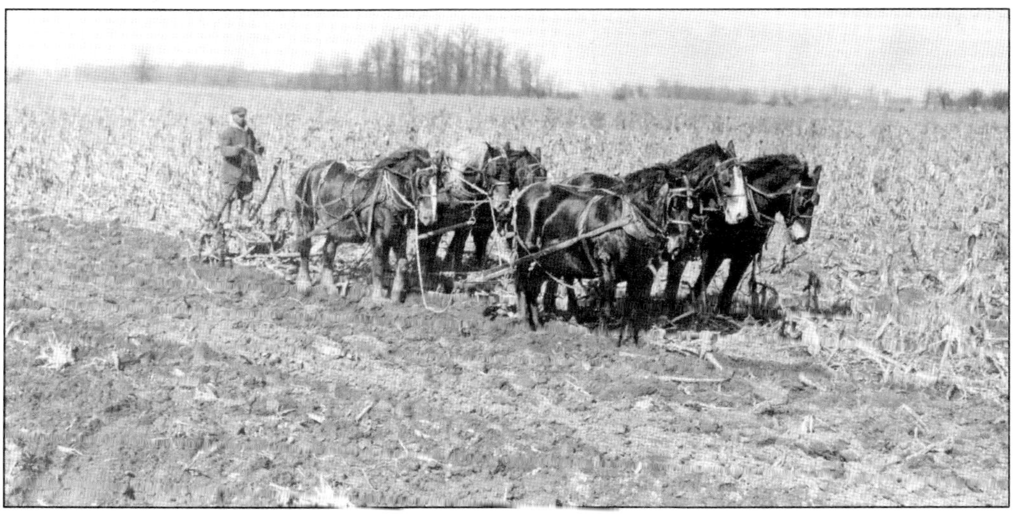

This farm scene is labeled "Ray Engle, 1931, 50 yrs ago." It may have appeared in the newspaper column called "50 Years Ago." The 1930 census lists Ray Engle, who was a Hamilton Township farmer, with a wife, Madie, and a daughter, Lucille. In this photograph, the farmer appears to be standing on a wheeled plow or cultivator with a team of six horses. (Larry Campbell.)

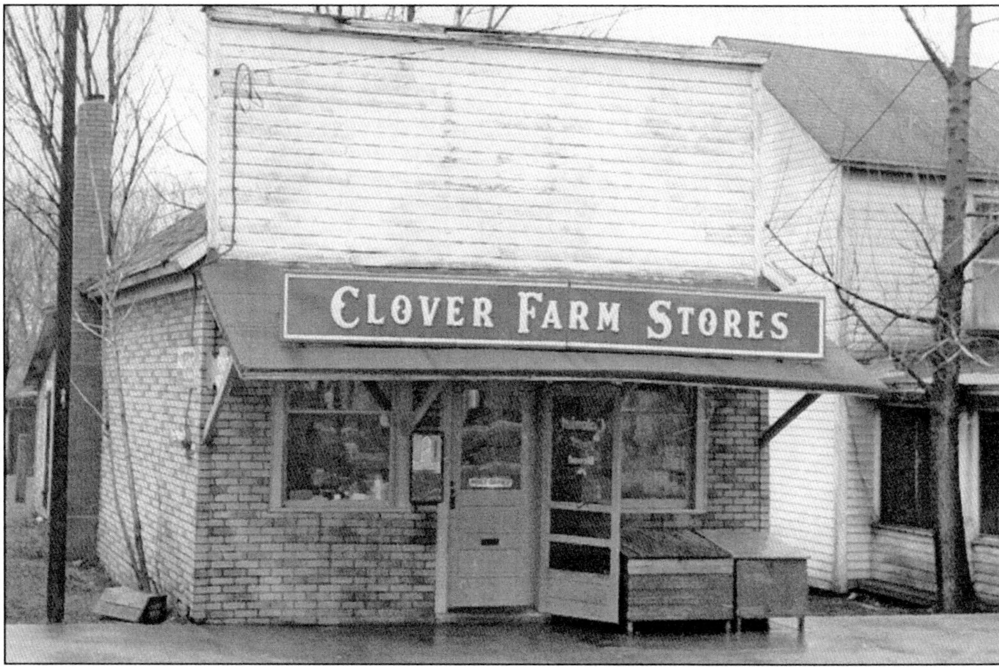

In Desoto, this Clover Farm store would have been the convenience store of its time, with its prefabricated sign showing it to be part of a known brand. The bins probably contained potatoes and seasonal produce. In addition to being a store, the post office sign on the door shows the building to have a second important function for the village and surrounding area. (Jeffrey Koenker.)

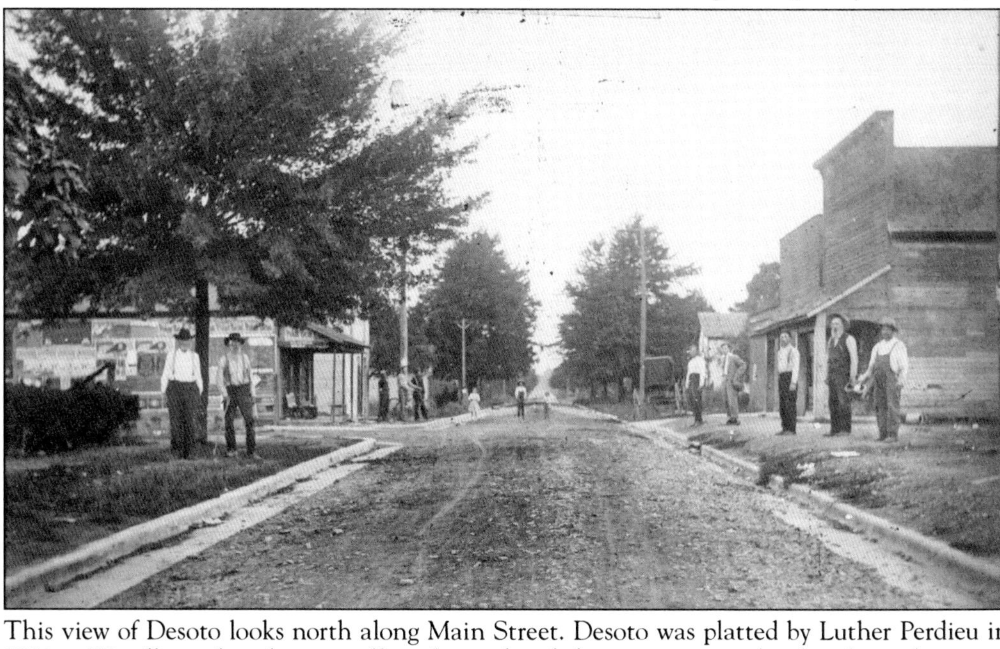

This view of Desoto looks north along Main Street. Desoto was platted by Luther Perdieu in 1881 as Woodlawn, but the post office objected and the proprietor and railroad people agreed on Desoto. The village had a church, a school, and a railroad station as well a combination store and post office. The post office existed from 1881 to 1978. (Minnetrista Heritage Collection, Muncie, Indiana.)

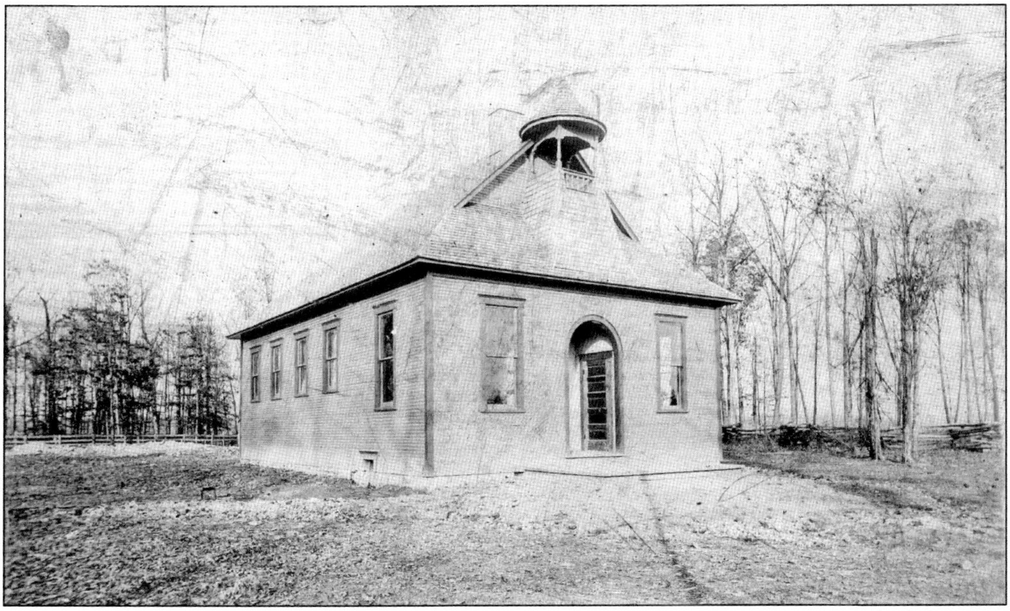

This one-room school at Desoto varied somewhat from the usual pattern with its arched doorway and a conical bell tower directly over the door. The chimney is located behind the bell tower. There is a small opening on the left side of the school that was probably used to resupply wood for the stove. (Jeffrey Koenker.)

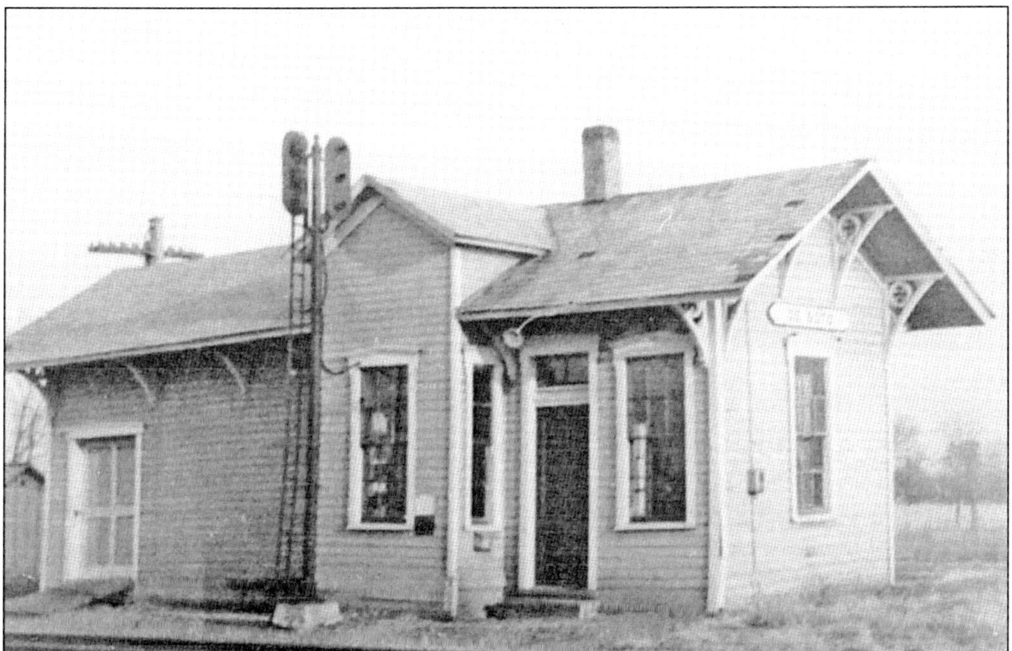

The Lake Erie & Western Railroad station was the visible emblem of Desoto's success, built as it was on the railroad line. Desoto was a thriving little community in the early 20th century. In modern days, it is the location of Desoto School. (Jeffrey Koenker.)

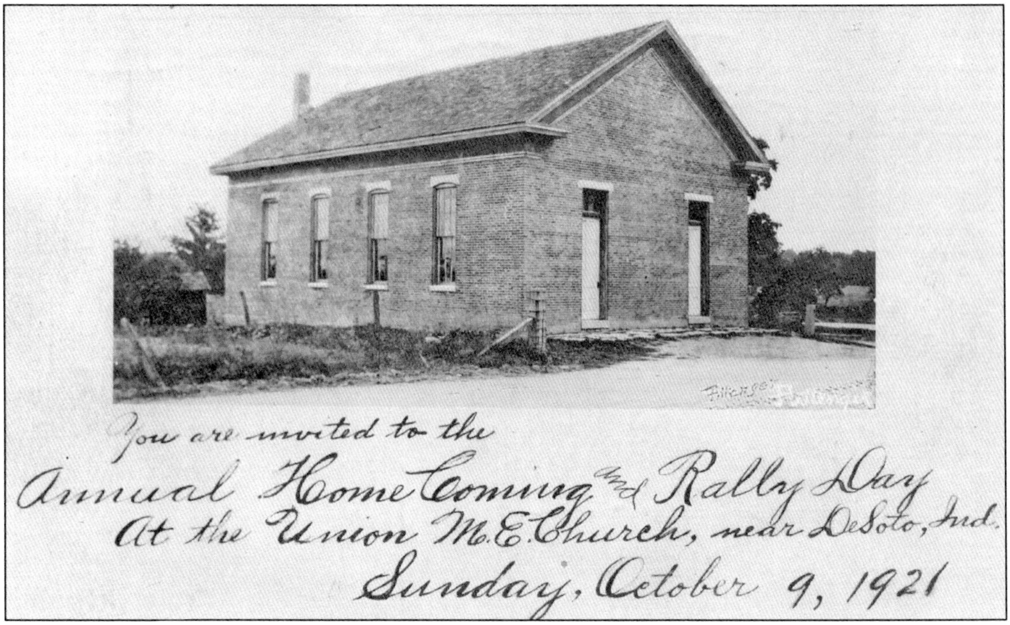

The Union Methodist Episcopal Church at Desoto met in a frame building from about 1845. In 1870, that structure was replaced by a plain brick building. This photograph was used on the invitations to the "Home Coming and Rally Day" held at the Union Methodist Episcopal Church on Sunday, October 9, 1921. (Jeffrey Koenker.)

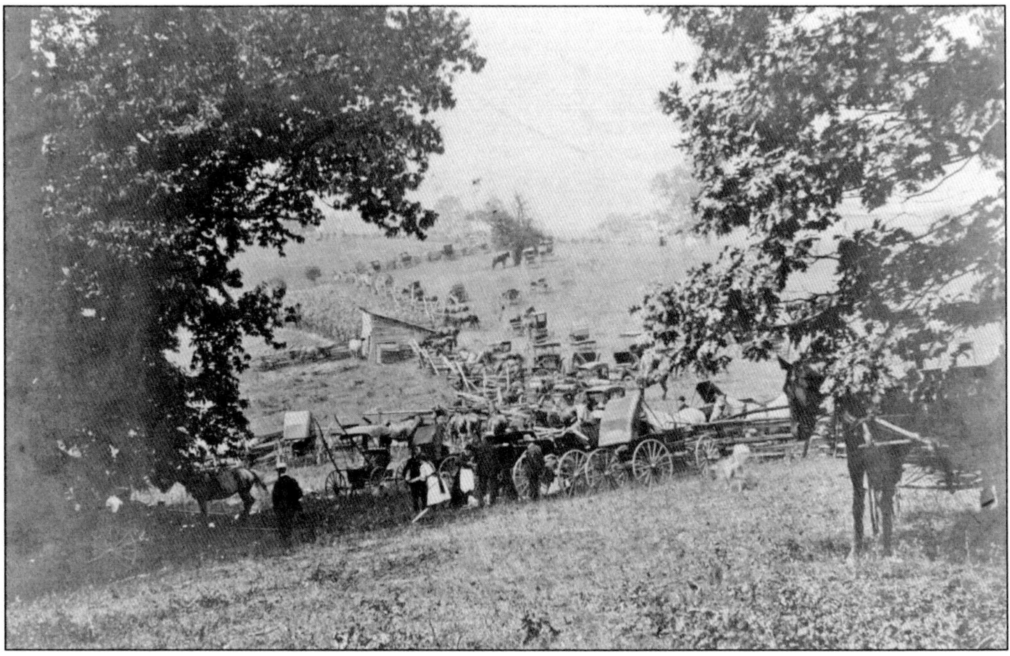

This field full of horses with buggies and wagons reminds people that vehicles must be parked, whether horse-drawn or horseless. The photograph is labeled that it was taken at "Claude Jones' grandson's farm, Delaware County, Indiana." The gathering could have been for any of several events, such as a grange meeting, a farm institute meeting, or a church camp meeting. (Minnetrista Heritage Collection, Muncie, Indiana.)

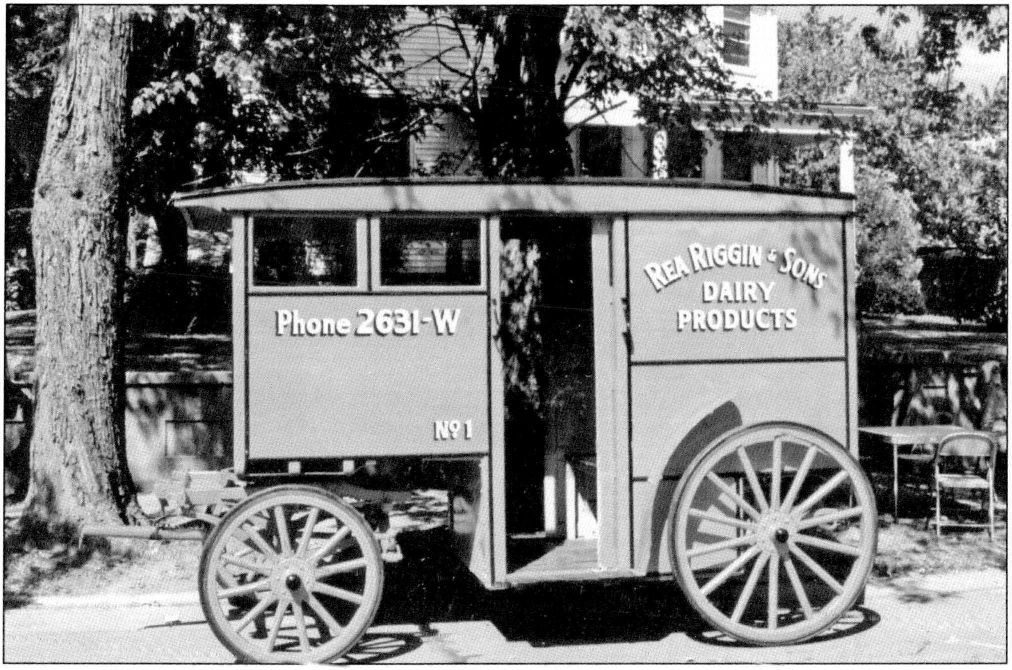

This restored Riggin Dairy delivery wagon takes people to the time when one of the services offered in towns and cities was delivery of milk to the home. Customers commonly acquired an insulated box that would hold the bottles of milk and keep them cool on summer mornings. Of course, the milk came in glass bottles that needed to be rinsed and returned to the dairy for reuse. (DCHS.)

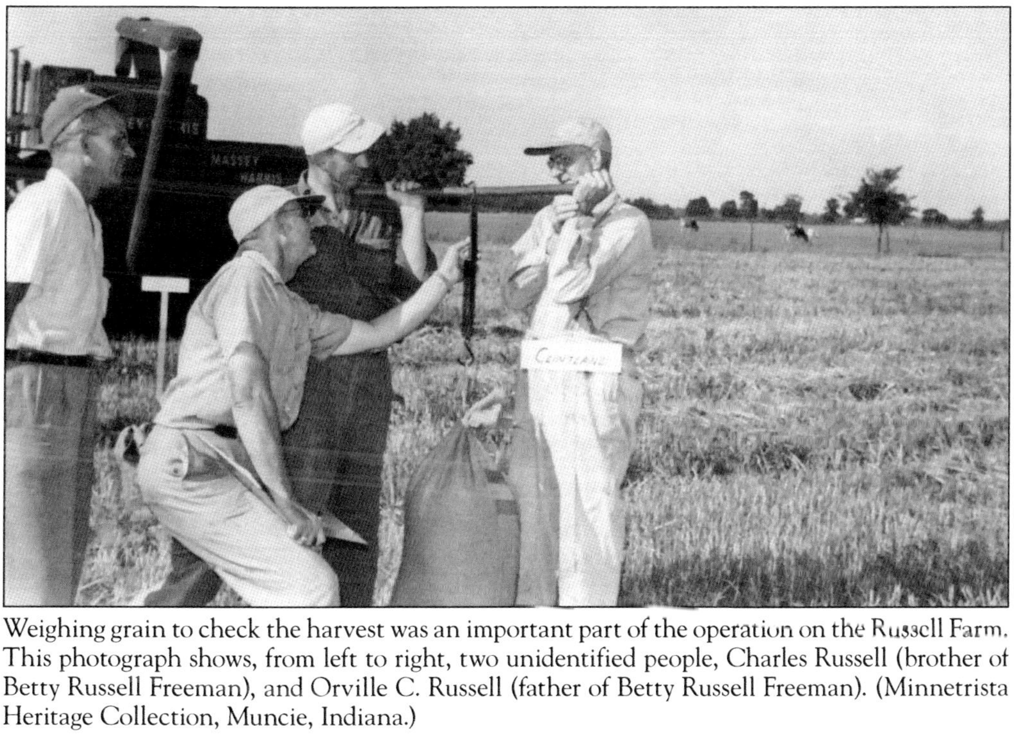

Weighing grain to check the harvest was an important part of the operation on the Russell Farm. This photograph shows, from left to right, two unidentified people, Charles Russell (brother of Betty Russell Freeman), and Orville C. Russell (father of Betty Russell Freeman). (Minnetrista Heritage Collection, Muncie, Indiana.)

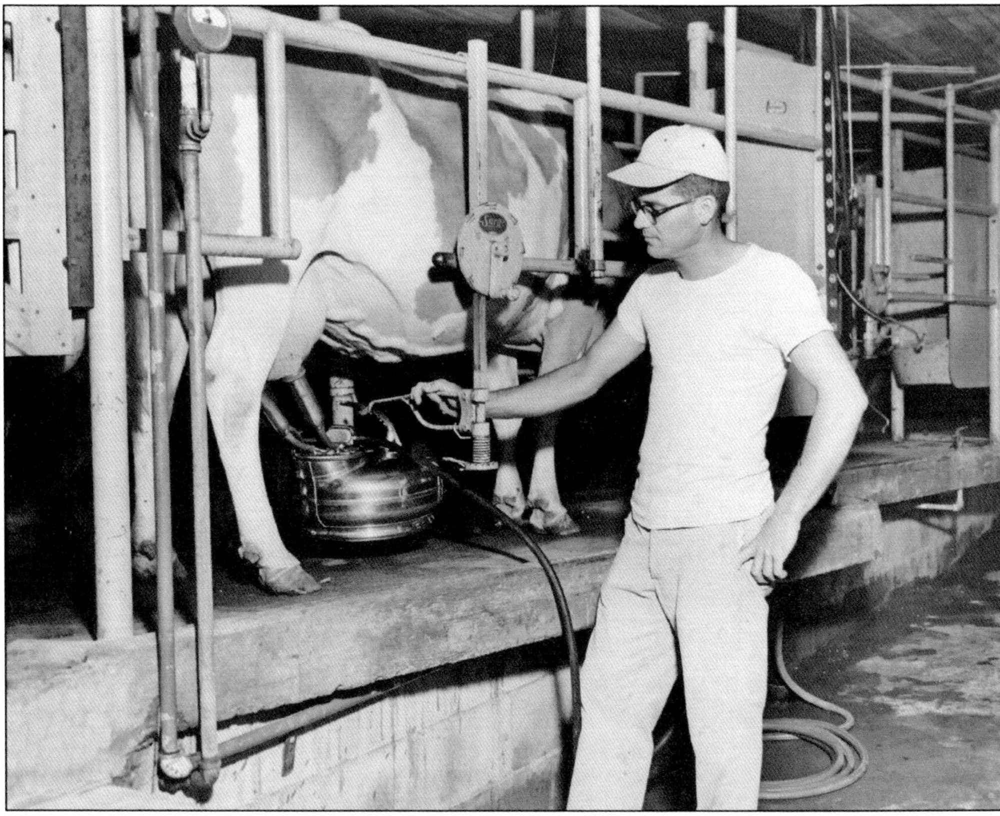

In this photograph, Vernon Freeman is demonstrating a milking machine—probably a surge milker, which was widely used from the 1920s until in the 1960s when the pipeline milking systems became available. (Minnetrista Heritage Collection, Muncie, Indiana.)

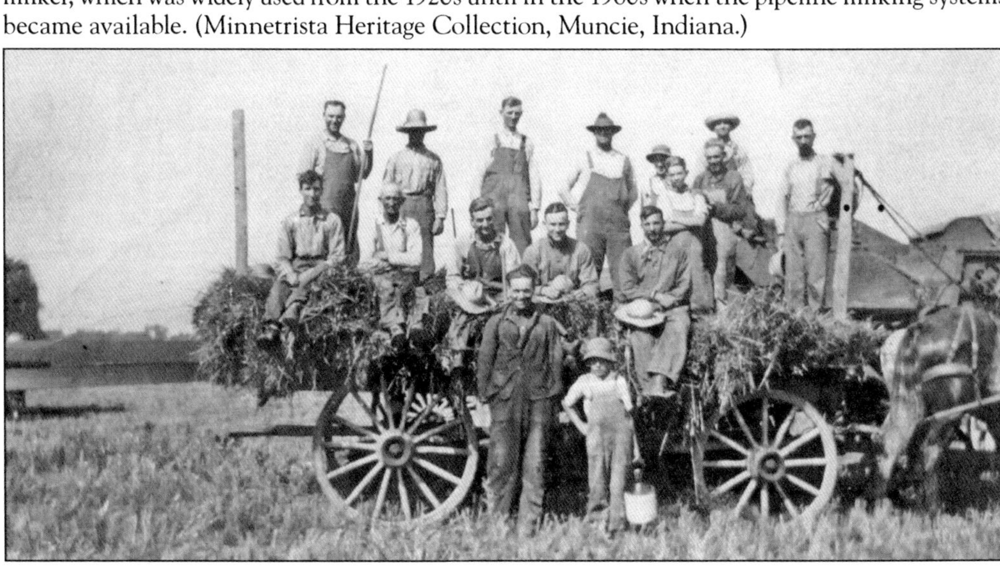

This threshing crew was photographed on the Freeman farm. They appear to be gathering the cut wheat to take it from the field to the threshing machine. The only member of the crew identified is Ernest Freeman, who was second from right sitting down. (Minnetrista Heritage Collection, Muncie, Indiana.)

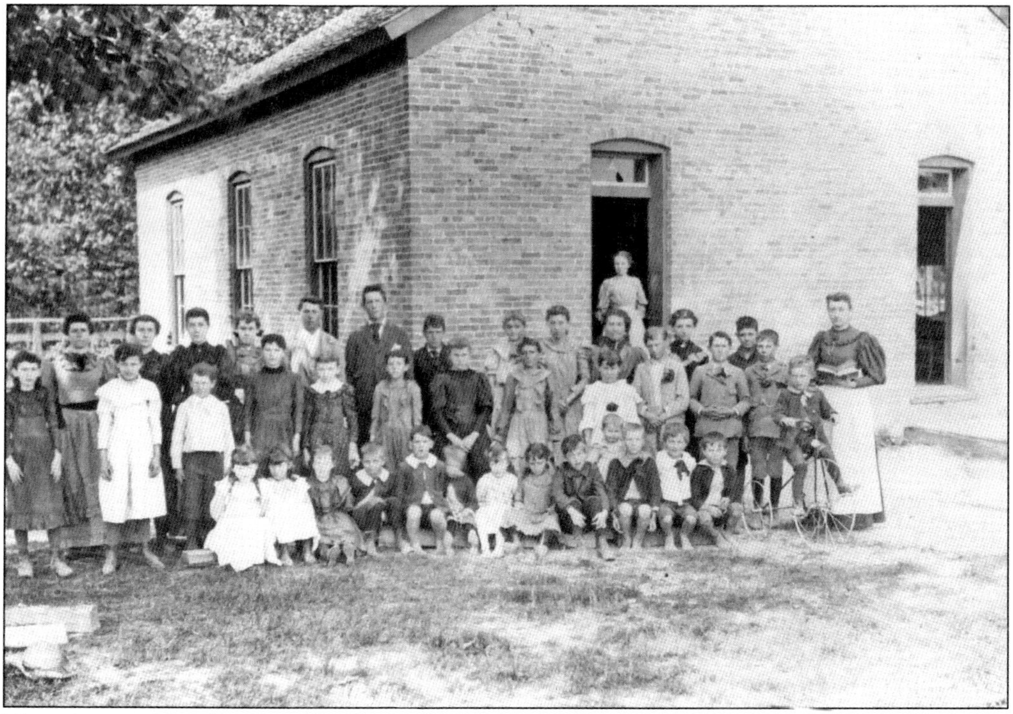

This photograph of Tabor School in Liberty Township is labeled "Grandma Stella Watt with students." Tabor School was District School 9 in Liberty Township, west of Smithfield. The nearby Mount Tabor Cemetery is on both sides of the road, but the church is no longer standing. Stella Watt died in 1948, having lived all her life near Smithfield. (Michael Mavis.)

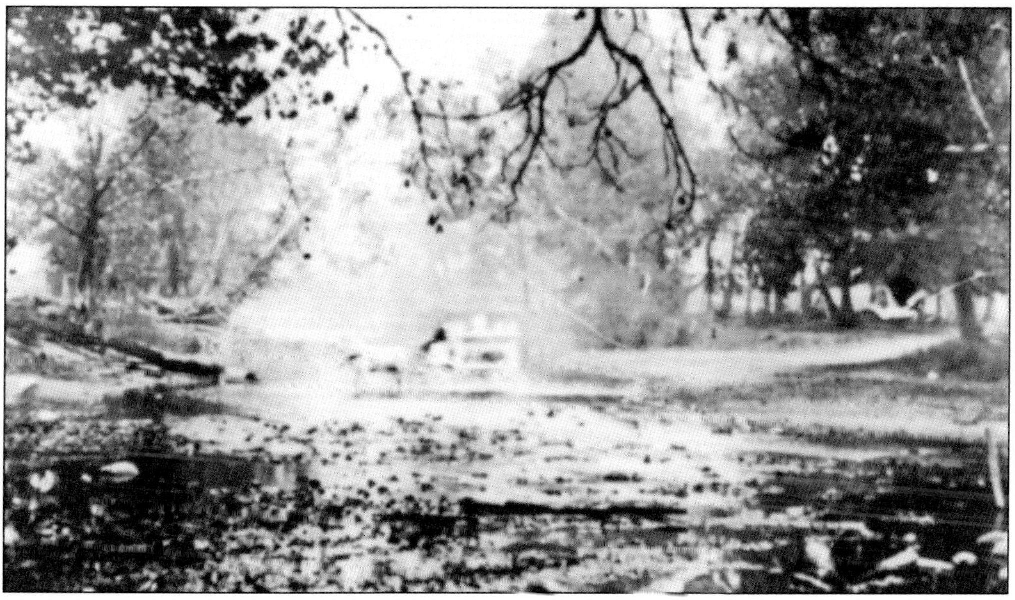

The horse-drawn Meeks mortuary carriage was probably photographed in the 1890s, according to David Meeks, as it crossed the ford at Inlow Springs with some mortuary paraphernalia on the top of the carriage. The Inlow Springs were located in Liberty Township, near where Inlow Springs Road crosses White River today. (Meeks Mortuary, Gordon Cox.)

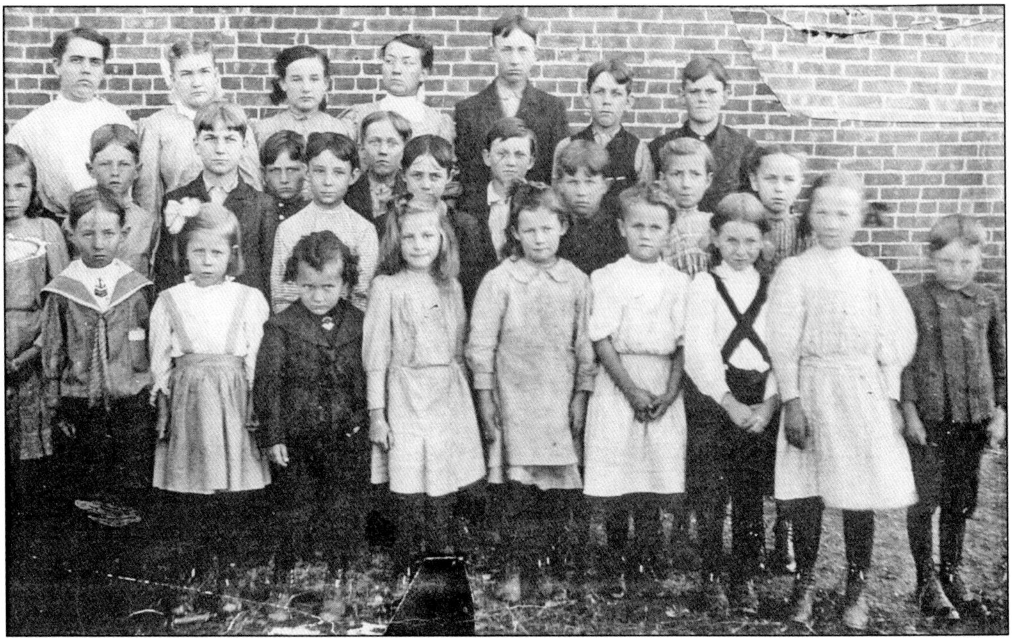

This 1907 Macedonia school photograph shows the students with O'Letha Oxley, their teacher. In the first row, beginning with the girl with a bow in her hair, are, from left to right, Ermal Chalfant, George Gibson, Virgie Reese, Mary Gibson, Lamon West, Ethel Hutchison (mother of Norma Jean Qualkinbush Reavis), Mary Priddy, and Lowell Fry. Macedonia was a few miles east and south of Cowan. (J. Paul and Norma Jean Reavis.)

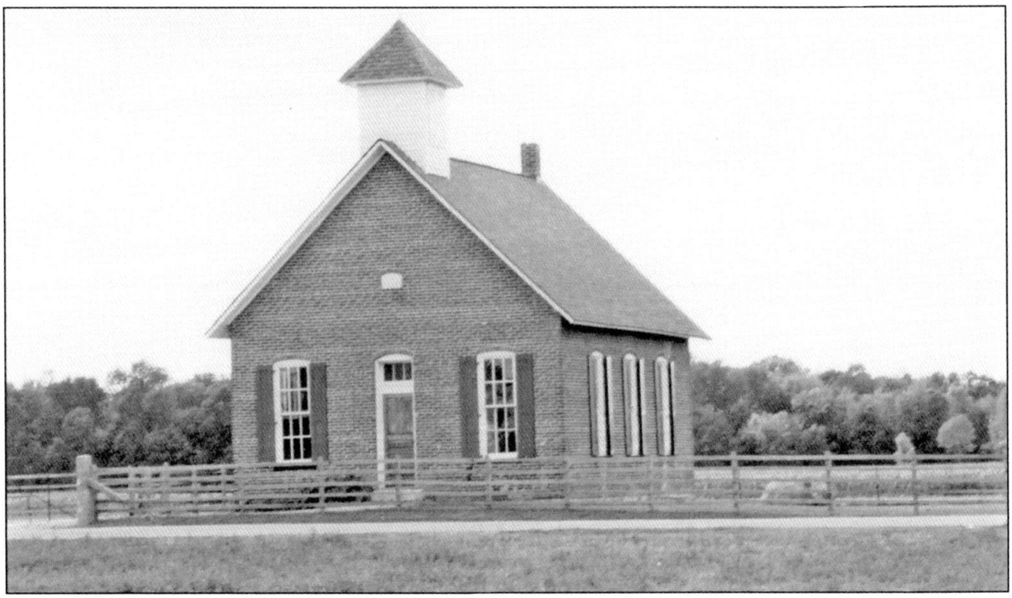

Corinth School in Monroe Township was originally District School 3 and was catty-corner from Corinth Church of the Brethren on the 1887 atlas. The school was restored by Dr. Norman Miller a few years ago, and there are lesson plans to be used with a class to demonstrate the one-room school experience. (DCHS.)

The Mount Zion Church, located on the Eaton-Wheeling Pike, is well preserved and maintained, as is its companion cemetery. Originally the site of a log church, a brick church was built in 1867. The land for church and cemetery was donated by Richard Craw, whose family were pioneers in Union Township. (Photograph by Thomas R. Tomlinson.)

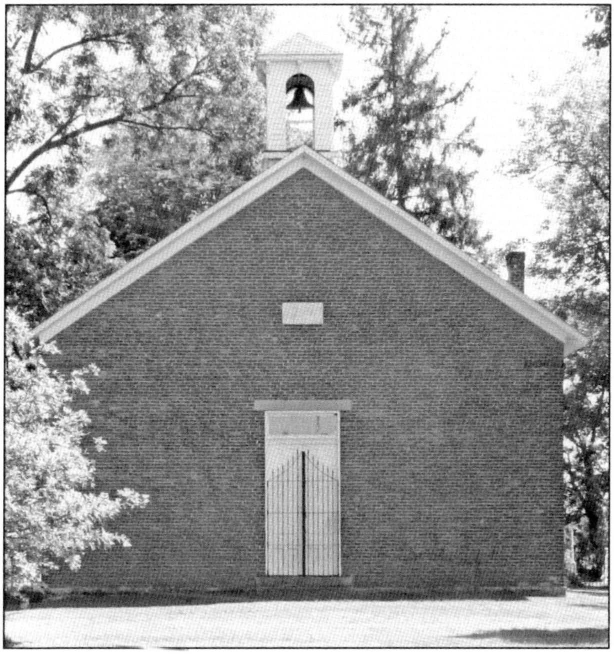

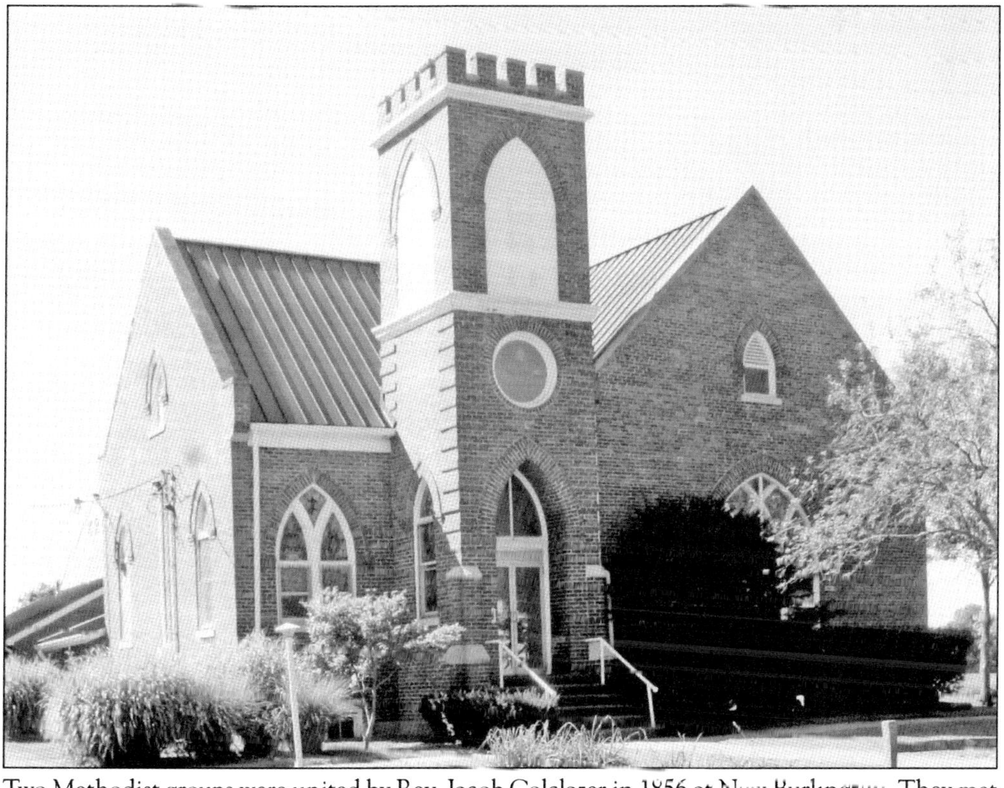

Two Methodist groups were united by Rev. Jacob Colclazer in 1856 at New Burlington. They met in a Presbyterian church, which became a Methodist church when the Presbyterians combined with another group. When that building became unsafe, a frame structure was erected in its place. The current building is made of brick. (DCHS; photograph by Thomas R. Tomlinson.)

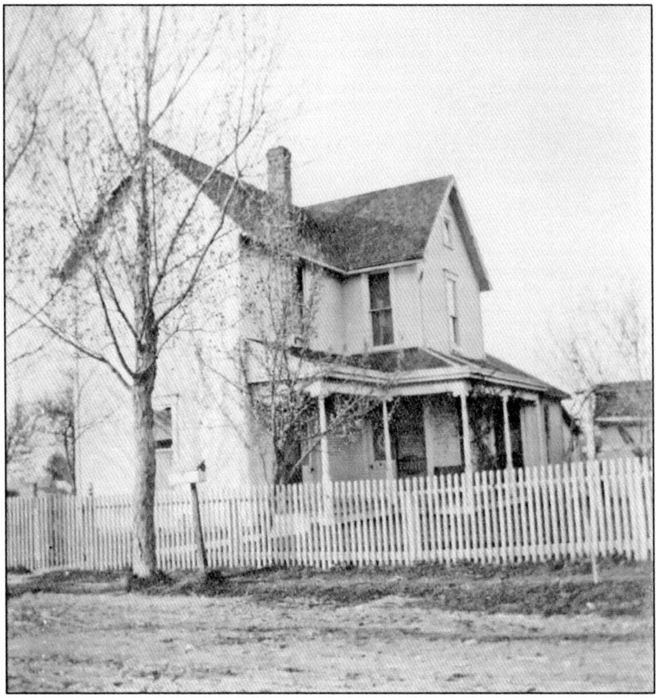

Dr. John N. Bell, a popular physician in New Burlington, was the grandfather of Rita Winters, a popular columnist for the *Muncie Star* for many years. Dr. Bell's office was in his house, which was common for small-town doctors. He died in 1928. (Minnetrista Heritage Collection, Muncie, Indiana.)

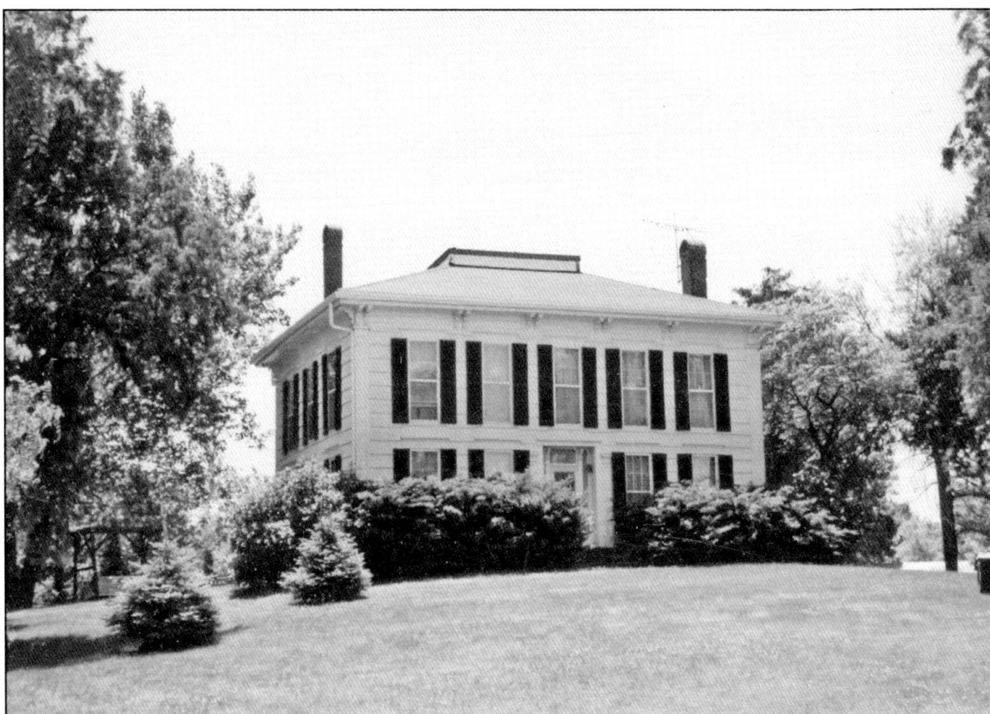

Dr. Samuel Jump was a well-known and respected physician who lived in this house at the south edge of New Burlington. He settled in New Burlington in 1848 after studying and working with another physician, as was then the custom. His medical equipment and other memorabilia is on display in the collection of the Moore-Youse Home Museum. (DCHS.)

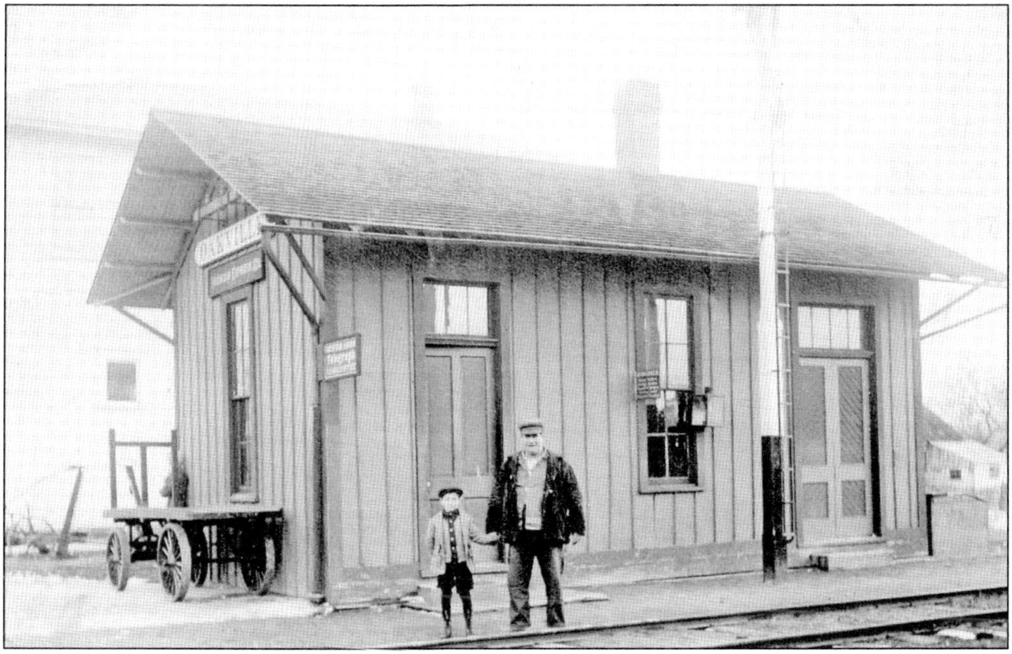

Oakville was on the Lake Erie & Western Railroad, one of the three earliest railroads in the county. The station house was a block north of Main Street along the west side of the railroad in the 1887 atlas. This little station house is long gone now but once represented a feature that made Oakville a thriving village. (Michael Mavis.)

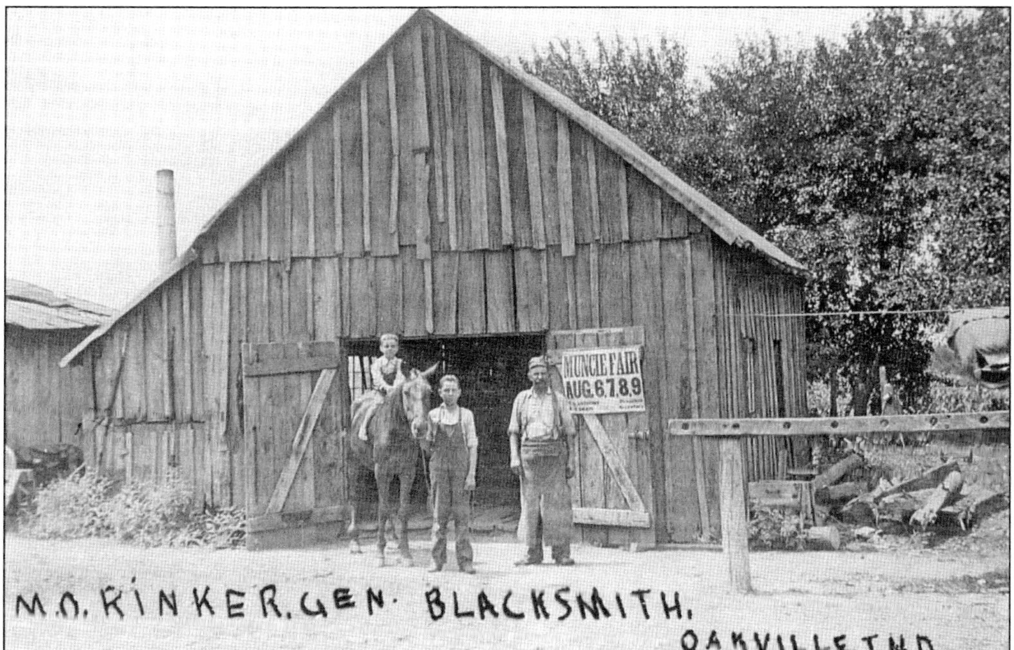

Marion O. Rinker was listed in the 1920 census as a blacksmith who owned his shop. He was 51 years old and was listed with his wife, Margaret; a son, age 13; and a daughter, age 10. The Muncie Fair sign is for the county fair at the Delaware County Fairgrounds in Muncie. (Jeffrey Koenker.)

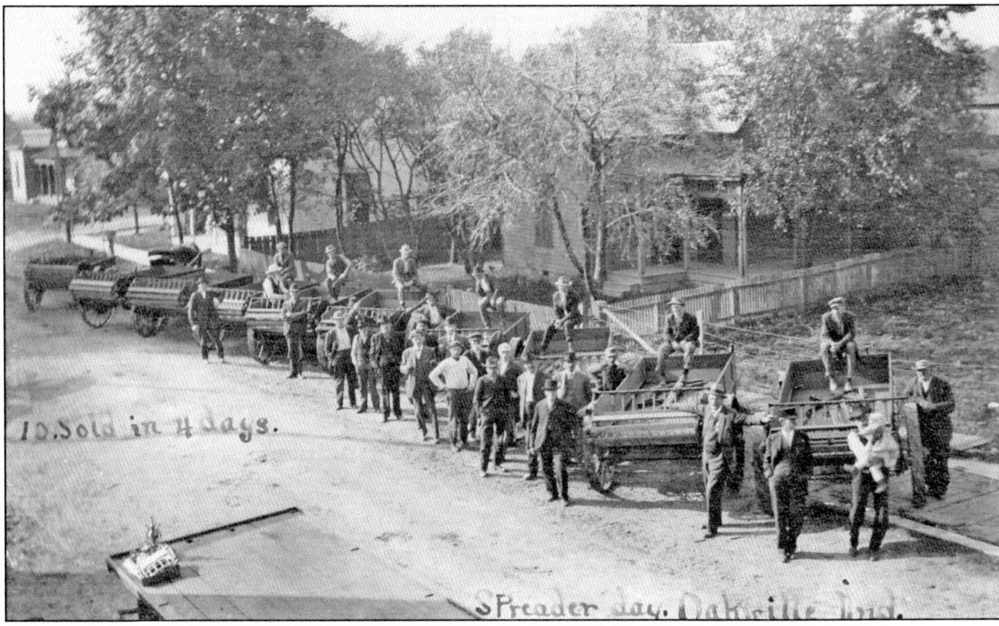

Selling 10 manure spreaders in four days was no doubt an accomplishment in those times. It is not known who manufactured these implements, but Jeremiah Holsinger of Oakville was listed in the 1907–1908 directory as carrying "farming implements," among other items. In the directory of 1919–1920, G.W. Teeter of Oakville is listed as carrying "agricultural implements." (Jeffrey Koenker.)

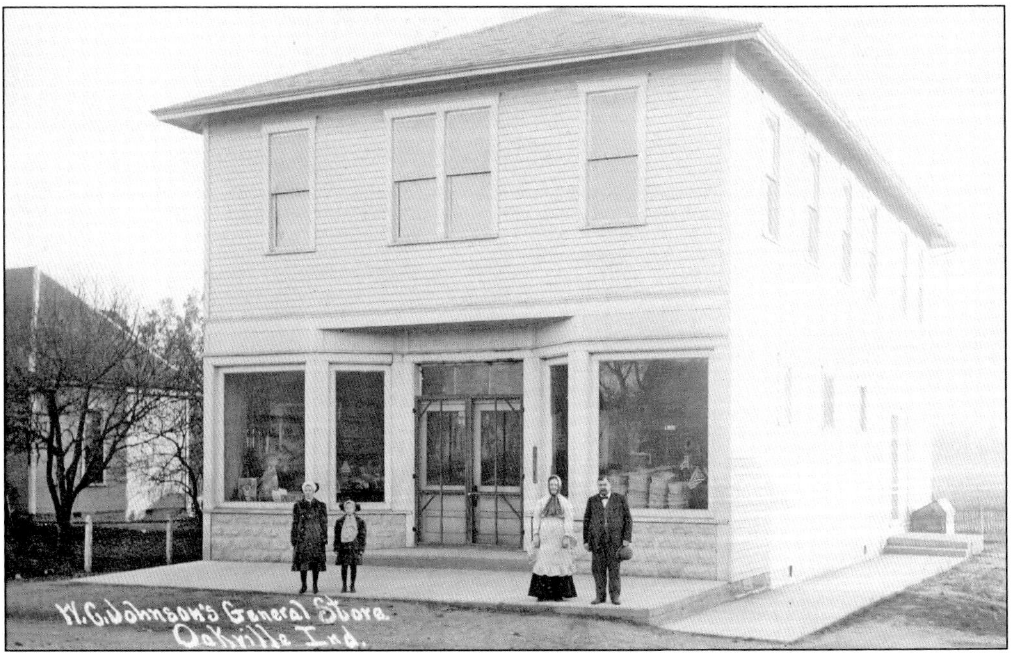

This postcard reads "W.C. Johnson's General Store." Willard C. Johnson is listed in the 1910 census as a merchant with a general store. In addition to his wife, there are three children ranging from age 9 to age 16. Other postcards show that the store was on Main Street, east of the railroad track. (Jeffrey Koenker.)

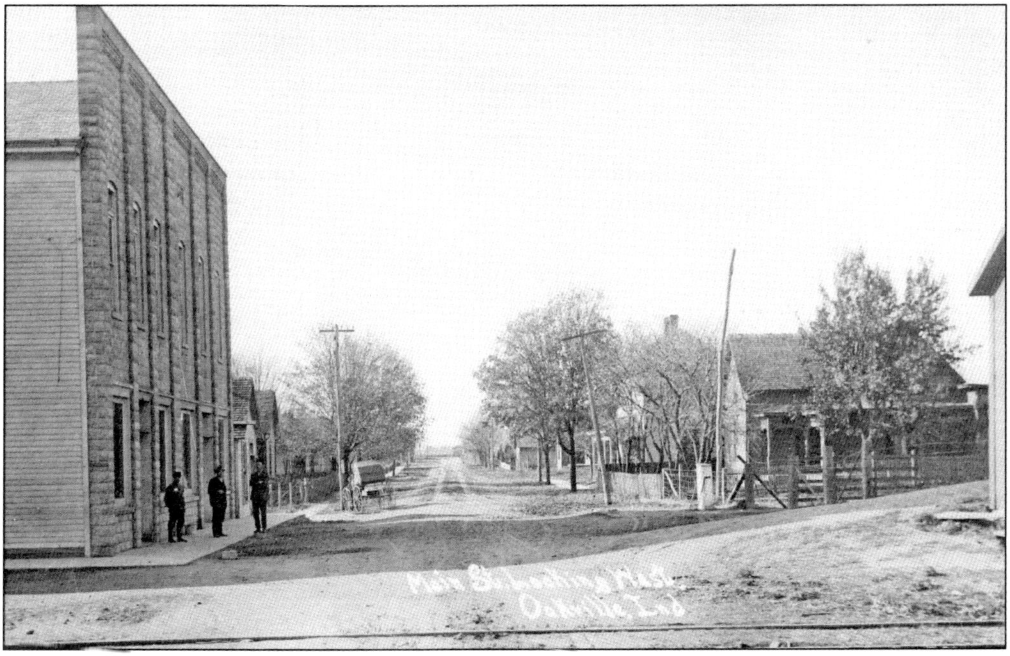

This postcard is postmarked 1911. In this view with the railroad in the foreground, the General Store would be on the left and east of the railroad if it were within view. Oakville is located close to the Henry County line in southern Delaware County. (Jeffrey Koenker.)

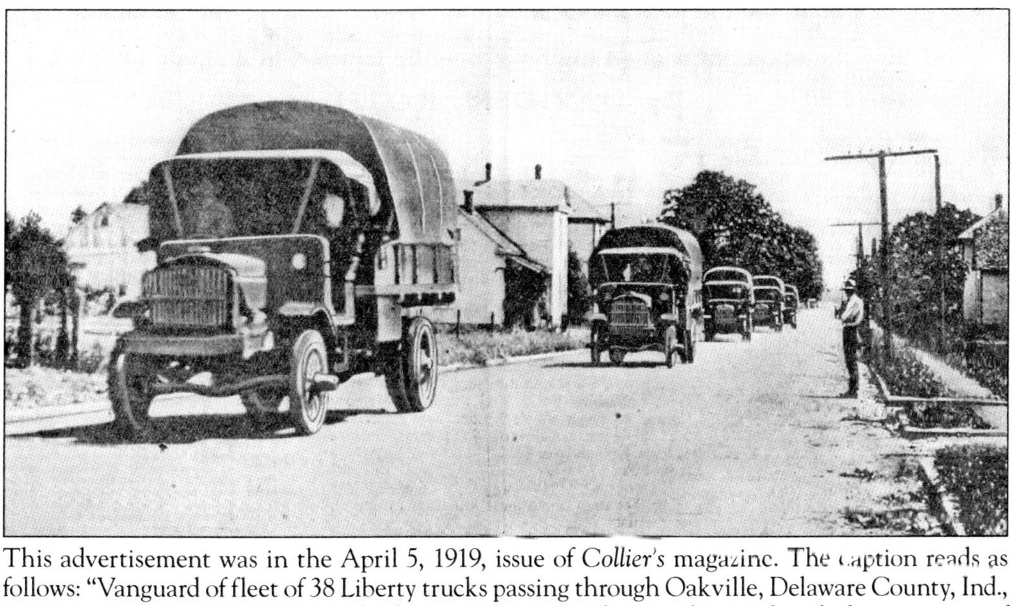

This advertisement was in the April 5, 1919, issue of *Collier's* magazine. The caption reads as follows: "Vanguard of fleet of 38 Liberty trucks passing through Oakville, Delaware County, Ind., in August 1918, over Tarcia Road built in 1916. Note perfect condition of road after two years of hard service." (DCHS.)

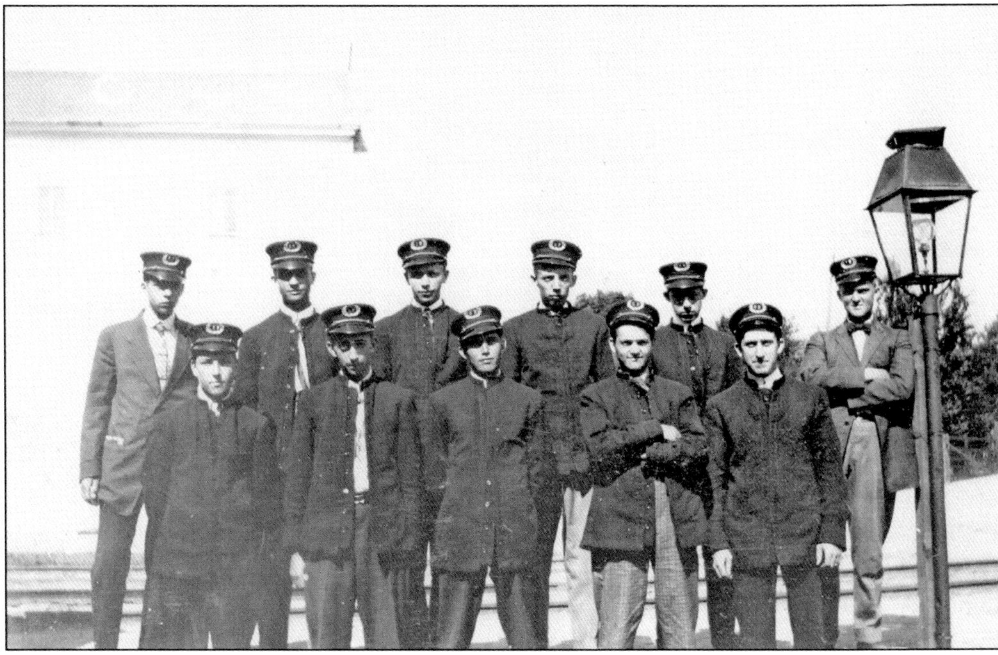

The Oakville band was organized in 1906 under the direction of Charles Kern. As word of the band spread, members came from the surrounding area, including Cowan and Springport. They rehearsed in the Knights of Pythias lodge hall and in 1909 played at the Middletown Fair. They disbanded about 1912. (Michael Mavis.)

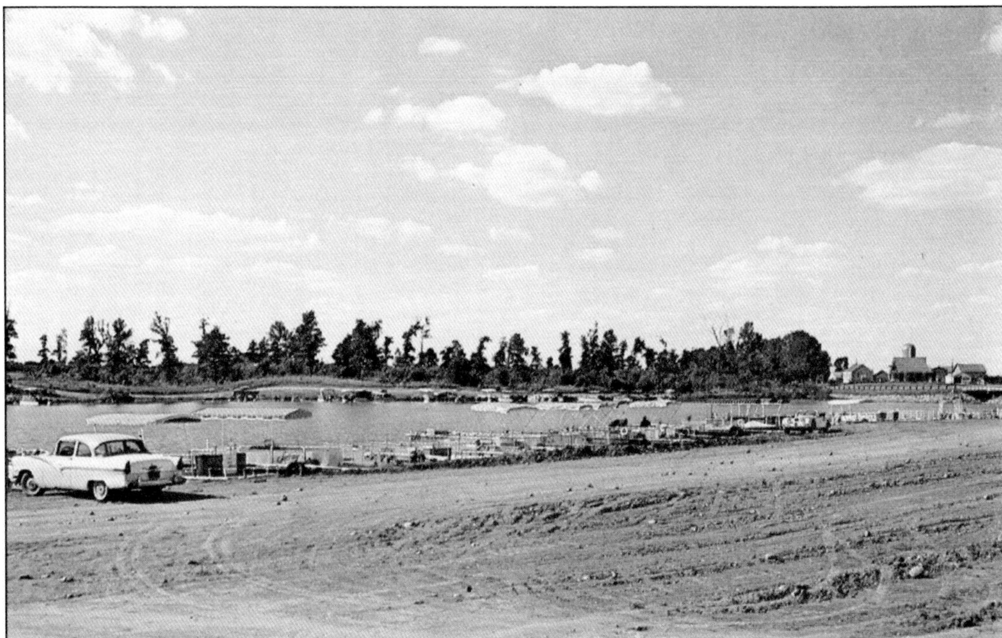

Construction work was in progress on the Prairie Creek Reservoir when this photograph was taken. The view shows the causeway at the north end in the background. The reservoir and park contain about 1,275 water acres and 750 land acres. It was developed in 1954 by the Muncie Water Works and is leased by the City of Muncie. (Muncie Public Library.)

This image appeared in *Our Country* by John S. Ellis. The home and store of Eli Walradth was at Hasel, here said to be Old Mount Pleasant. Described as being in the northeast quarter of section 19, it may have been a little to the west of the present village of Mount Pleasant. Waldradth ran the post office at Hasel from 1896 to 1901. (DCHS.)

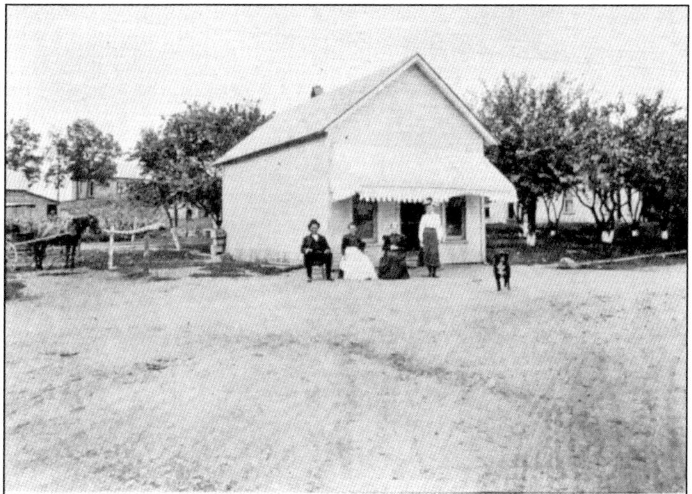

HOME AND STORE OF ELI W. WALRADTH,
Hasel, (Old Mt. Pleasant). Perry Township.

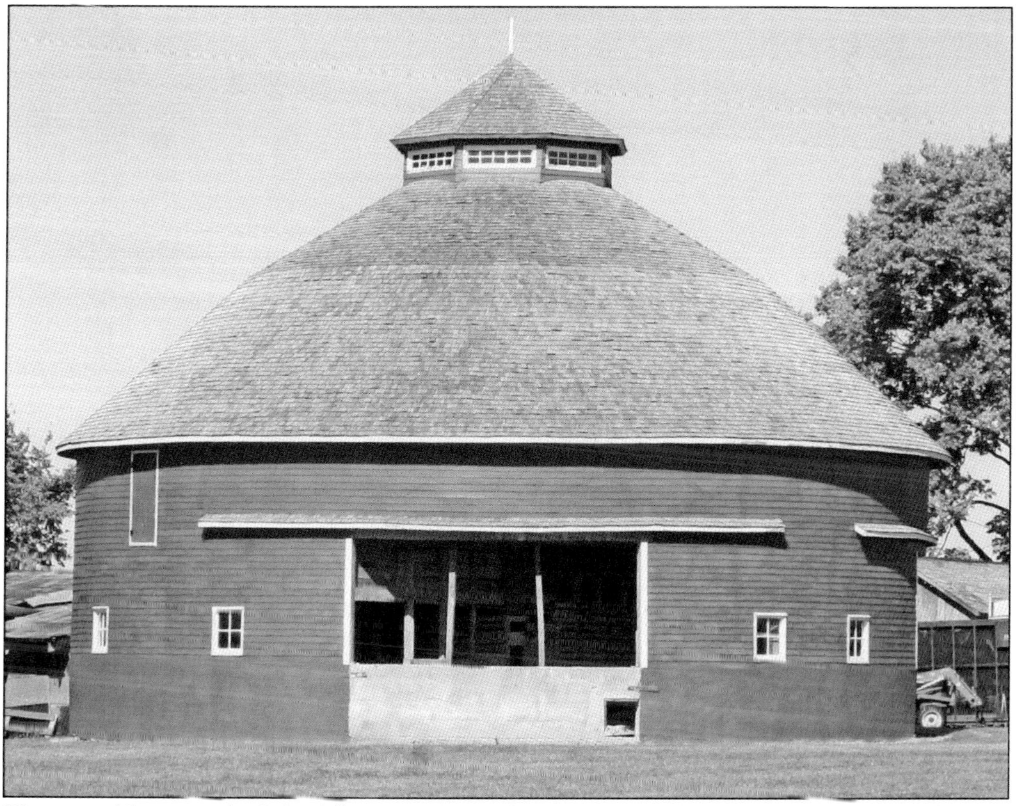

This round barn was built by Albert Keesling, whose great-grandson Douglas Keesling still owns and maintains the barn. It was built with a four-foot concrete foundation, cypress walls, and cedar shingles on the roof. There is a concrete silo 30 feet high in the center with a haymow in the top loft. Recent restoration work included new cypress walls and cedar shingle roof. (Photograph by Thomas R. Tomlinson.)

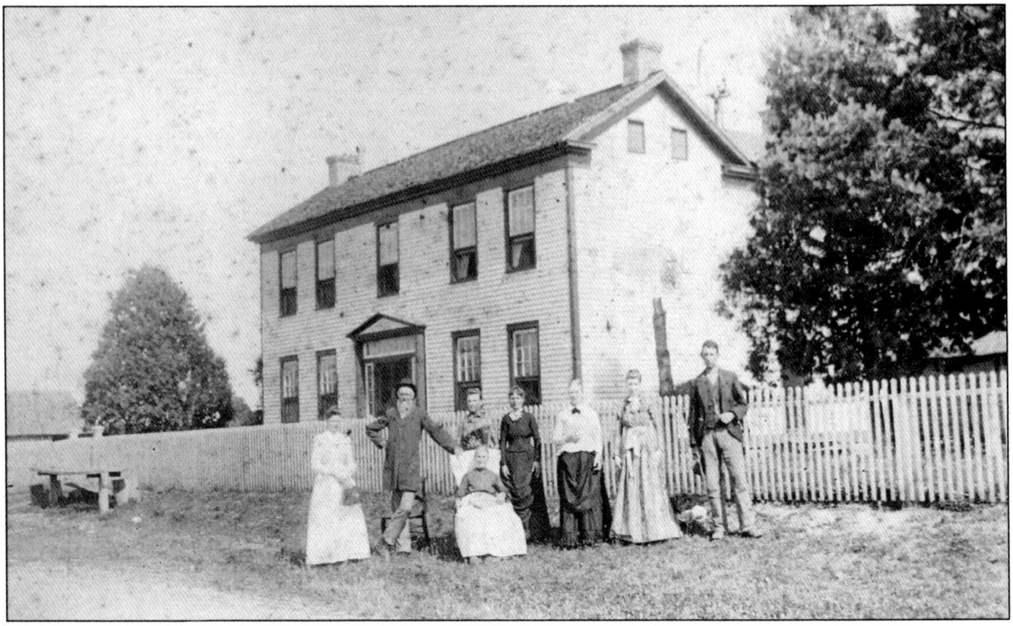

This photograph is labeled "Family scene at Whitney's Ford, Perry Township, Delaware County, Ind." Lafayette Whitney and Phineas Whitney owned land in section 32 along White River, in northern Perry Township next to the Liberty Township line. The 1887 atlas shows a road crossing the river to the north from Whitney land, where the ford would have been before a bridge was built. (Michael Mavis.)

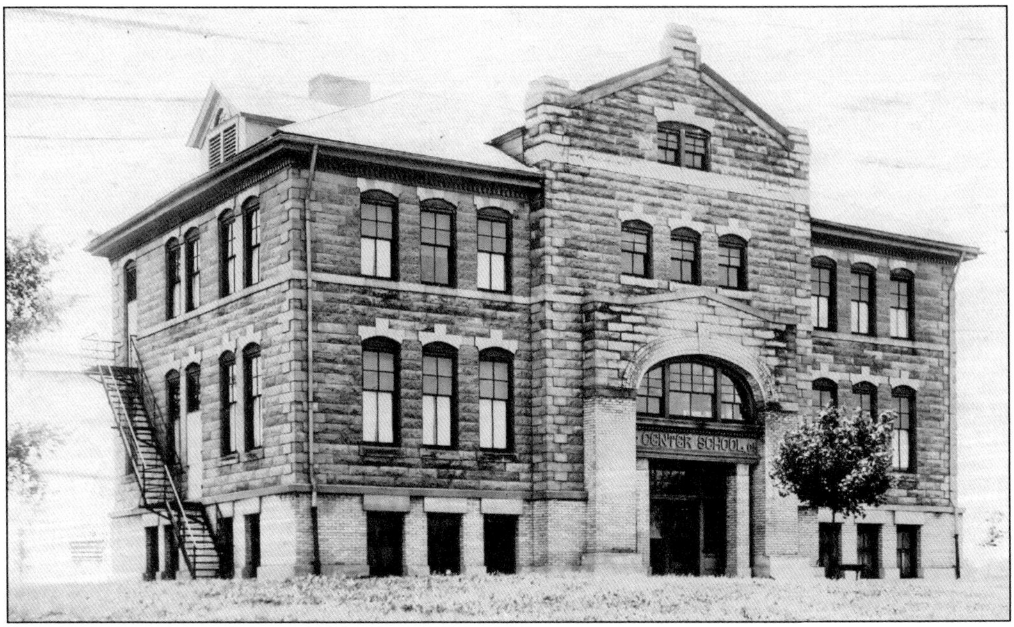

This school building was said to be the first public structure in the county to be constructed of cement blocks. The new Center School building was a consolidation replacing two older school structures. It was planned to be open by November 10, 1905, but construction was delayed and it opened in February 1906. Center School served about 160 pupils from the northeastern part of Perry Township. (Jeffrey Koenker.)

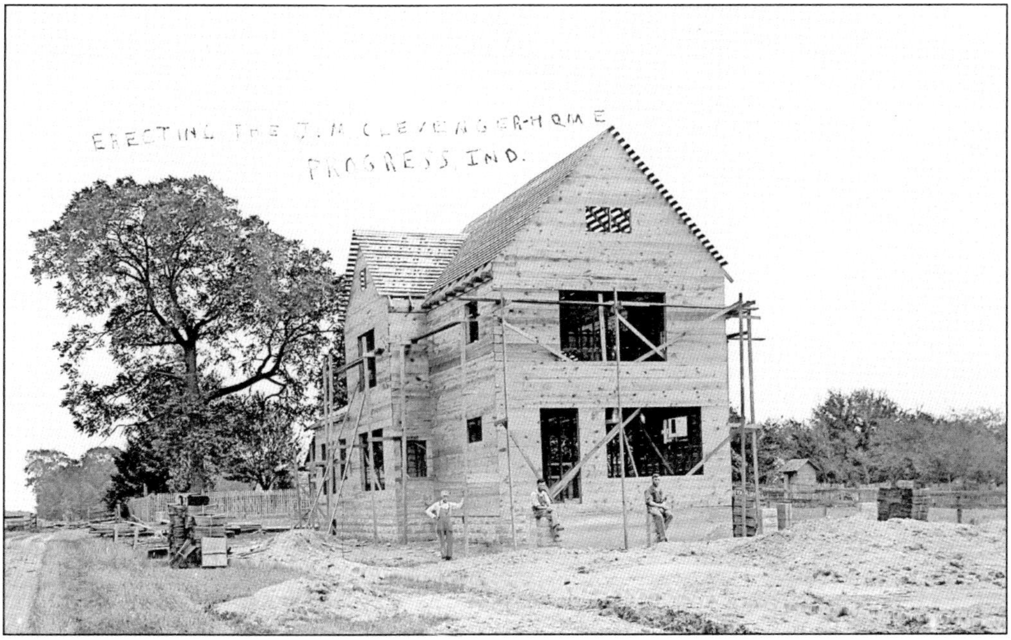

This new house under construction shows the methods of the time. The community of Sharps, named for the pioneer family, changed its name to Progress when a railroad came through in 1899. The Sharp family also owned a gas well that supplied six houses in the village. (Jeffrey Koenker.)

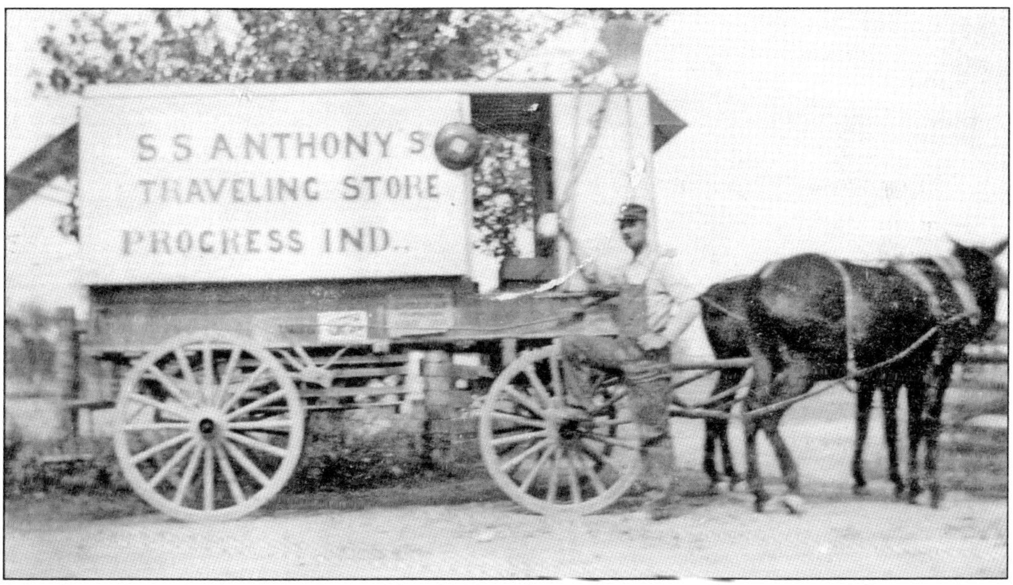

This huckster wagon was welcomed by the people in the surrounding countryside. Travel was difficult and time consuming. The arrival of the wagon broke the monotony of the day for the housewife who came to see what was available. Among the more essential items for sale, there was often a tempting choice of ribbon or lace. (Jeffrey Koenker.)

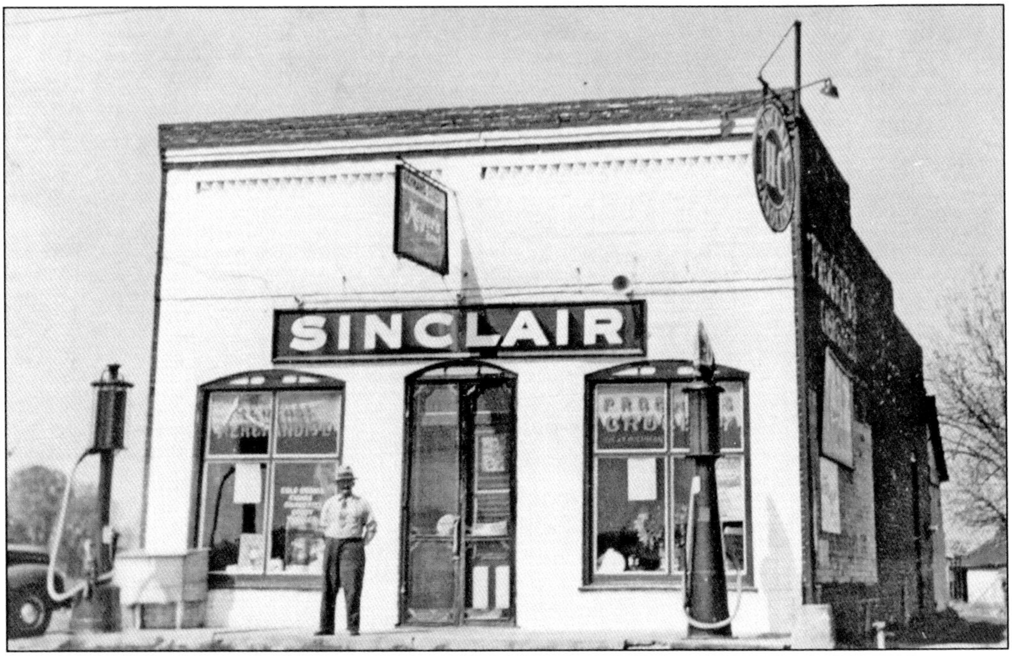

This c. 1930 photograph shows a store in Progress. General Merchandise and Grocery are on signs in the two windows. The two gas pumps indicate it was a filling station also. Such versatility was probably a requirement for keeping a business going in the villages of the county. (Rev. Gary McManus.)

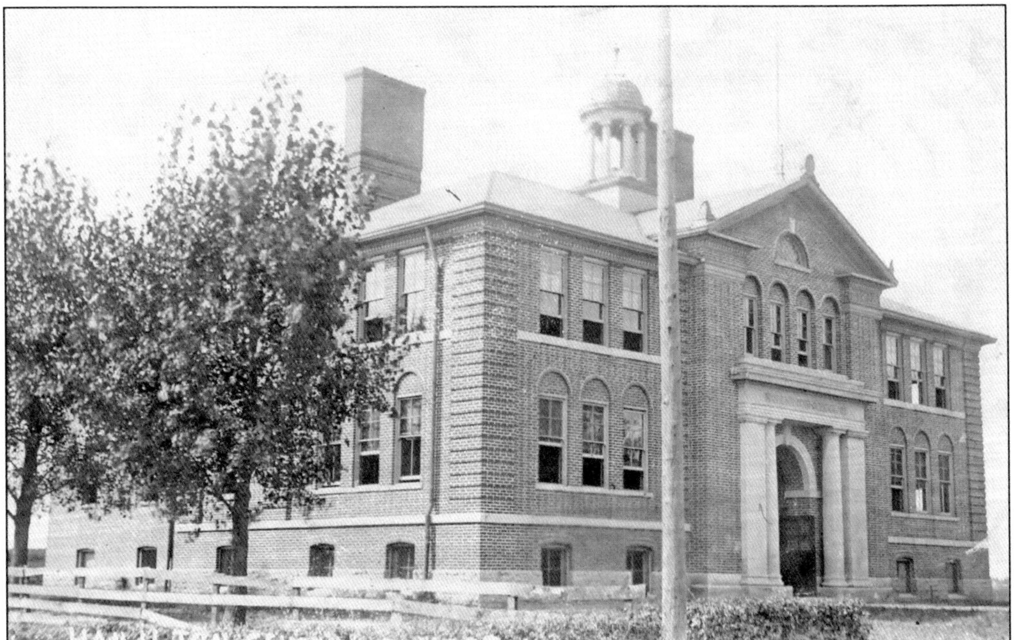

Hamilton Township began school district consolidation in 1899. The new building expanded from two rooms to four rooms. In 1901, six of the district schools were merged with Royerton School, which was a great advance in consolidation. The consolidated school brought students in from an area of 20 square miles. (Jeffrey Koenker.)

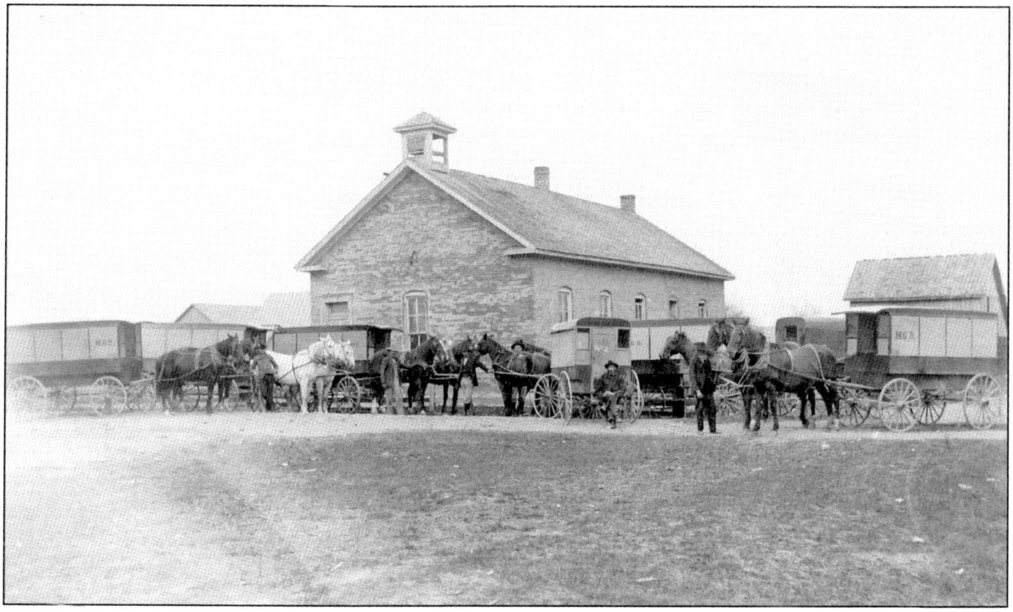

Hamilton Township was the first school in the county to adopt the principle of consolidation. The practicality of transporting children by wagon was proven by using two one-horse wagons to transport 10 or 12 children from each district to the Royerton School. After consolidation, seven wagons were used for conveying 129 students, with transportation costing about 7¢ each. (Jeffrey Koenker.)

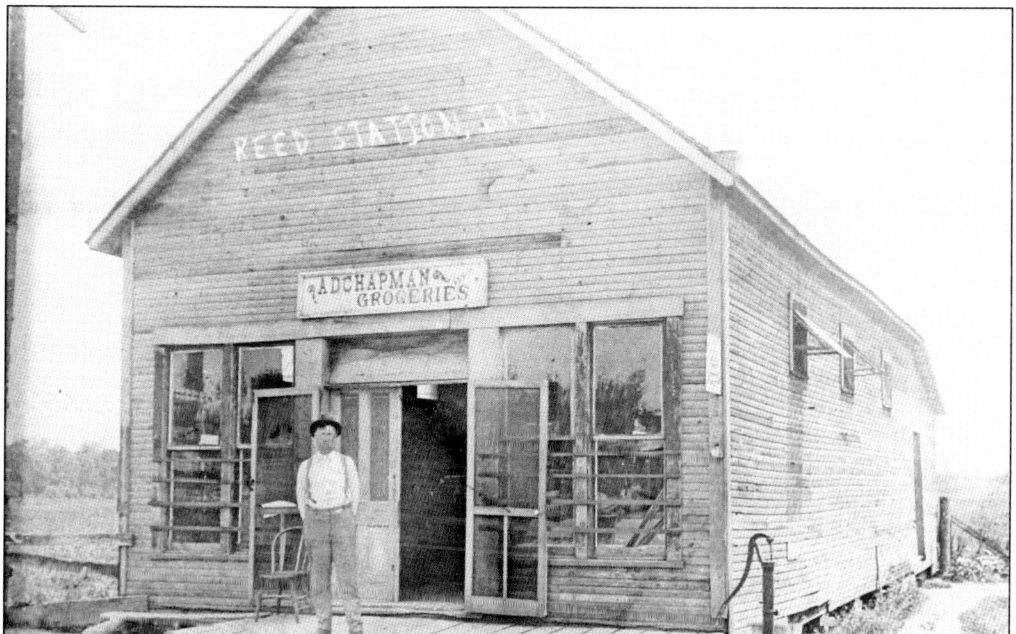

Reed Station, or Reed, as it was sometimes called, was platted in 1877. It had a livery stable, a blacksmith, and a justice of the peace. At one time, there were two groceries. The Chapman grocery, on the north side of Jackson Street, was also the post office. Chapman also had a huckster wagon, with groceries, soap, and other items welcome to his rural customers. (DCHS.)

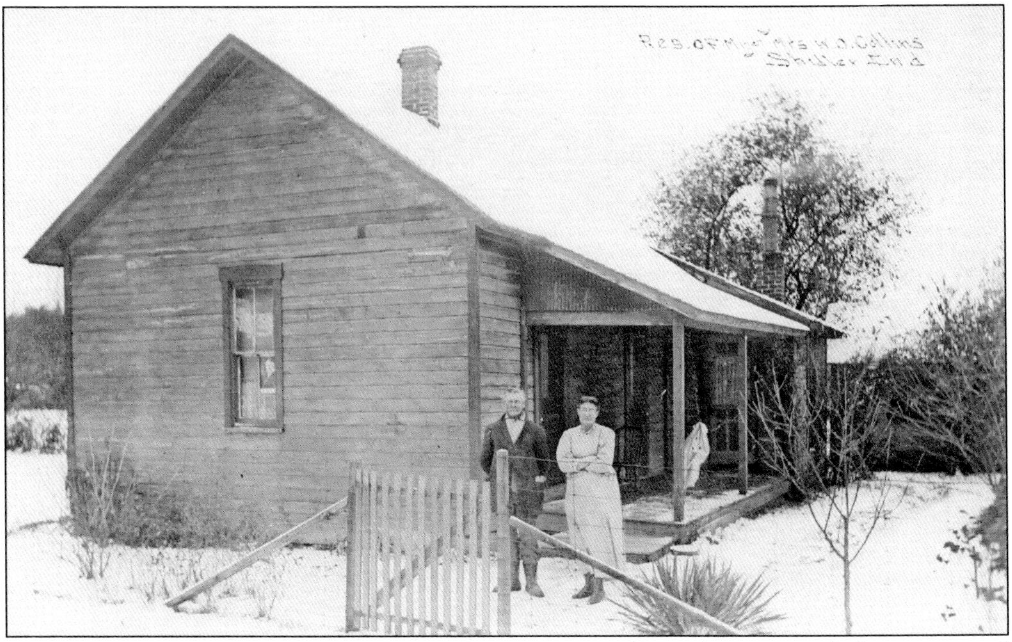

This postcard of the "Residence of Mr. and Mrs. W.O. Collins" shows a sturdy house in good repair. The couple has braved cold weather and snow for this photograph of their neat little home. On the porch to the right, a cloth is hanging over a vine. There appears to be a photograph of a person in one of the panes of the front window. (Jeffrey Koenker.)

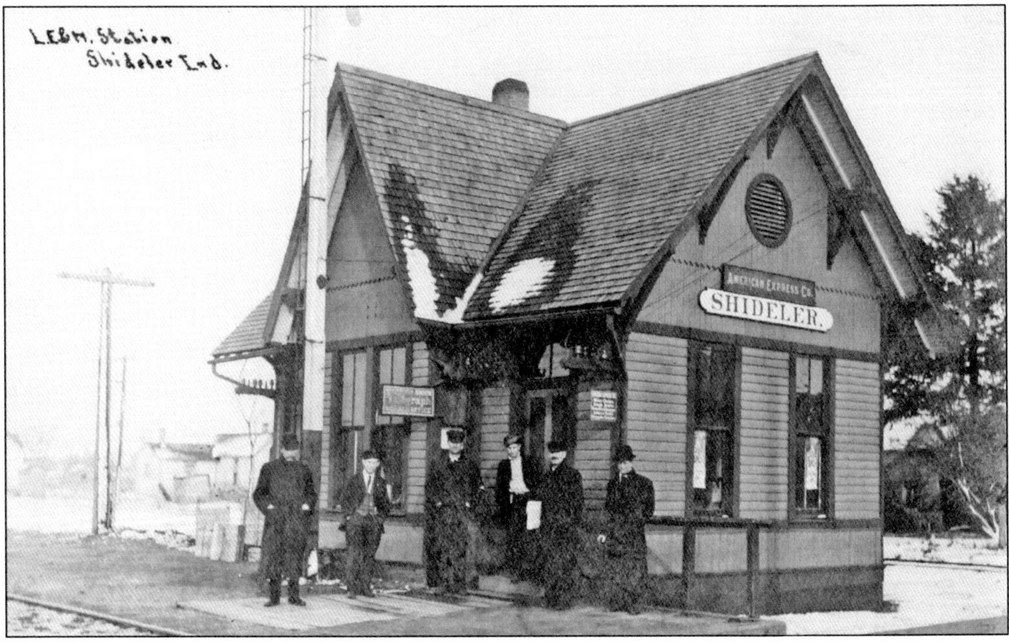

The Lake Erie & Western Railroad depot is shown on the west side of the railroad, about two blocks south of Main Street, on the 1887 atlas. Shideler became a shipping point and developed a small business center. Isaac Shideler was the proprietor of a store and served as postmaster at about this time. A gas well was drilled in Shideler in 1888. (Minnetrista Heritage Collection, Muncie, Indiana.)

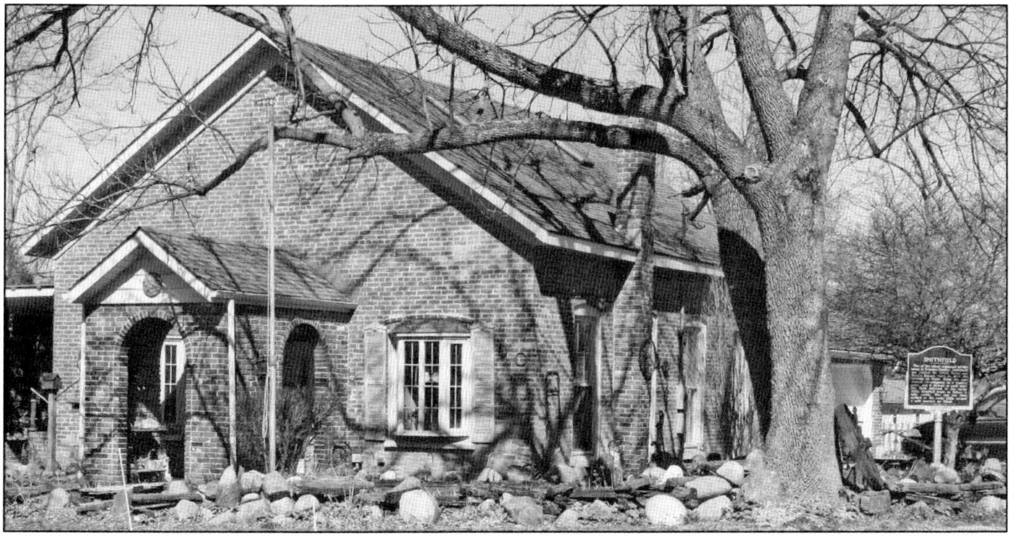

The schoolhouse at Smithfield is a landmark in the county, a reminder of the village settled here. Smithfield was on an early road laid out from Windsor in Randolph County to Muncie brought settlers to the township by 1829. In the 1850s, the railroad line—on which Selma was laid out—drew people and commerce to Selma, and Smithfield began to fade. (DCHS; photograph by Thomas R. Tomlinson.)

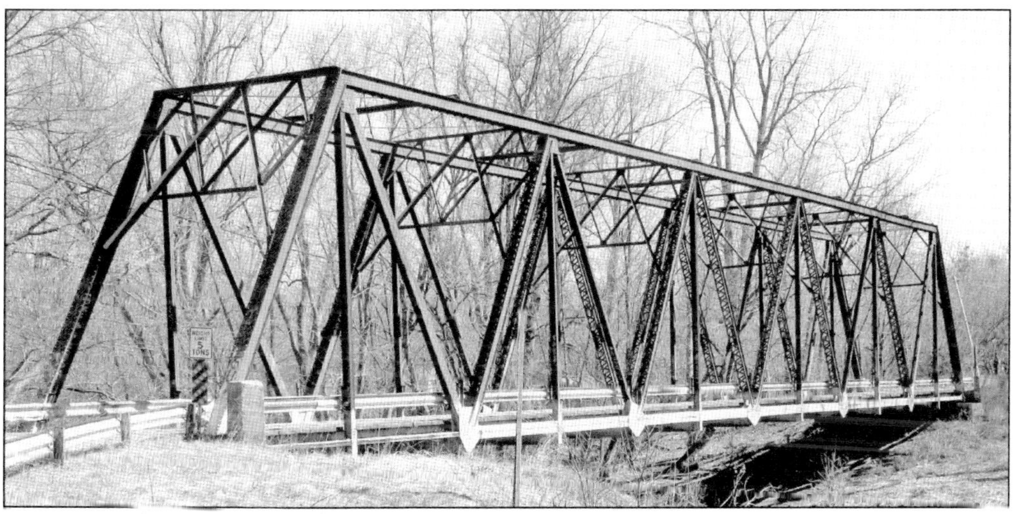

The Smithfield Bridge is one of six iron bridges remaining in the county. It was built by the Indiana Bridge Company in 1908. This steel through truss bridge has been determined to be eligible for the National Register of Historic Places by the Indiana Department of Transportation. Although the bridge was washed downstream in the 1913 flood, it remained intact and was soon returned to the original location. (DCHS; photograph by Thomas R. Tomlinson.)

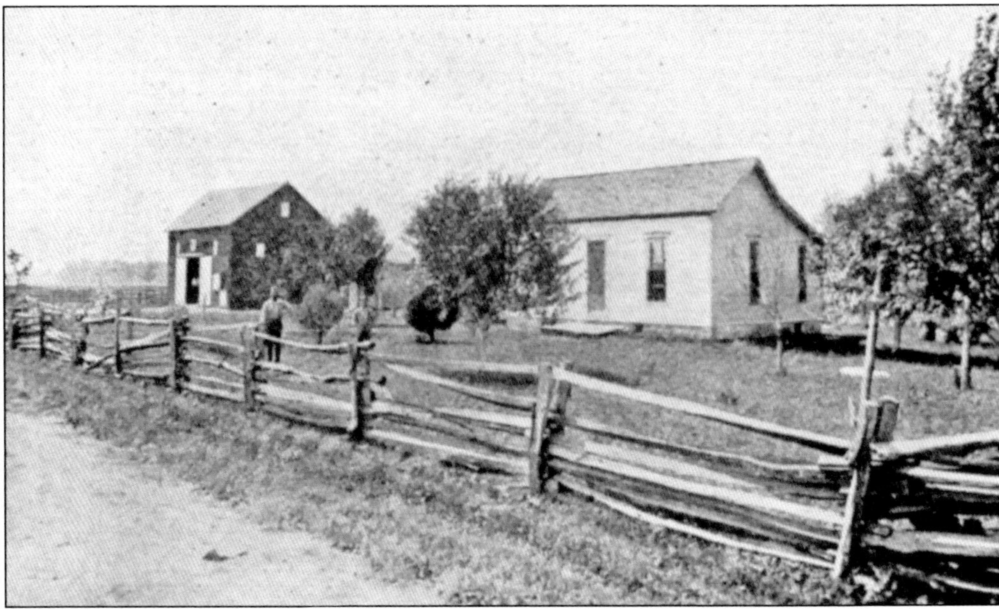

This photograph from the John Ellis book *Our County* shows the homestead of the Mason family in the late 1890s. They lived on the Selma-Albany road about two miles north of Selma. The zig-zag rail fence was common during this period and continued to be used up through World War II. Wire fences required special tools, especially for postholes and stretching the fence. (DCHS.)

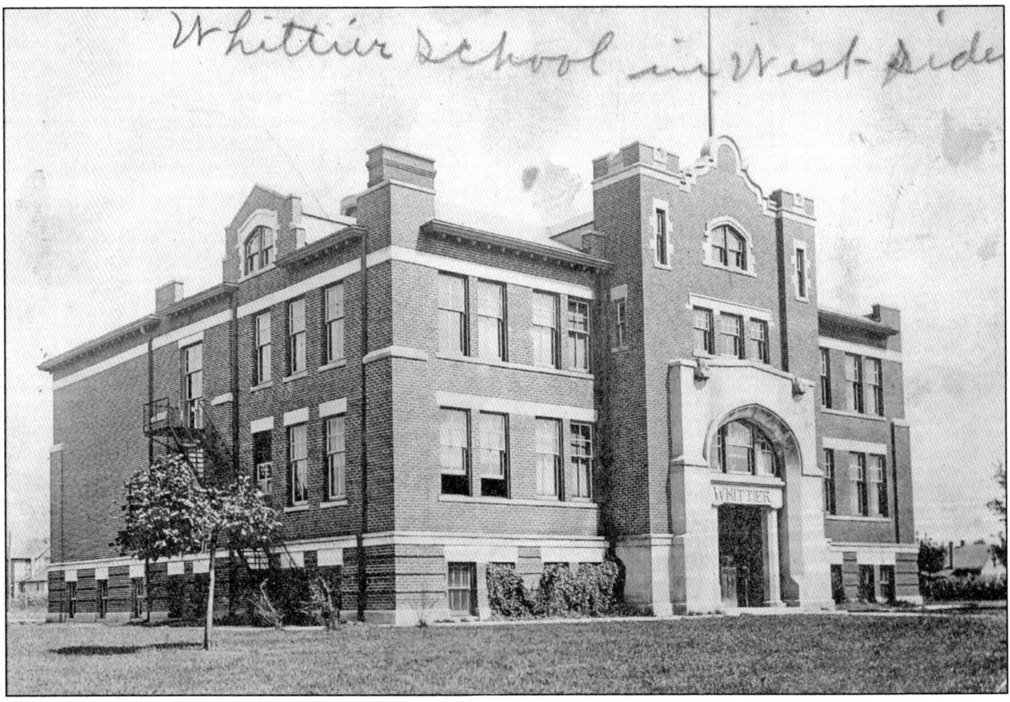

Whittier School was on the site now occupied by the College Avenue United Methodist Church in Muncie. The school was originally a township school and was built before Normal City became part of Muncie. The 1921–1922 *Emerson's Muncie City Directory* described it as a "grade training school for Indiana State Normal." Whittier School had grades one through eight only. (DCHS.)

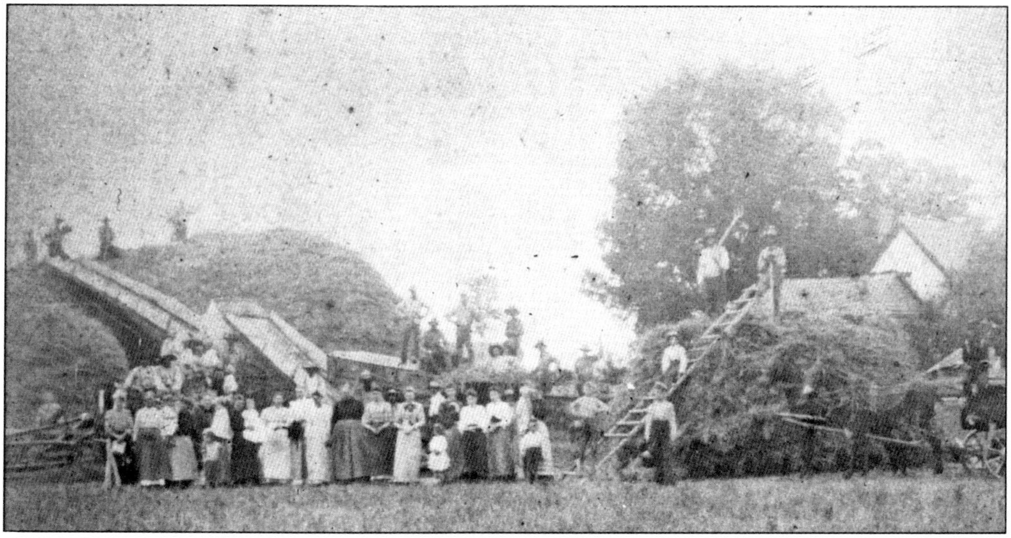

A threshing crew required food, and it took many women to prepare for and serve the large crews. The preparation and the baking were done as much ahead as possible. The day's cooking was supplemented by the neighbors' stoves, and all hands available dished up and served. (DCHS.)

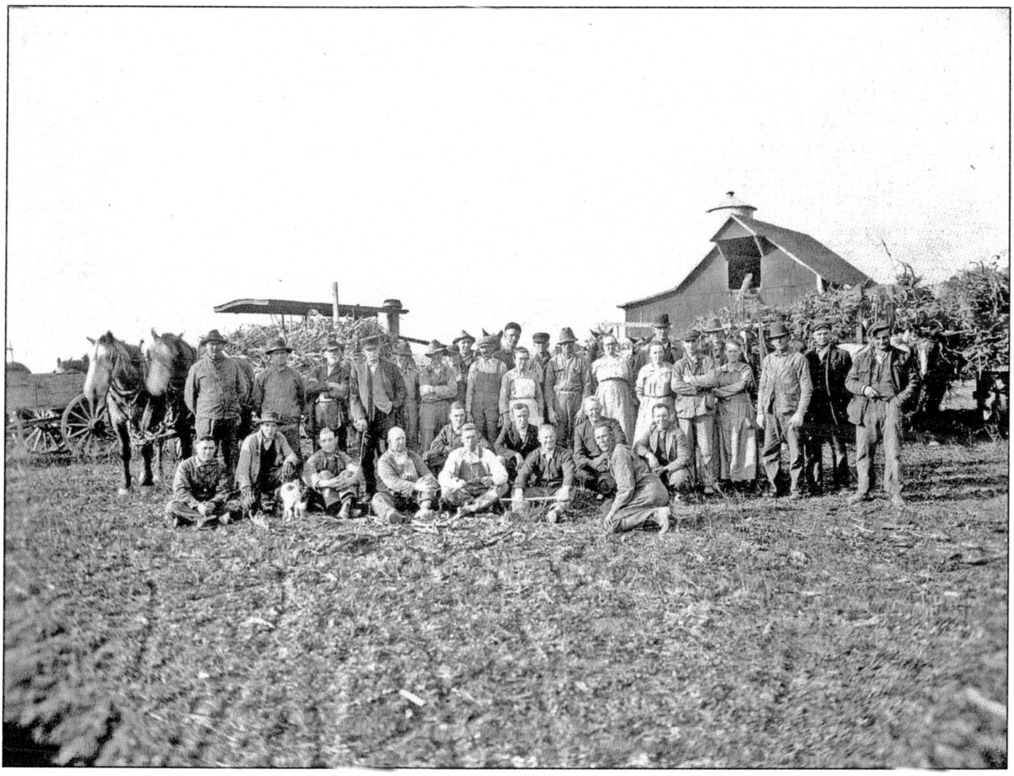

This threshing crew covered the jobs that needed to be done. Grain would have been cut, maybe by horse-drawn mower, in preparation for threshing day. Then the grain stalks were gathered into sheaves, or bundles, and loaded onto wagons in the field. The wagons were pulled to the thresher and unloaded into it. New loads of grain kept the thresher going as continuously as possible. (DCHS.)

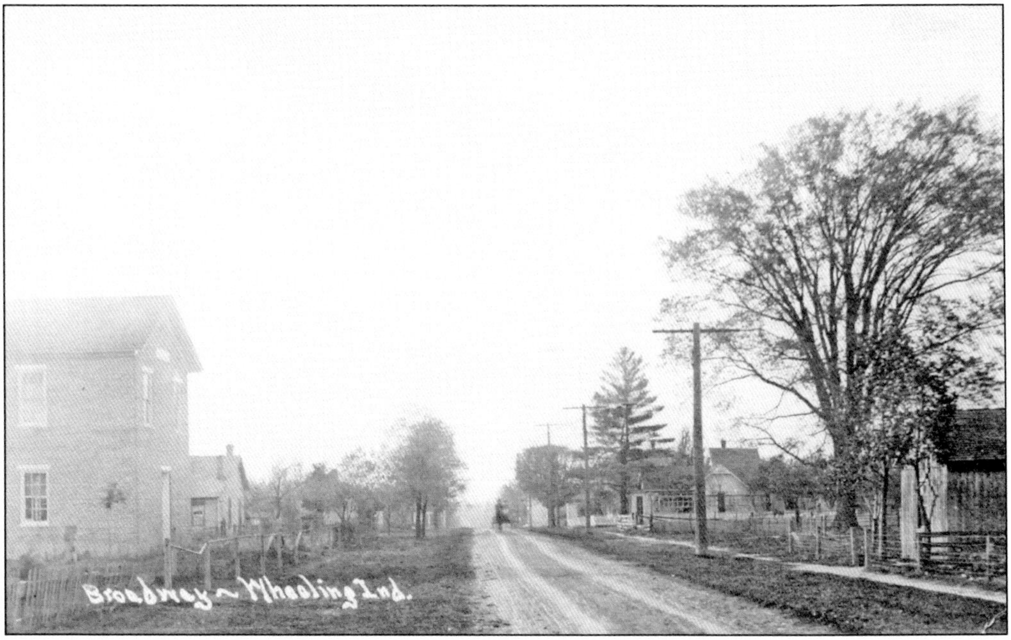

This Wheeling street was part of the Albany-Jonesboro Pike, later the Wheeling-Eaton Pike. Mud streets and roads were dusty and rutted at times. The gravel roads of the 1860s were a great improvement. Local citizens formed companies that built the new roads and collected tolls for such improved roads. The county later took over the gravel roads, and taxes provided for their upkeep. (Jeffrey Koenker.)

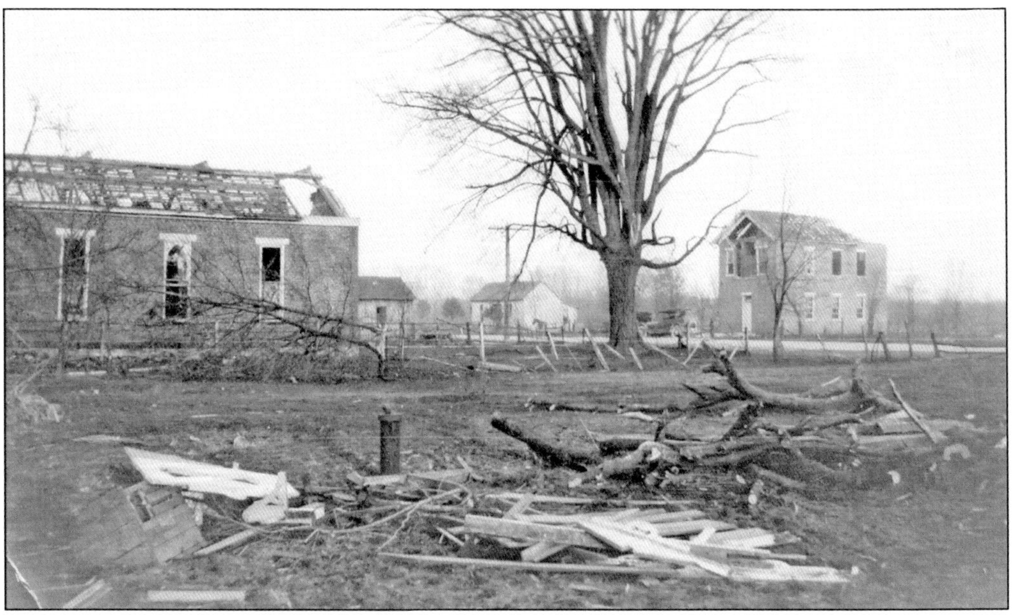

The tornado of April 1922 struck Wheeling, where it did extensive damage to the buildings, including the Methodist Episcopal Church roof at left and the IOOF hall at right. The school was also badly damaged. The Hastings family of Wheeling was away from home, which was fortunate since only the kitchen floor of their house remained after the storm. (Jeffrey Koenker.)

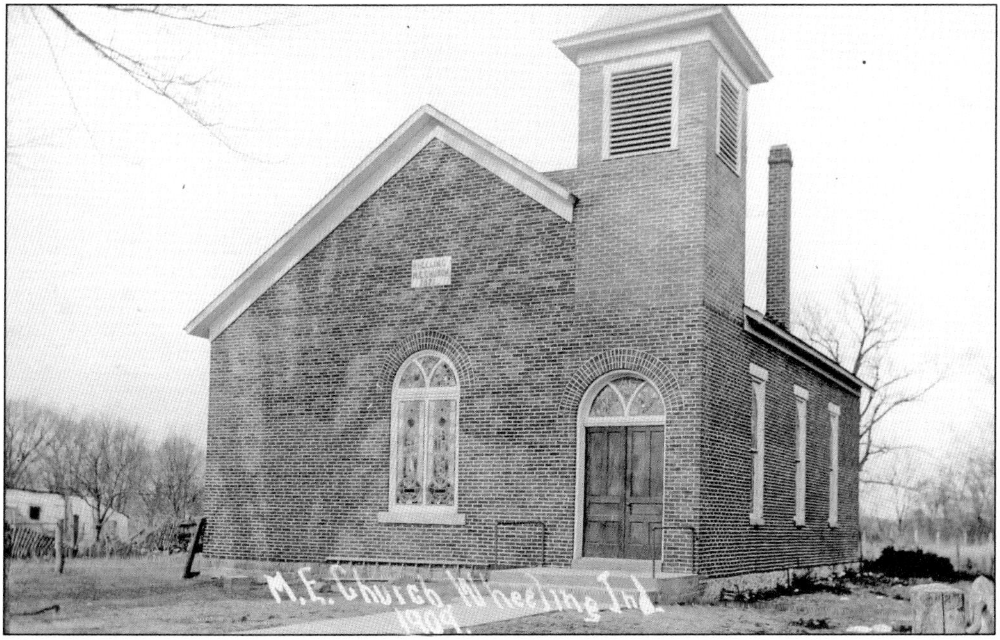

The church was repaired, and the roof replaced after the 1922 tornado. It has been kept in good repair since. Services are still held in this church, and it looks as it did in this 1909 photograph. Other buildings have changed and trees have died, with a new landscape in place. (Jeffrey Koenker.)

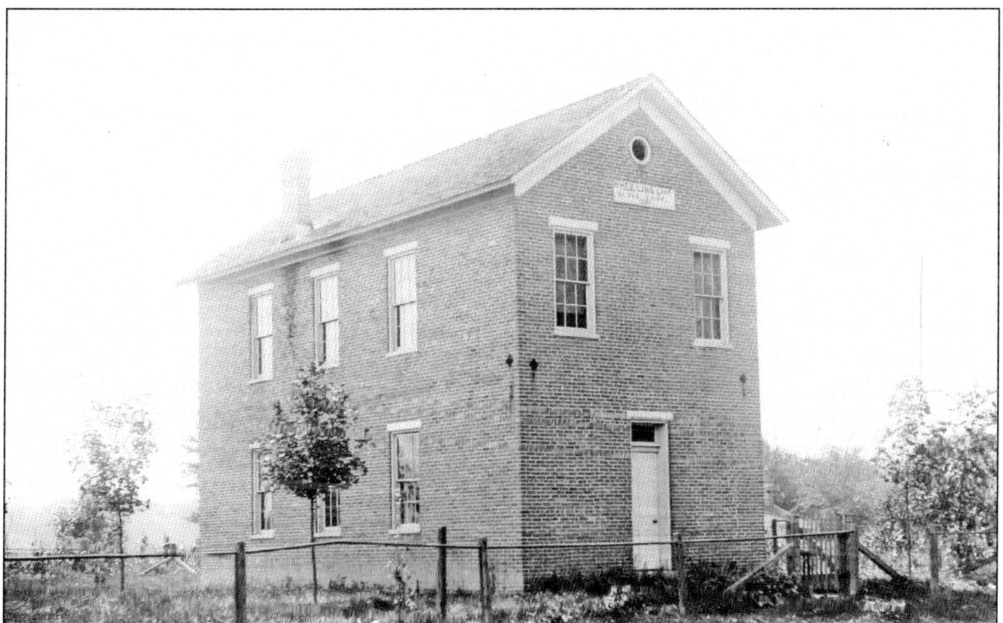

The Wheeling IOOF lodge was established in 1869. In 1871, they added a story to the local schoolhouse and met in the room, so constructed, above the school. Later, they built the lodge hall pictured here. It also was repaired after the storm of 1922 and stood until about the 1980s when it was torn down. (Jeffrey Koenker.)

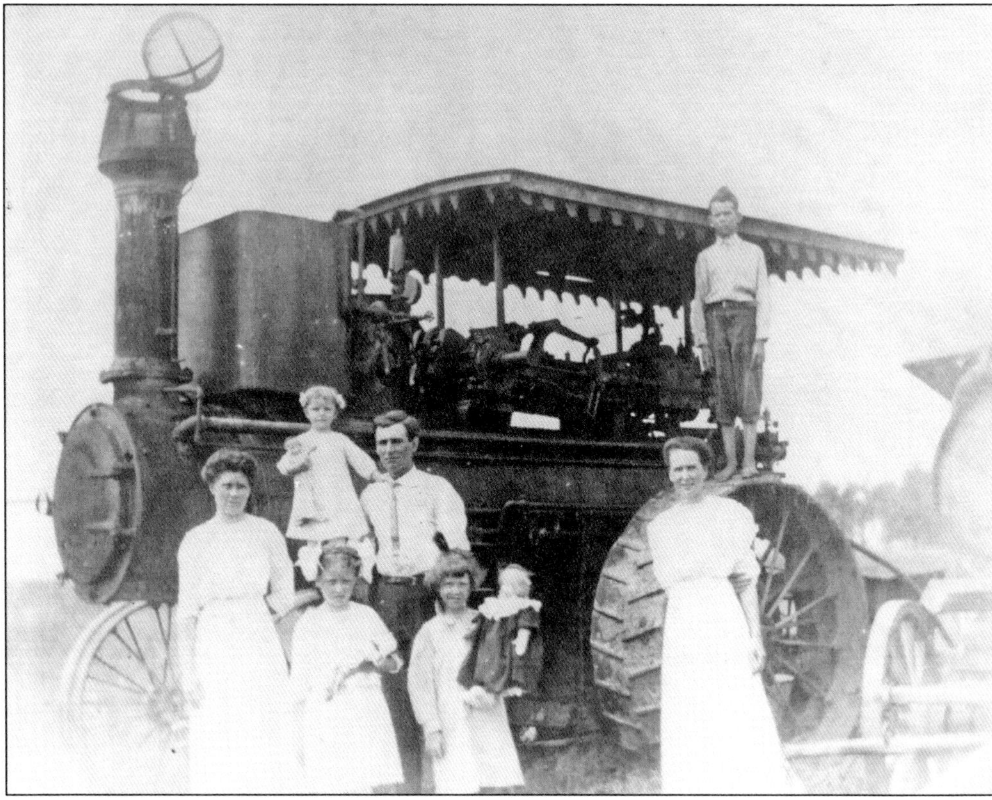

Glenn Snider and his family pose in front of their steam engine. Snider may have had a large harvest of his own as well as working as a thresher man, taking his equipment to the farms around to do custom threshing. Custom threshing made a living for many farm families. (DCHS.)

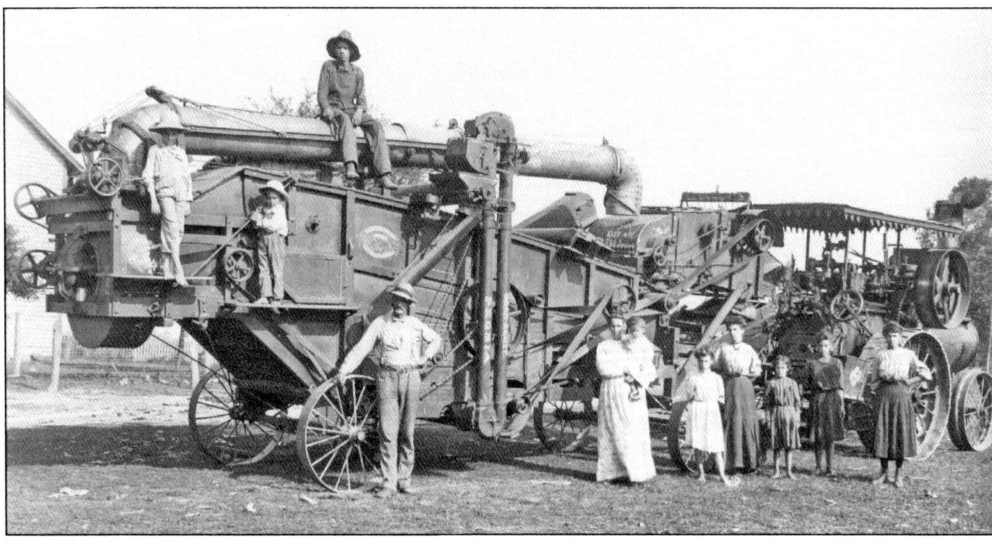

Elmer Bilby and his family came to Delaware County about 1906 and settled in the Gaston area. He apparently did custom threshing for farmers in the area. This photograph shows the entire family, including the children's dollies, standing beside the family's major investments: a steam engine and threshing machine. (DCHS.)

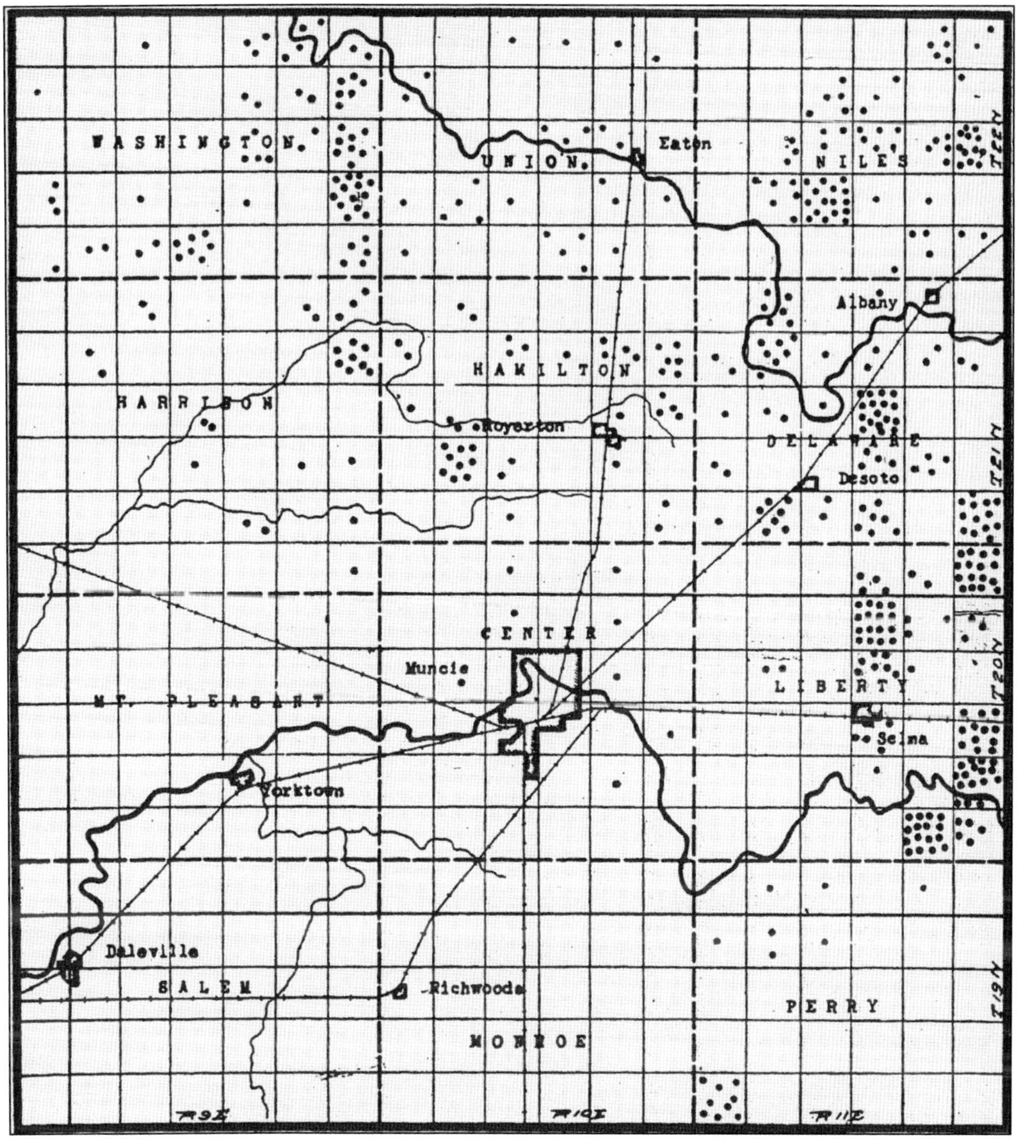

This 1922 map of the county from the Indiana Department of Conservation's Publication No. 21 shows the location of abandoned gas and oil wells. The eastern tier of townships was oil bearing, and the remainder of the county "gas territory." The southwestern part of the county had very few wells. The townships and towns are marked, except for Gaston in lower Washington Township near seven abandoned gas wells. A few of the villages are also shown. The outline of Muncie shows the core of the town before many of the suburbs were added. (Muncie Public Library.)